Choosing Outcomes
and Accommodations
for Children

Choosing Outcomes and Accommodations for Children

A Guide to Educational Planning for Students with Disabilities

Second Edition

by

Michael F. Giangreco, Ph.D.
University of Vermont
Burlington

Chigee J. Cloninger, Ph.D.
University of Vermont
Burlington

and

Virginia Salce Iverson, M.Ed.
Vermont State I-Team
Hinesburg

·P A U L·H·
BROOKES
PUBLISHING Cº

Baltimore • London • Toronto • Sydney

Paul H. Brookes Publishing Co.
Post Office Box 10624
Baltimore, Maryland 21285-0624

All royalties from the sale of this book will be donated to nonprofit agencies that address human needs.

Typeset by Edington-Rand, Inc., Cheverly, Maryland.
Manufactured in the United States of America by
Versa Press, East Peoria, Illinois.

All examples in this book are composites. Any similarity to actual individuals or circumstances is coincidental, and no implications should be inferred.

Partial support for the preparation of this book was provided by the U.S. Department of Education, Office of Special Education and Rehabilitative Services, under the funding categories 1) Innovations for Educating Children with Deaf-Blindness in General Education Settings, CFDA 84.025F (H025F10008); and 2) Research Validation and Implementation Projects for Children Who Are Deaf-Blind, CFDA 84.025S (H025S40003), awarded to the University Affiliated Program of Vermont at the University of Vermont. The content of this book reflects the ideas and positions of the authors and does not necessarily reflect the ideas or positions of the U.S. Department of Education; therefore, no official endorsement should be inferred.

COACH Student Record Forms can be purchased separately in packages of three. To order, contact Paul H. Brookes Publishing Co., Post Office Box 10624, Baltimore, Maryland 21285-0624; 1-800-638-3775; *http://www.pbrookes.com.*

Library of Congress Cataloging-in-Publication Data

Giangreco, Michael F., 1956– .
    Choosing outcomes and accommodations for children: a guide to educational planning for students with disabilities / by Michael F. Giangreco, Chigee J. Cloninger, Virginia Salce Iverson.—2nd ed.
      p. cm.
    Rev. ed. of: Choosing options and accommodations for children (COACH). © 1993.
      Includes bibliographical references and index.
      ISBN 1-55766-323-8
      1. Handicapped children—Education—United States.   2. Mainstreaming in education—United States.   3. Home and school—United States.   4. Quality of life—United States.
5. Inclusive education—United States.   I. Cloninger, Chigee J., 1946– .   II. Iverson, Virginia Salce, 1951– .   III. Giangreco, Michael F., 1956– . Choosing options and accommodations for children (COACH).   IV. Title.
LC4031.G5 1998
371.9′046′0973—dc21   97-19992
    CIP

British Library Cataloguing in Publication data are available from the British Library.

CONTENTS

ABOUT THE AUTHORS

Michael F. Giangreco, Ph.D., Research Associate Professor, Department of Education, University Affiliated Program of Vermont, University of Vermont, 499C Waterman Building, Burlington, Vermont 05405-0160

Michael F. Giangreco has spent more than 20 years working with children and adults in a variety of capacities including special education teacher, community residence counselor, camp counselor, school administrator, educational consultant, university teacher, and researcher. Dr. Giangreco received a bachelor's degree from the State University of New York–College at Buffalo and graduate degrees from the University of Vermont and the University of Virginia. He received his doctoral degree from Syracuse University and has been a faculty member at the University of Vermont since 1988.

His work and educational experiences have led Dr. Giangreco to focus his research, training, and other work activities on three interrelated aspects of educating students with and without disabilities in their local general education schools: 1) individualized curriculum planning, 2) adapting curriculum and instruction, and 3) coordinating support services in schools. Dr. Giangreco is the author and editor of numerous professional publications, including *Vermont Interdependent Services Team Approach (VISTA): A Guide to Coordinating Educational Support Services* (Brookes Publishing Co., 1996) and two volumes of *Quick-Guides to Inclusion: Ideas for Educating Students with Disabilities* (Brookes Publishing Co., 1997, 1998) and is a frequent presenter of educational issues and strategies. Based at the College of Education and Social Services and the University Affiliated Program of Vermont, he has applied his work in numerous schools across North America. His work has been advanced by the feedback and input of innumerable students (with and without disabilities), parents, teachers, administrators, related services providers, and other colleagues.

Chigee J. Cloninger, Ph.D., Research Associate Professor, Department of Education, University Affiliated Program of Vermont, University of Vermont, 499C Waterman Building, Burlington, Vermont 05405-0160

Chigee J. Cloninger has been a teacher of children and adults with and without disabilities for many years. Even in leadership or research positions, teaching, in the sense of bringing about change, has been a key component to Dr. Cloninger's work. She is Coordinator of the Vermont State I-Team, a statewide training and technical assistance team providing intensive special education supports to children and youth with disabilities, educational personnel, and families. She is also Director of the Vermont State Project for Children and Youth with Deafblindness and a teacher in the Intensive Special Education

Master's Program. A national presenter on issues pertaining to students with intensive educational needs, Dr. Cloninger is interested in creative problem-solving approaches, communication, and learning processes for individualized education and leadership.

Virginia Salce Iverson, M.Ed., Educational Consultant, Vermont State I-Team, R.R. 1, Box 550, Northwest Region, Hinesburg, Vermont 05461

Virginia Salce Iverson has worked in the field of education for more than 25 years as a teaching assistant, an educator, an administrator, and a consultant. In addition to teaching fifth grade, she has taught special education across the continuum of placements, including institutions, special schools and classes, and inclusive classrooms from preschool through high school. Ms. Iverson also teaches courses at the university level and presents nationally on issues related to inclusive education. She is an educational consultant for the Vermont State I-Team for Intensive Special Education for which she provides consultation, training, and technical assistance to teams of educators, parents, and related services providers on behalf of students with intensive special education needs. Ms. Iverson is primarily interested in blending systematic instruction with inclusive practices for students with severe disabilities.

WHAT'S NEW
IN THIS EDITION OF COACH

This latest edition of COACH has many changes and improvements based on 1) ongoing field testing in schools; 2) feedback from a variety of people who have used COACH; and 3) a series of research studies, including

- A *national expert validation* of COACH (Giangreco, Cloninger, Dennis, & Edelman, 1993)
- An *analysis of students' IEP goals* (Giangreco, Dennis, Edelman, & Cloninger, 1994)
- A study of the *use and impact* of COACH (Giangreco, Edelman, Dennis, & Cloninger, 1995)
- An individual case study documenting the impact of COACH on a student's *valued life outcomes* (Edelman, Knutson, Osborn, & Giangreco, 1995)
- A *cross-cultural review* of COACH (Dennis & Giangreco, 1996)

All of these sources have been combined to update and improve COACH.

Here are some of the major changes you will find in this edition:

- A brief document entitled *Questions and Answers for Parents About COACH* (see Appendix A) has been developed to share with parents so you can orient them to COACH more easily and efficiently.
- Although COACH forms still may be photocopied (see Appendix B), they are now also available as *preprinted, individual student records.*
- A *Preparation Checklist* has been added to the forms.
- The *Family Interview* has been updated in content and format to improve its effectiveness and ease of use (e.g., valued life outcome questions and learning outcomes lists have been updated; nonessential steps have been eliminated).
- The *valued life outcomes* have been updated, including a new option in which family members are asked if they want to answer questions about each valued life outcome area.
- To improve the clarity of the instructions, a new format has been used. For each step in COACH you will find a detailed *description* followed by *directions* that include 1) a briefly stated *purpose* (explaining the meaning of the step), 2) *instructions* (providing you with the *essentials* of what to do), and 3) *helpful hints* (a set of additional pointers to assist you).
- Changes to facilitate use of COACH in *cross-cultural situations* have been embedded within the background information, instructions, and forms.

- The instructions and formats for the *additional learning outcomes* (formerly Breadth of Curriculum) and *general supports* have been changed although their intended purposes have remained the same.
- A checklist, *Organizing and Informing the Instructional Planning Team*, has been added; and the *scheduling matrix* has been revised.
- Now there are new instructions and forms available to 1) develop annual goals and short-term objectives, 2) facilitate *lesson planning*, and 3) evaluate a student's educational program using the *evaluation of impact process*.

We are very excited about the updates to COACH and hope you find them useful. Good luck!

Michael, Chigee, & Ginny

A BRIEF HISTORY OF COACH (1982–1997)

The history of COACH dates back to 1982, when Michael F. Giangreco was studying and working in Charlottesville, Virginia, where he created an unnamed planning tool to assist in the design of individualized habilitation plans for adults with disabilities who were living in the community. This was the core of what would eventually become COACH. At this same time, Michael's future colleagues, Chigee J. Cloninger and Virginia (Ginny) Salce Iverson, were working in New York and Vermont, respectively.

In 1985, Michael revised this planning tool for use in public school programs for students with disabilities and gave it the acronym COACH, which at the time stood for Cayuga–Onondaga Assessment for Children with Handicaps in recognition of the place where it was being developed, Cayuga and Onondaga counties of central New York state. COACH was distributed by the National Clearing House of Rehabilitation Training Materials at Oklahoma State University from 1985 to 1992.

Five different versions of COACH were developed by Michael between 1985 and 1989 based on field testing in schools and feedback from consumers. The first five versions of COACH were Michael's attempts to combine and operationalize four major sets of information:

1. The ecological inventory approaches pioneered by Lou Brown and many of his colleagues at the University of Wisconsin (Brown et al., 1979; Brown, Nietupski, & Hamre-Nietupski, 1976)
2. Information about curriculum planning learned from Wes Williams at the University of Vermont
3. Information about the Creative Problem-Solving process learned from Sidney Parnes and his colleagues at Buffalo State College
4. What was learned in his roles as a community residence counselor, summer camp counselor, special education teacher, hospital education consultant, and special education coordinator

In October 1988, when Michael joined the faculty at the University of Vermont, he was excited to learn, first-hand, about the work that many of his new colleagues were doing. As a member of the Vermont State I-Team at that time, he learned about the work that was being done by Ginny Iverson and Chigee Cloninger on the *Vermont Integration Planning Process* (VIPP), most notably their development of a scheduling matrix, program-at-a-glance, and lesson adaptation plans. During the early and mid-1980s, Ginny had been working on educational planning processes to facilitate inclusion of students with severe disabilities in general education classes; Chigee added her input to this work when she joined the I-Team in 1987. Their work on these planning processes, summarized in VIPP, complemented and extended the existing versions of COACH, so, beginning in 1990, key components of VIPP were incorporated into COACH. At the time, all three were members of the Vermont State I-Team and they used their experiences in many of Vermont's schools to further develop COACH. New sections were added and existing sections were constantly being revised. Around this time they were also conducting interviews with parents who had children with severe disabilities (Giangreco, Cloninger, Mueller, Yuan, & Ashworth, 1991). These interviews and their work in schools that were including students with severe disabilities in general education classes led to changes in COACH that helped add to its unique character. For example, additions to COACH focused on planning in the context of general education classes. Also, starting in 1991, the context for individual curriculum selection in COACH evolved from considering the current and future status of frequented environments to considering the current and future status of *valued life outcomes* that had been identified through interviews with parents.

As COACH use expanded nationally, a decision was made to publish COACH through Paul H. Brookes Publishing Company. In essence, COACH was moving from an "underground" type of document that most people discovered by word of mouth to one that would become "above ground," making it more widely and readily accessible. At this time we decided to change the name of COACH while retaining the acronym, which had become familiar to many people in the field. So in late 1992 COACH was published as *Choosing Options and Accommodations for CHildren: A Guide to Planning Inclusive Education* (Giangreco, Cloninger, & Iverson, 1993).

Since 1992, COACH use has continued to expand across North America, and the authors and other colleagues have had the opportunity to conduct a series of research studies to learn more about COACH. This second Brookes edition of COACH incorporates what has been learned since 1992. You will notice that the COACH acronym has been retained, but again the name has changed slightly to *Choosing Outcomes and Accommodations for CHildren: A Guide to Educational Planning for Students with Disabilities*. Like its predecessors, this version of COACH reflects the authors' efforts to provide you with information that reflects the input of the thousands of individuals from whom they have learned over the years in their quest to keep COACH current, relevant, and grounded in the values and practices that support students with disabilities, their families, and those who care about their education and lives.

ACKNOWLEDGMENTS

The people who deserve special thanks for the development of this edition of COACH are too numerous to mention. Many of the most significant contributors were educational team members who participated in our research efforts or have been part of our training efforts, including parents, students, special educators, general educators, and related services providers. Thanks also go to the many university faculty and students who offered their insights. We also would like to acknowledge and thank all those who contributed to earlier versions of COACH, particularly our colleagues at the University of Vermont, members of the Vermont State I-Team, and staff of the Cayuga–Onondaga Board of Cooperative Educational Services in Auburn, New York.

To
all the students, families, and school folks
who have taught us so much

Thank you!

Choosing Outcomes
and Accommodations
for Children

Section I

INTRODUCTION

COACH (Choosing Outcomes and Accommodations for CHildren: A Guide to Educational Planning for Students with Disabilities) will enable teams to make an efficient front-end expenditure of their time that will pay off by actually *saving time* throughout the school year. Parents and professionals will join together to plan, implement, and evaluate appropriate educational programs for students with disabilities.

COACH is a planning tool designed to identify the contents of a student's educational program and strategies for implementing this program in general education settings and activities. COACH is a set of field-tested steps that turn ideas about inclusive education into actions that your team can take.

COACH is divided into two major parts, which are listed briefly here and described in more detail in Section III of this manual. **Part A (Determining a Student's Educational Program)** includes a *Preparation Checklist* plus 1) a *Family Interview* to determine family-selected learning priorities, 2) *Additional Learning Outcomes* to select a broader set of learning outcomes in addition to those selected by the family, 3) *General Supports* to determine what needs to be done to or for the student, 4) an approach for translating priority learning outcomes into individualized education program (IEP) *Annual Goals*, 5) a *Program-at-a-Glance* to summarize a student's educational program, and 6) an approach to developing *Short-Term Objectives.*

Part B (Strategies and Processes to Implement a COACH-Generated Educational Program) includes steps for 7) *Organizing and Informing the Instructional Planning Team* to ensure that educational plans are effectively carried out; 8) *Scheduling for the Student with Disabilities in the Classroom* to ensure that students' needs are addressed within typical classroom routines; 9) *Planning and Adapting Instruction* to ensure instructional plans are developed and implemented to address student needs and participation in class activities, even when their goals are different from those of their classmates; and 10) *Evaluating the Impact of Educational Experiences* to determine the extent to which educational efforts are having an impact on student learning and valued life outcomes.

WHAT YOU CAN GET OUT OF COACH

Based on our experiences and research, here is what COACH can offer when it is used effectively (Dennis & Giangreco, 1996; Giangreco, Cloninger, Dennis, & Edelman, 1993; Giangreco, Dennis, Edelman, & Cloninger, 1994; Giangreco, Edelman, Dennis, & Cloninger, 1995):

- COACH can provide a process for individualized educational planning in inclusive settings.

  It's a combination of structure, but flexibility . . . so we can tailor it to everyone's individual needs.

  special educator

- COACH can provide an organized way to assist in making complex decisions.

  I very much liked . . . [COACH] because it's a very directed and organized way to be able to discuss things that are sometimes difficult to discuss.

  special educator

- COACH can encourage team members to think about how education can influence valued life outcomes for a student.

- COACH can encourage parents and professionals to think about educational planning in new ways.

  It enabled you to think about things that you would not have considered before.

  parent

- COACH can provide a constructive forum for professionals and parents to listen to each other and clarify expectations.

  [It] spurred on some conversations I don't think would have come up if we had not been doing COACH.

  special educator

- COACH can increase family involvement in educational planning.

  I think COACH really gave an opportunity for her parents to have an articulate way to contribute to her educational life, and for us as a team to hear from them.

  special educator

- COACH can assist families in focusing on learning priorities for their child.

  Of everything we've tried, and we've tried lots of different approaches over the years with Sandra of coming up with IEP goals, this [COACH] just gave us so much assistance in really getting what we wanted for her and helping us crystallize what we really did want.

  parent

- COACH can add clarity and relevance to the IEP, helping to focus and shorten the document.

The ones [IEPs] developed in my experience without using COACH were unrealistically huge, disjointed, were not necessarily focused on the family's identified priorities and goals, and were unmanageable. . . . They did not seem to have the personal focus. "What would this young person and his or her family like to accomplish this year?"

special educator

- COACH can help team members agree on a shared set of goals for the student rather than a different set for each discipline (e.g., physical therapy, speech-language pathology, special education) represented on the team.

I firmly believe in the process and just thought it was extremely challenging and exciting, and it made a much better educational program for the child. It was just a very satisfying way to work because you felt you had a road map of where you wanted to be and a way to get there. We were seeing progress every time we met. . . . it was Joe's progress and you had a piece in it, no matter what it was, and that was really exciting and kept us all going.

physical therapist

- COACH can facilitate meaningful inclusion in general education settings and activities.

If she needs something, if she needs help opening the paint, I mean, she'll tap one of the other kids and hand them the jar like, "you know, I can't get this cover off!" And they have gotten so they've been as excited as I have. "Hey, it's like Holly wants me to open it! Holly asked me to do it! She asked me to do it! She's communicating!"

parent

- COACH can assist in clarifying a student's participation in general education curriculum, classes, and activities.

We use it [Program-at-a-Glance] every day. There's a pretty discrete number [of learning outcomes] that we're trying to address; this has let everyone be able to remember what is being worked on.

classroom teacher

- COACH provides strategies for students with disabilities to have increased access to the general education curriculum.

Looking at the regular education curriculum, I think people were really surprised; . . . it made a big difference when people look at the elementary curriculum and say, "Wow! . . . there's a lot here that we can be focusing on."

special educator

- COACH can clarify the types of general supports that need to be provided to or for the student and can help distinguish the difference between supports that need to be provided to or for a student and a student's learning outcomes.

- COACH can facilitate pursuit of valued life outcomes for students (e.g., meaningful relationships, participation in meaningful activities in various places).

He went to dances, he went to games, he was just part of it. He was a kid in the 6th or 7th grade. It was just exciting to see that; things that people generally take for granted.

parent

- COACH can enhance relationships between families and professionals.

[The parents] were very surprised to be involved in the process; they thought it was wonderful. I think they felt they were valued as part of the team.

special educator

- COACH can assist in facilitating family interviewing in cross-cultural situations.

One of the major reasons cited for nonparticipation of minority families is the imbalance of power in the parent–professional relationship. All too often, professionals assume that, because of their expertise, they have solutions to a problem and do not consult families for their opinion and knowledge.

educator

- COACH can provide opportunities for professionals to view families more favorably.

I was impressed with how well this mother knows her child. I was very impressed with her present goals and expectations for the future, and I didn't necessarily have that understanding of the mom up until going through COACH with her the first time.

special educator

- COACH can provide opportunities for professionals to share more decision-making control with families.

Even though it was initially like, "Oh, this [sharing control with families] is hard for me!" . . . because of the way I saw it follow through, the way it made the IEP smoother, the way it made our team work so much better, it made me feel real good. It just made a big difference overall and [in] the whole relationship with parents. I can honestly say that they are part of the team now.

special educator

- Overall, COACH can be an important piece of providing appropriate and quality education when used in conjunction with other exemplary practices, such as inclusive placement, collaborative teamwork, participation in shared activities with peers who do not have disability labels, active learning, and use of necessary supports.

I certainly have come out of every COACH learning things about children and their families that have helped me do a better job as an educator.

special educator

CONCEPTUALIZING EDUCATIONAL PLANNING FOR STUDENTS WITH DISABILITIES WHO ARE IN GENERAL EDUCATION CLASSES

One of the most common, and potentially challenging, aspects of planning for the inclusion of a student with significant disabilities in general education is having a way to think about it that makes sense. People often ask, "How can a student with severe disabilities be included in general education class activities when the content being taught is different from what this student needs?" This is a legitimate question to ask and demonstrates a desire to ensure the integrity of each student's education.

It is often incorrectly assumed that grade-level placement is synonymous with curricular content—in other words, that all fifth-graders must do the same fifth-grade work. Rather, grade-level placement and individual curricular content should be independent of each other (Giangreco, Cloninger, Dennis, & Edelman, 1994). For example, students in the same fifth-grade class can be functioning below or above the designated "fifth-grade level" and still receive appropriate, quality education *if their individual learning needs are addressed.* Even in classes in which there are no students with labeled disabilities, it is a myth that all students in a particular grade function at the same level in all academic areas. In fact, the general education movement toward multigraded classrooms, and corresponding strategies to accommodate learners at various levels of functioning, lends support to the premise that teachers must be prepared to accommodate wider variance among students. Purposeful heterogeneous grouping of students can be desirable and beneficial as students learn from each other in a diverse learning community. As we explore ways of including students with significant disabilities, we are learning approaches that benefit all the students in our schools. Inclusive education, although prompted by the presence of students with disabilities, is about educational access, equity, and quality for *all* students; it is not exclusively a disability issue.

In the following sections we define what we mean by the term *inclusive education*, provide a framework for conceptualizing inclusive options, and describe two ways of approaching curricular and instructional planning when a student's learning goals differ significantly from those of his or her classmates (i.e., multilevel curriculum and instruction, curriculum overlapping).

Defining Inclusive Education

People have used the term *inclusive education* in so many different ways, we felt it was important to explain what we mean by it in the context of COACH. Inclusive education means (Giangreco, Baumgart, & Doyle, 1995):

- *All* students are welcomed in general education. The general education class with support is the first option considered, regardless of disability type or severity.
- Students are educated in classes where the number of those with and without disabilities is proportional to the local population (e.g., 10%–12% have identified disabilities).
- Students are educated with peers in the same age groupings available to those without disability labels.
- Students with varying characteristics and abilities participate in shared educational experiences while pursuing individually appropriate learning outcomes with necessary supports and accommodations.
- Shared educational experiences take place in settings predominantly frequented by people without disabilities (e.g., general education classroom, community worksites).
- Educational experiences are designed to enhance individually determined valued life outcomes for students and therefore seek an individualized balance between the academic/functional and social/personal aspects of schooling.
- Inclusive education exists when each of the previously listed characteristics occurs on an ongoing, daily basis.

We will know that inclusive education has fully arrived when designations such as the "inclusion school," the "inclusion classroom," or the "inclusion student" are no longer needed as part of our educational vocabulary. To paraphrase Biklen and Knoll (1987), inclusion survives as an issue only so long as someone is excluded.

Inclusion Options

Within general education classes and activities, the participation of students can be broadly characterized along two dimensions: 1) the *program*—what is taught (e.g., curriculum, annual goals, learning outcomes); and 2) the *supports*—what is provided to assist the student in accessing and achieving his or her educational program (e.g., materials, teaching strategies, personnel) (Giangreco & Meyer, 1988; Giangreco & Putnam, 1991). As shown in Figure 1, there are four basic options in this approach for including students in general class activities using the learning outcomes you will generate from COACH. It is important to recognize that these four options should be considered fluid rather than static. Individual students may use some or all of these options throughout the course of a school day or even within a single lesson or activity, flowing back and forth between options as needed.

Option A—No Accommodations Required

Option A exists when a student is pursuing the general education program that is readily available to any student and

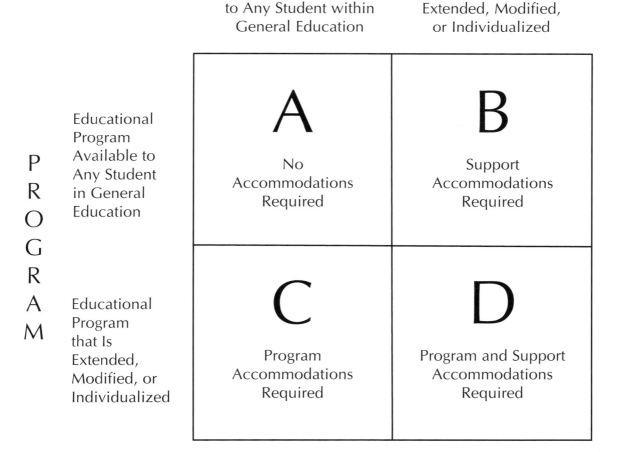

Figure 1.   Inclusion options within general education environments and activities. (Adapted from Giangreco & Putnam, 1991.)

can pursue that program given the supports available to all students. Clearly, the supports available in schools vary, and what is typically available in one may not be in another. *However, as general education becomes more inclusive, what historically has been an accommodation becomes typical.* Many students, even those with severe disabilities, have portions of the school day or parts of activities when they require no accommodations. Part of our responsibility is to identify these opportunities and expand on them. All too often, with the most benevolent of intentions, we provide support to students even when they do not need it (Giangreco, Edelman, Luiselli, & MacFarland, in press-a). By relying more on natural supports (Nisbet, 1992) and providing supports that are "only as special as necessary" (Giangreco, 1996c), we can provide students with the appropriate and socially valued opportunities to receive their education.

Option B—Support Accommodations Required

Option B exists for students who require extended, modified, or otherwise individualized supports while having access to and pursuing the general education program. For example, a student who is deaf may require an interpreter, a student who is blind may require reading materials in braille, or a student with motor difficulties may require a tape recorder to "take notes" in order to participate in the general education program.

Option C—Program Accommodations Required

Option C exists when a student requires extension, modification, or individualization to the content of his or her educational program but does not require specialized supports. For example, a teacher may adjust the amount of production (e.g., 5 new spelling words instead of 10), the level of content (e.g., asking questions at the student's level), or the type of content (e.g., selection of different subject content), without needing unusual or specialized supports to do so. Like Option A (no accommodations required), this option encourages educational teams to consider the use of natural supports.

Option D—Program and Support Accommodations Required

Option D exists at times when a student needs extension, modification, or individualization of both the educational program and the supports to access and participate in class activities. This fourth option, while necessary for some students, should be considered only after exhausting possibilities using Options A, B, and C. When using this option, it is crucial to be aware that few, if any, students require this option full time. We should be observant for opportunities to educate students using other options that allow them the most normalized opportunities.

Educational Program Adjustment

When using Option C or D, there are two very basic ways to think about adjusting a student's educational program: 1) multilevel curriculum and instruction and 2) curriculum overlapping.

Multilevel Curriculum and Instruction

Multilevel curriculum and instruction refers to teaching a diverse group of learners within a shared activity in which students have different individually appropriate learning outcomes within the same curriculum area (e.g., social studies) (Campbell, Campbell, Collicott, Perner, & Stone, 1988; Giangreco & Putnam, 1991). Whereas one student may be learning at a basic knowledge or comprehension level, another student simultaneously may be working on an application or synthesis level. For example, second-grade students might play a small-group social studies board game devised by their teacher to learn about their neighborhood, town, and state. The teacher prepares a set of 10 game cards for each student that target individual learning outcomes. For one student the game cards require applying knowledge about the roles of community helpers (e.g., police, firefighters, store clerks, postal workers) by moving game pieces to respond to scenarios on cards (e.g., "Move your player to the place where you might go if you wanted to send a card to your grandmother for her birthday"). For another student the game cards require learning to answer questions about where he or she lives (e.g., street address, telephone number, recognizing neighbors). A third student is using map skills such as north, south, east, and west to respond to questions (e.g., "If you started at the bookstore and went two blocks north and one block east, where would you be?"). In this example, all the students have social studies learning outcomes that have been individually selected to match their level of functioning and needs.

Multilevel curriculum can include variations across subject content, level of learning outcomes pursued, or both. For example, in a seventh-grade social studies class, the subject content throughout the year focuses on American history from the Revolution through the Civil War. The team for Joseph, a student with disabilities, decided that the subject content should be the same for him, but the level of learning outcomes should be adapted. In other words, his studies would focus on American history but be adapted to an appropriate level (e.g., historical people, places, and events). In Joseph's math class they are studying algebra. His team decided that the subject content for Joseph should be basic computation (e.g., adding, subtracting), and that the level and quantity of the learning outcomes needed to be adapted. In both classes Joseph is working on learning outcomes within the same curricular area as his classmates.

Curriculum Overlapping

Curriculum overlapping refers to teaching a diverse group of students within a shared activity in which students have different, individually appropriate learning outcomes that come from two or more curriculum areas (e.g., a student is pursuing communication learning outcomes in a science activity while other students have science learning outcomes). For example, in a high school biology class, lab teams of three students each are assembling a model of a human heart. Two of the students have goals related to the identification, anatomy, and physiology of the human heart. The third student, who has severe disabilities, participates in helping to assemble the model heart but is working on communication and social skills (e.g., taking turns, following instructions, describing events, maintaining socially acceptable behavior). Curriculum overlapping can also address other general education curriculum areas. For example, it was mentioned previously that Joseph, a seventh-grade student with disabilities, was participating in social studies and math via multilevel curriculum. His team agreed that his participation in French class would be through curriculum overlapping. In French class he would be exposed to French words, language, and culture, but there would be no expectation of competencies in French. The team agreed that participation in French class provided opportunities to pursue learning outcomes identified from his seventh-grade English class pertaining to listening, speaking, reading, writing, and spelling. For example, his spelling words from English class could be duplicated in French and he could practice reading and writing both sets, use them in sentences, and read them orally.

Curriculum overlapping occurs when learning outcomes from two or more curriculum areas are overlapped within the same activity. Opportunities for both curriculum overlapping and multilevel curriculum and instruction are abundant in classrooms in which students participate in active learning.

PRINCIPLES FORMING THE BASIS OF COACH

This section describes six guiding principles on which COACH is based:

1. Pursuing valued life outcomes is an important aspect of education.
2. The family is the cornerstone of educational planning.
3. Collaborative teamwork is essential to quality education.
4. Coordination among support service providers is essential to appropriate education.
5. Using problem-solving methods improves the effectiveness of educational planning.
6. Special education is a service, not a place.

Becoming aware of these foundational principles should assist teams in determining whether they wish to use COACH. It can also help team members develop a common framework for their work. Although COACH offers explicit instructions for its use, it also requires skillful adaptation to adjust to the varied circumstances in which it is used. Our research and common sense tell us that, if you adapt COACH in ways that match its underlying principles, you are more likely to have positive outcomes. Conversely, if you adapt COACH in ways that do not match its underlying principles, you are less likely to have positive outcomes (Giangreco, 1996a; Giangreco, Edelman, et al., 1995). By understanding the principles on which COACH is based, team members put themselves in the best position to get the most out of COACH.

Principle 1: Pursuing Valued Life Outcomes Is an Important Aspect of Education

A common belief shared by many people who care about the education of children, including those with disabilities, is that students' lives should be better as a result of having been in school. COACH includes a set of *valued life outcomes* that are based on information collected from parents who have children with severe disabilities. These valued life outcomes are designed to facilitate student independence and interdependence, as well as pursuing personal growth by expanding access, creating new opportunities, developing individual abilities, and providing ways to contribute to one's community (Giangreco, Cloninger, et al., 1993; Giangreco, Cloninger, Mueller, Yuan, & Ashworth, 1991; Giangreco, Edelman, et al., 1995). The valued life outcomes in COACH include

- Being safe and healthy
- Having a home, now and in the future
- Having meaningful relationships
- Having choice and control that match one's age and culture
- Participating in meaningful activities in various places

Clearly, these valued life outcomes will hold different meanings to different families depending on a variety of factors, such as where they live, their family configuration, and their cultural beliefs and practices. Valued life outcomes are equally applicable, whether or not a student has a disability (Dennis, Williams, Giangreco, & Cloninger, 1993). Although each family will pursue valued life outcomes for their child in unique ways, COACH is one of the few planning approaches that explicitly links selection of curriculum to individually determined valued life outcomes. By selecting curriculum based on valued life outcomes, we are encouraging people to look beyond splintered skills and provide a curricular focus that has meaning to the family. Without an emphasis on valued life outcomes, students with disabilities are at risk of completing their education without meaningful outcomes. "After years of public education, youth with severe disabilities all too often exit school unemployed, without basic skills, lonely, isolated from peers, and disenfranchised from the larger society" (Giangreco & Snell, 1996, p. 100).

Although there may be some general agreement about what constitutes valued life outcomes, how to best assess, plan for, and pursue these outcomes through education remains debatable. One approach suggests that increasing independence in performing daily living skills will lead to valued life outcomes. Although this may be true in some situations, there is no guarantee that skill development necessarily leads to improvement in a person's valued life outcomes. For instance, teaching banking skills to a student who will have little opportunity or need to use them may have no impact on that individual. Conversely, for a young adult with a job, learning to use an automated teller machine may offer him or her more choice, control, and independence. As self-advocate Norman Kunc said,

> For me I guess the key is the difference between what I call "ease of living" and "quality of life"; many people confuse the two. Ease of living would be something to minimize the physical struggle, time, or energy that has to be expended in daily tasks. But just because life gets easier doesn't necessarily mean that my quality of life has improved.
>
> Norman Kunc (Giangreco, 1996b, p. 7)

Another approach holds that a student's valued life outcomes can be improved when people without disabilities provide necessary supports by applying inclusionary knowledge, skills, and attitudes—this does not require the person with a disability to change.

> Ironically, developing relationships, the opportunity to make contributions to your community, even fun itself is taken away from people with disabilities in the name of trying to get them to function better to pre-

sumably improve the quality of their lives. So I didn't get to go to regular school and then I missed the opportunity to make friends. Why? Because professionals were trying to improve my quality of life by putting me in a special school where I am supposed to learn to function better. So they take away the opportunity for me to have friends and subsequently they actually interfere with the quality of my life.

Norman Kunc (Giangreco, 1996b, p. 7)

COACH is based on the assumption that pursuit of valued life outcomes is based on an individually determined combination of 1) having students learn relevant skills and 2) providing students with necessary supports. This assumption establishes expectations that all students can learn. At the same time, it does not presume that people with disabilities need to become less disabled in order to be valued and have a good quality of life. By approaching our students as individuals with unique characteristics and focusing on their attributes rather than perceived deficits, we hope to advance valued life outcomes for students by facilitating their learning as well as our own.

COACH provides a method for exploring a student's current situation and the family's hopes for future directions related to valued life outcomes. The student, as part of the family, may be included in the process as determined by the family. Often factors such as the age of the child and the culture of the family influence these decisions.

COACH encourages families to clarify their vision for the student's current and future valued life outcomes. Having the family establish this individualized vision of what they value sets a meaningful context for educational planning. The following sections describe each of the five valued life outcomes included in COACH. Each family will attach a different meaning to each valued life outcome based on their own circumstances and beliefs. Although each child shares some characteristics with all other children and shares other characteristics with some other children, each child also has characteristics that are uniquely his or her own (Speight, Myers, Cox, & Highlen, 1991). Thus individualization is required to ensure that educational planning yields meaningful outcomes (Edelman, Knutson, Osborn, & Giangreco, 1995). These descriptions offer examples of how some families have interpreted the valued life outcomes and do *not* infer that a family using COACH must match any of the examples. It is also crucial to remember that valued life outcomes are pursued both by developing skills of the student and by providing supports from those who interact with the student.

Being Safe and Healthy

Personal safety and health are foundational outcomes. Like all valued life outcomes, safety and health can be enhanced by the supports we provide for people as well as skill development on the part of the person. The range of how families interpret this valued outcome is vast. One family may be concerned that their child needs to drink more liquids by mouth to avoid the need for tube feeding. Another is concerned about their inquisitive child being burned by a hot stove. A third may be concerned that their very friendly child will be a target of "stranger danger" or sexual abuse.

Frequently, safety and health issues overlap other valued life outcomes or are embedded within them. For example, learning pedestrian skills may address 1) *access* to new activities and places, 2) *safety* to avoid being hit by a car, and 3) expanded *choices.* Learning to respond to an emergency alarm improves *safety* and may increase a person's *access* to certain types of living arrangements. We can affect people's personal health and wellness through the foods they eat, the care we take to ensure that their specialized equipment is properly fitted, or the fitness activities we teach them.

Safety and health frequently must be balanced with choice and control. With new choices come new physical and emotional risks to safety, ranging from the pain of a broken leg to the pain of a broken heart. The balance between safety/health and choice/control should be determined individually by each family and should include the student. Our research on COACH indicates that this valued life outcome was situationally important to families (Giangreco, Edelman, et al., 1995). Although all families are generally concerned about their children's safety and health, typically these issues were major concerns only to families in situations in which the child had chronic health problems or there was an imminent safety threat (e.g., busy streets, gang violence).

Having a Home, Now and in the Future

"Home" means a place of belonging, security, safety, and privacy where you can feel free to be yourself. Like health and safety, our research on COACH indicates that having a home, now and in the future, was situationally important to families (Giangreco, Edelman, et al., 1995). This tended to be of concern in circumstances in which the family perceived an imminent need. One such situation occurs with older students for whom community living is an option. For example, Jaimie had a wonderful home growing up with her parents, brothers, and sisters, but both Jaimie and her parents hope that, as a young adult, she will be able to live in an apartment with a friend as a roommate. Jaimie's experiences living on her own can be enhanced by learning certain skills, such as responding to a smoke alarm, preparing her own food, and being able to make purchases. Because the valued life outcome of having your own home can also be realized through supports provided to people with disabilities, Jaimie's opportunity to live in her own apartment need not be predicated on her skill development. Supports (e.g., attendant care) can be provided so that living on her own or with a roommate becomes a reality regardless of her skill development. Families may pursue community living options for their children out of concern regarding who will advocate for their children after they are gone and out of fear that their children will be institutionalized.

In other cases in which an imminent need was perceived related to having a home, families questioned their capacity to cope with their child's behaviors or characteristics (e.g., lack of sleeping through the night, aggressive or destructive behaviors, high physical care needs). In these types of situations, the balance of having the student learn new skills and receive supports again can come in to play. For example, a teenager who routinely destroys parts of the family's home needs to learn new skills to address his needs more constructively; being able to raise this child at home may be facilitated by supports provided to the family (e.g., respite care, counseling). Another teenager who has severe physical disabilities, and who has grown to a mature adult size, may be able to live at home more easily and more enjoyably if she learns certain skills (e.g., assisting in personal care) or by receiving needed supports (e.g., adaptive equipment). These types of issues are critical for some families and not for others.

Having Meaningful Relationships

When we think about the most important things in life, relationships with other people are at or near the top of the list. We all need other people in our lives. The range of relationships most people have is quite diverse, including immediate or extended family relationships, friendships, relationships that revolve around specific interests (e.g., choir, softball team), and relationships with co-workers, acquaintances, and others. By developing various types of relationships with others, we seek to experience an important range of human emotions, such as love, kinship, and companionship. By interacting with others, we learn from them and also learn more about ourselves. People with disabilities deserve access to the same range of relationships available to people who do not have disabilities. This is most likely to occur when people with disabilities have opportunities to live, work, play, and go to school with people who do not have disabilities but also who are not restricted from interacting with others who have disabilities. Too many people with disabilities have not been given the opportunities to develop a full range and network of relationships, which sometimes puts undue pressure on the smaller existing network of family and friends. Being with other people in a variety of ways is, in part, the essence of the human experience, regardless of our varied characteristics.

Having Choice and Control that Match One's Age and Culture

Some people with disabilities have less personal choice and control than people without disabilities who are the same age. For example, it is not unusual to observe youngsters with severe physical or cognitive disabilities who have little or no control over important, or even mundane, aspects of their daily lives. Someone else may decide what they eat, what they wear, where they go, how long they stay, whom they will see, when they will get out of a wheelchair, what they will play with, where they will work, or whether they will work at all. Such lack of control may lead to passivity, whereby the person becomes resigned to his or her plight, lacking the will to challenge others' control over aspects of life that many people without disabilities take for granted. For others, lack of choice and appropriate control may result in challenging behaviors, such as aggression.

What is considered an appropriate level of choice and control varies in different cultures depending on factors such as age, sex, and religious beliefs. In some cultures giving children age-appropriate choice and control is considered highly desirable. In other cultures it is the parents who are expected to remain in control; child choice may be viewed in some cultures as disrespectful or rebellious (Dennis & Giangreco, 1996). A common theme that cuts across cultures is that children are given increasing choice and control, along with corresponding responsibilities, as they are prepared for adulthood. Because people with disabilities are sometimes viewed as "eternal children" (Wolfensberger, 1970), as they grow they sometimes are not afforded the same choices and control made available to their peers without disabilities. This perpetuates an unproductive cycle of limited expectations and opportunities for people with disabilities. Providing people with disabilities chronologically age-appropriate levels of choice and control is consistent with Donnellan's (1984) *criterion of the least dangerous assumption.* If we are not sure about the motivations or intentions of an individual, we are safer to err on the side of providing opportunities for choice and control rather than summarily denying those choices.

Participating in Meaningful Activities in Various Places

Having a variety of activities to do and places to do them is part of what separates a boring existence from an interesting life, even when the person's level of participation is partial (Ferguson & Baumgart, 1991). "Meaningful activities" refers to activities that are valued both by society and by the individual. An individual can demonstrate that he or she values an activity by showing a preference for or interest in the activity on an ongoing basis, highlighting the importance of actively teaching choice making. Activities may be intrinsically valued by the person, as in the fun of swimming, or may have some secondary value to the person, as in earning money in exchange for work. Parents of children with severe disabilities tell us their children's lives improved through their participation in meaningful activities in places frequented by people without disabilities (e.g., school, extracurricular activities, work, community recreation facilities, friends' homes) (Edelman et al., 1995; Giangreco, Cloninger, et al., 1991; Giangreco, Edelman, et al., 1995).

Principle 2: The Family Is the Cornerstone of Educational Planning

One aim of COACH is to assist families in becoming better consumers of education and related services, as well as partners in the educational process. We use the term *families* with the recognition that it means many different things, such as two-parent families, single-parent families, blended families with stepchildren, adoptive families, and multigenerational families. This emphasis on consumerism and partnership is based on the following five tenets.

Families Know Certain Aspects of Their Children Better than Anyone Else

Although school personnel get to know their students throughout a 6-hour school day, this is only a fraction of the students' entire day. The rest of the day, as well as weekends, holidays, and school vacations, presents a more complete picture of a student's life. As educators, we must remind ourselves that we spend only about half of the year with our students, seeing them less than a third of each of those days. Parents, siblings, and others are present for much of the students' nonschool time. Nonschool time provides key information that has educational implications, such as the nature of the student's interests, motivations, habits, fears, routines, pressures, needs, and health. By listening to families, educators can gain a more complete understanding of the students' lives outside school.

Families Have the Greatest Vested Interest in Seeing Their Children Learn

In our professional eagerness to help children learn, we sometimes convey a message to parents that teachers care more about their children than they do. Of course, this is rarely the case. It can be dangerous to make assumptions about a parent's intentions based on certain behaviors. One study of parents of children with multiple disabilities sheds light on why some mothers and fathers withdraw from the educational process (e.g., choose not to attend educational meetings). As one parent said, "It doesn't matter what I say because they [professionals] are going to do what they want anyway" (Giangreco, Cloninger, et al., 1991, p. 20). COACH addresses this problem by providing a forum and a process for families to share their ideas and encourages professionals to listen.

Families Should Be Approached in Culturally Sensitive Ways

Approaching families in culturally sensitive ways is becoming increasingly important as professionals work with more children and families who have varied cultural backgrounds (Harry, 1992; Lynch & Hanson, 1992):

> For me, this is the essence of culturally sensitive practice; not that professionals need to know particular details of all cultural groups; this being in fact impossible and tends to lead to stereotyping, but rather that they are open to different belief systems, and capable of listening in a nonjudgmental way to concerns that may surprise or even shock them. Next, they must be able to collaborate with families in such a way as to respect their cultural framework, while simultaneously honoring their own.
>
> Beth Harry (Dennis & Giangreco, 1996, pp. 110–111)

Based on feedback from special educators from various cultural groups, Dennis and Giangreco (1996) suggest the following principles and guidelines to facilitate family interviewing in culturally sensitive ways (e.g., COACH Part A, Step 1: Family Interview):

- Appreciate the uniqueness of each family.
- Be aware of the influence of your role as a professional.
- Acknowledge your own cultural biases.
- Seek new understandings and knowledge of cultures.
- Develop an awareness of cultural norms.
- Learn with families.
- Seek help from "cultural interpreters" before the interview.
- Ascertain literacy and language status of family members.

- Involve family members in planning interviews (e.g., time, place).
- Preview the interview with family members (e.g., Appendix A: Questions and Answers for Parents About COACH).
- Adapt the time frame to meet the needs of the family.
- Carefully examine the nature of the questions you ask.

The Family Is Likely to Be the Only Group of Adults Involved with a Child's Educational Program Throughout His or Her Entire School Career

Over the course of a school career, a student with special education needs will encounter so many professionals that it will be difficult for the family to remember all of their names. Some of these professionals will work with the child for a number of years, others for a year or less. Eventually, even the most caring and competent among them will depart because they are professionals who are paid to be part of the student's life (Falvey, Forest, Pearpoint, & Rosenberg, 1994). However, all of these professionals will bring with them unique skills and ideas that can have a positive effect on the child and family. Although such diversity of ideas and personal energy can be helpful and invigorating if it is well coordinated, the varying input of professionals could prove harmful if it is so territorial or chaotic that it does not contribute to developing a cohesive plan or direction. Professionals are encouraged to build on an ever-evolving, family-centered vision for the child, rather than reinventing a student's educational program each year as team membership changes. Throughout the student's school career, the family is most likely to be the only human constant. Powell and Gallagher (1993) remind us that, typically, brothers and sisters are the people with whom we have our longest relationships, longer than with our parents or friends. Therefore, when we think about the family, we need to consider the child, parents, siblings, and potentially others (e.g., grandparents, aunts and uncles) who are integral family members. COACH is designed to assist families in clarifying and articulating their own vision for themselves and their children.

Families Have the Ability to Positively Influence the Quality of Educational Services Provided in Their Community

Historically, families have been responsible for improving access to educational and community-based opportunities for their children with disabilities (Turnbull, Turnbull, Shank, & Leal, 1995). In the 1950s and 1960s, when schooling was unavailable to many children with disabilities, parents created schools. Families were a driving force behind the passage of the Education for All Handicapped Children Act of 1975 (PL 94-142), which mandated free, appropriate public education for all children. Families were influential in the reauthorization of PL 94-142 as the Individuals with Disabilities Education Act of 1990 (IDEA, PL 101-476). They continued to advocate for the reauthorization of IDEA in 1997. Active groups that include many families (e.g., The Arc, SAFE—Schools Are For Everyone), as well as individual families (e.g., *Sacramento City Unified School District v. Rachel H.*, 1994; *Oberti v. Board of Education of the Borough of Clementon School District*, 1993), continue to be influential in improving education for students with disabilities. Undoubtedly, families will continue to play a vital role in improving educational services for all children.

Families Must Live with the Outcomes of Decisions Made by Educational Teams, All Day, Every Day

People should be involved in making decisions that will affect their lives. When families do not do what professionals have prescribed, this may be an indication that the family was inadequately involved in the decision-making process. As professionals, when we make decisions we must constantly remind ourselves that they are likely to affect other people besides the child and to have an effect outside the school. COACH encourages families to be part of the process of deciding what their children's educational program will look like because they know what the child and family need, what is most important to them, and what they can handle. In our experience, when given the opportunity to participate in educational planning using COACH, families are invaluable in determining appropriate educational experiences and do an excellent job of pinpointing priorities.

Principle 3: Collaborative Teamwork Is Essential to Quality Education

COACH is predicated on family members and school professionals working together as a team (Thousand & Villa, 1992). Teams typically include the student, parents, classroom teacher and assistant(s), special educators, related services providers, and others (e.g., principal, bus driver) as needed. The nature of each member's participation should be individually determined. Teamwork requires two or more members, distribution of labor agreed to by the team, sharing of resources, effective communication, ongoing interactions, and consensus decision making. Ironically, you can have all these important teamwork characteristics and still not have a team. If these aspects of teamwork are to be effective, they must be applied within "an ever-evolving *shared framework*, which consists of a set of beliefs, values, or assumptions about education, children, families, and professionals to which team members agree" (Giangreco, 1996c, p. 4). In addition, teamwork needs to be applied to a set of *shared student goals* agreed to by the team. By establishing common student goals, teams can avoid the problem of each member having her or his own separate goals. When team members establish common student goals, they pull in the same direction for the student, rather than pulling in different directions.

Teams should include "those who will be most directly affected," rather than "everyone who might be affected." Sometimes teams become so large that planning and decision making are unnecessarily complicated. Teams can reduce the number of people involved in regular team meetings by designating a *core team* consisting of people who have the most ongoing involvement with the student, an *extended team* that includes the core team plus those members who have less frequent involvement with the student, and *situational teams* consisting of individually determined combinations of team members to address specific issues or concerns. In other words, everyone does not need to be involved in everything. By clarifying who are core members, extended members, or situational resources to the team, everyone's time is used more efficiently.

Principle 4: Coordination Among Support Service Providers Is Essential to Appropriate Education

One of the most common questions asked about COACH planning is, "Where are the therapy goals?" The short answer is, "There aren't any therapy goals in COACH." That does not mean that some students do not need support services or that support services are unimportant. On the contrary, some students can access and participate in their educational program only if they are given appropriate supports. So for some children, services such as occupational therapy, physical therapy, and speech-language pathology are essential.

Within COACH, the role of specialized supportive services is designed to match the definition of "related services" provided in the Individuals with Disabilities Education Act Amendments (1997), which states that related services should be provided "as may be required to assist a child with a disability to benefit from special education" (20 U.S.C. §§ 1400[Sec. 602][20]). Related services are provided as a support to a student's educational program if they are needed educationally, not as a parallel service. All too often, each professional establishes his or her own set of goals based on the orientation of his or her discipline, leading teams down a path likely to be educationally fragmented and disjointed (Giangreco, Edelman, & Dennis, 1991). To provide effective education, supportive services need to be coordinated in ways that account for the interrelationships that exist among the disciplines so as to avoid unnecessary and undesirable service gaps, overlaps, and contradictions (Giangreco, 1996c).

One way COACH addresses these issues is to encourage the development of shared educational goals that are discipline free. Discipline-free goals are family-selected learning outcomes free of the orientations of the various professional disciplines (e.g., physical therapy, occupational therapy, speech-language pathology). Discipline-free goals typically do not use professional jargon, whereas goals that are not discipline free often do use discipline-specific jargon. For example, the goal

Maria will point to pictures on her communication board to make requests for preferred people, toys, and food, and getting out of her wheelchair at school and at home.

is discipline free when we know that it was selected as a priority learning outcome during the Family Interview in COACH. This goal includes a functional, observable behavior as well as a context in which the behavior will occur.

The following examples of IEP goals are *discipline specific,* not *discipline free* (Giangreco, Dennis, et al., 1994):

The student will improve postural stability and increase antigravity of head, trunk, and extremities.

The student will initiate correction to midline when displaced laterally while prone or sitting astride a horse or bolster.

These examples 1) are stated as nonfunctional subskills, 2) were selected by specialists based on the orientation of their discipline, 3) are jargon filled, and 4) do not include a context for use.

Once a student's educational program has been determined (i.e., discipline-free annual goals, additional learning outcomes from an educational perspective, general supports), it then becomes appropriate for team members to ask, "In what ways are related services required to assist the student in accessing or participating in his or her educational program?" Making decisions about which related services are needed, what functions they need to serve, how they should be provided (e.g., indirectly), how frequently they are needed, and a variety of other issues is beyond the scope of COACH but is addressed in a companion manual called *Vermont Interdependent Services Team Approach (VISTA): A Guide to Coordinating Educational Support Services* (Giangreco, 1996c). Additional resources on the use of support services in inclusive classrooms are also available (e.g., Dunn, 1991; England, 1994; McEwen, 1995; Orelove & Sobsey, 1996;

Rainforth & York-Barr, 1997; York, Giangreco, Vandercook, & Macdonald, 1992).

Principle 5:   Using Problem-Solving Methods Improves the Effectiveness of Educational Planning

Developing a relevant educational program for a student with disabilities can be a challenge or, in another sense, a problem to be solved. Professionals with good intentions often seek input from families but fail to provide families with methods to help them make important decisions. Use of open-ended questions such as, "What would you like to see on Anthony's IEP this year?" or "What are your priorities for Kendra?" can work for some families. However, all too often this open-ended approach results in parents deferring to professionals or making selections that do not necessarily represent their top priorities. This may occur because families are faced with trying to prioritize hundreds of options without any strategies to help them organize and sort this vast array of possibilities. Using problem-solving methods cannot guarantee positive results, but it will improve the odds.

One unique feature of COACH is its use of the Osborn-Parnes Creative Problem-Solving (CPS) process (Osborn, 1953; Parnes, 1988, 1992). Aspects of CPS are embedded in COACH to help families select the most important learning outcomes to be included on their children's IEPs. Once a person or group has identified the general problem (e.g., planning an appropriate educational program for Robert), they can use the remaining steps of CPS. These include

- Fact Finding (gathering information)
- Problem Finding (clarifying the problem)
- Idea Finding (brainstorming a quantity of ideas in an atmosphere of deferred judgment, using idea joggers)
- Solution Finding (selecting the best ideas based on criteria)
- Acceptance Finding (making a plan, refining it, and taking action)

Although COACH does not employ a classic application of the CPS process, it retains many of the key features (e.g., certain types of fact finding, selecting solutions based on criteria). The following sections describe how key concepts of the Osborn-Parnes Creative Problem-Solving process are embedded in COACH.

Deferring Judgment

The steps of COACH establish a pattern in which at certain times participants defer judgment and at other times they actively make judgments. This creates opportunities for team members to share information in an atmosphere of trust, without fear of being criticized or interrupted. Furthermore, it allows for consideration of ideas that might be lost if judged and discarded prematurely.

Alternating Between Divergent and Convergent Steps

An overarching characteristic of CPS is the alternating use of divergent and convergent thinking phases. The *divergent* aspects encourage the problem solver to explore information and ideas broadly by extending in different directions from a common point (the problem to be solved). *Convergent* aspects encourage analysis of the divergent data to make decisions and select solutions. COACH alternates between divergent and convergent thinking within each of its steps and substeps. Part A, Step 1 (Family Interview) begins divergently by setting a context and considering many possibilities. The Family Interview culminates with the selection of the top priorities for inclusion on the IEP. Step 2 (Additional Learning Outcomes) includes divergent steps to consider a wide variety of learning outcomes and culminates with the selection of learning outcomes in addition to those identified as priorities. Step 3 (General Supports) begins by considering a wide array of supports in various categories and culminates in the selection of those that are individually appropriate for the student. Divergent and convergent components are present in other steps of Part A (e.g., Step 4: Annual Goals, Step 6: Short-Term Objectives). Part B of COACH (Strategies and Processes to Implement a COACH-Generated Educational Program) also employs CPS divergent/convergent approaches to assist with organizing and informing the instructional planning team (Step 7), scheduling (Step 8), planning and adapting instruction (Step 9), and evaluating educational impact (Step 10).

Multiple Opportunities and Various Perspectives

COACH helps families select priorities by providing opportunities for parents and other team members to consider the large number of curricular possibilities from various perspectives, in increasingly smaller and different sets, multiple times, prior to final selection. In traditional approaches, such as asking, "What would you like to see on Miguel's IEP this year?", parents have a single chance to respond. Through COACH, by the time a learning outcome has been selected as a priority for the IEP (Part A, Step 1.5), it has been considered by the family from six to nine different times, in different sets of items. This increases the likelihood that families will select learning outcomes that truly are priorities for their children. Similarly, in the rest of Part A, and in Part B, multiple opportunities are offered for team members, including the family, to consider many options before making final selections.

Principle 6: Special Education Is a Service, Not a Place

All over the United States, and around the world, the underlying principles of inclusive education and the practical applications of it have become increasingly available to students with disabilities and the teams who educate them (Downing, 1996; Stainback & Stainback, 1996; Thousand, Villa, & Nevin, 1994; Villa & Thousand, 1996). The Individuals with Disabilities Education Act Amendments (1997) states that "The term 'special education' means specially designed instruction" (20 U.S.C. §§ 1400[Sec. 602][23]). The law also requires each state to establish procedural safeguards

> *to assure that, to the maximum extent appropriate, children with disabilities, including children in public or private institutions or other care facilities, are educated with children who are not disabled, and that special classes, separate schooling, or other removal of children with disabilities from regular education environments occurs only when the nature or severity of the disability is such that education in regular classes with the use of supplementary aids and services cannot be achieved satisfactorily.* (20 U.S.C. §§ 1400[Sec. 612][14])

We interpret this to mean that *special education is a service, not a place,* and that schools have a legal and educational responsibility to make a concerted effort to teach all children within general education, with necessary supplemental supports and services, before considering more restrictive options (Laski, 1991; Lipsky & Gartner, 1989; National Center for Inclusive Education and School Restructuring, 1995; Taylor, 1988).

- *The law does not say* children should be removed from regular class if they function at different levels than their classmates.
- *The law does not say* children should be removed from regular class if they have different learning outcomes from their classmates.
- *The law does not say* children should be removed from regular class if they require supports or accommodations.
- *The law does not say* children should be removed from regular class if they have a particular label (e.g., mental retardation, autism) at a certain level (e.g., severe).
- *The law does not say* children should be removed from regular class if the adults in the school are unaccustomed to the characteristics presented by the child.

In some schools, students with disabilities are never allowed initial access to general education classes because those making the decisions do so based on presumption rather than actual experiences with the child. How can we know whether a student will be successful in a general education class, given supports, if we have never provided him or her with that opportunity? What if a student has difficulties in general education class? Our first responsibility is to provide the needed supports, not automatically remove the student. As Norman Kunc (1996) reminds us, pursuing inclusive education is not just the right thing to do—people without disabilities need the perspective and diversity that people with disabilities have to offer.

We have moved beyond knowing whether inclusive education is viable; it has been demonstrated to be so in increasing numbers of schools over many years. Providing special education in general education environments will require a shift in how we think about educating diverse groups of students and how teachers operate. Special educators will no longer group students with special needs together in isolated areas for instruction. General educators will no longer automatically refer students with differing needs out of their classrooms to receive support. We will know inclusive education has truly arrived when students need not carry a label such as "disability" to receive the individualization they need to be educated. Rather, general educators, special educators, related services personnel, administrators, parents, students, and community members will work collaboratively to modify and adapt general education curricula, activities, and materials to meet the needs of diverse groups of students. When necessary, teams will identify supplemental curricula and develop ways of infusing it into general education class activities. COACH is a tool to help you navigate along this exciting road. Ultimately, this job will be easier and will be approached by all of us with greater enthusiasm and maybe even a greater sense of urgency when we truly value people with disabilities, consider them as equals to people without disabilities, and see their disabilities as diverse characteristics from which to gain new perspectives.

Section II

ANSWERING COMMON QUESTIONS ABOUT COACH

HOW DOES COACH FIT INTO IEP DEVELOPMENT?

COACH is meant to be used as *one part of an overall approach to planning* an appropriate education for a student with disabilities. Therefore, it is appropriately considered an IEP planning tool and has proven to be a useful component of transition planning (e.g., preschool to kindergarten; grade to grade; school to postschool). The information generated using COACH *is designed to develop an appropriate, individualized education program.* COACH is

- **Not designed to** determine eligibility for special education
- **Not designed to** provide a comprehensive assessment profile
- **Not designed to** assign grade or developmental levels
- **Not designed to** be used to the exclusion of other planning tools
- **Not designed to** justify segregation of students with disabilities

COACH is meant to assist in educational planning by

- Identifying family-centered priorities
- Identifying additional learning outcomes (e.g., general education)
- Identifying general supports to be provided to or for the student
- Identifying priorities into IEP goals and objectives
- Summarizing the educational program as a Program-at-a-Glance
- Organizing the planning team to implement the program
- Scheduling participation in general education classes/activities
- Planning and adapting lesson plans to facilitate learning
- Evaluating the impact of educational experiences

Typically, COACH is used to assist in the identification of IEP goals and objectives and to provide some information to document a student's present level of functioning in reference to selected goals and objectives. A companion process, VISTA (Vermont Interdependent Services Team Approach) (Giangreco, 1996c), is designed to be used by teams in IEP preparation to determine educationally relevant support services that are necessary to implement the educational program components identified using COACH.

The planning activities conducted using COACH and VISTA are then documented in the IEP. Figure 2 lists a sequence of major events that depict where and when COACH fits into IEP development. Although these events are presented sequentially, varying amounts of overlap are to be expected.

1. **Eligibility** for special education is determined.
2. A Student Planning **Team is formed.**
3. An **overall plan** to learn about the student's strengths, interests, and needs is developed. The team generates *descriptive information* about the student, *not separate goals from each discipline.*
4. **Educational program components** (priority learning outcomes/annual goals, additional learning outcomes, general supports) are determined using most of **Part A of COACH.**
5. The student's **educational placement** is determined. This should be the least restrictive option where the student can pursue his or her individually determined educational program. First consideration should always be given to the educational placement options the student would have if he or she did not have a disability label (e.g., general education class in neighborhood school), given supplemental supports and services.
6. **Related services** are determined that are necessary to support the student's educational program in the identified educational placement. The educational program (e.g., IEP goals) and the placement must be known prior to making informed related services decisions. Tools such as VISTA (Giangreco, 1996c) are designed to assist the team in making these decisions.
7. **Short-term objectives** are developed by subteams determined through related services decision making.
8. Information generated using COACH and other sources (e.g., speech-language evaluation; VISTA) is transferred to the **official IEP document.** Quality IEP planning is a process rather than a single event.
9. At this point the team knows what is to be learned, the student's placement, and who will be involved in supporting the program and how. It is now time to use **COACH Part B for more refined and ongoing planning.**

Figure 2.   Sequence of events for IEP development using COACH.

FOR WHOM SHOULD COACH BE USED?

COACH is designed for use with students ages 3–21 who are attending school and are identified as having moderate, severe, or profound disabilities. With modifications, components of COACH may be used with students who are older or who have mild disabilities. COACH does not attempt to duplicate general education curricular areas appropriate for students with mild disabilities who may be pursuing much or all of the general education curriculum. Use of COACH with children younger than 3 years old may be premature (Giangreco, Whiteford, Whiteford, & Doyle, 1997). Some people have successfully used COACH for older individuals or those with mild disabilities by substituting other curriculum listings of learning outcomes while retaining the COACH process steps.

HOW LONG DOES IT TAKE TO COMPLETE COACH?

Because COACH is a flexible tool, completion time varies widely. The *Family Interview (Step 1) can be completed in approximately 1 hour.* Completion time varies based on factors such as 1) the familiarity, experience, and skillfulness of the facilitator; 2) the number of family members involved in the interview (it typically takes slightly longer with two parents than one); and 3) the number of curriculum areas selected by the family for full review during the Family Interview (Step 1.2). It almost always takes longer for facilitators who are new to using COACH. In any case, if the Family Interview goes much beyond an hour and a half, it is likely there is some kind of facilitation problem. Table 1 presents an approximate breakdown of the time it takes to complete the various steps and substeps of Part A. The time it takes to complete Part B activities is more variable, in part because the activities in Part B are ongoing.

WHO CAN FACILITATE COACH?

COACH can be facilitated by any team member familiar with the process (e.g., special educator, general educator, school psychologist, guidance counselor, speech-language pathologist, family support professional). The team should agree on who will assume responsibility for facilitating the various parts of COACH. COACH can be facilitated by a person familiar with the student and family (to enhance individualization of the tool) or by a neutral party who is naive to the dynamics of the situation and therefore can minimize the potential for bias during question asking. Either approach can be effective; it depends on team choice and dynamics. A person familiar with the family and student must guard against asking questions to elicit parent responses that reflect the interviewer's opinions. A person unfamiliar with the family must be able to adapt questioning style, vocabulary, pacing, and so forth. As the authors of COACH, we have successfully facilitated COACH under both circumstances and have found that familiarity and skillfulness with COACH are essential to using the process effectively.

Table 1.   Time required to complete Part A of COACH

Step	Time range (minutes)
Step 1: Family Interview	**60–90**
Introducing COACH to Participants	5–10
Step 1.1: Valued Life Outcomes	10–15
Step 1.2: Selection of Curriculum Areas to Be Explored	5–10
Step 1.3: Learning Outcomes Lists	15–25
Step 1.4: Prioritization	12–15
Step 1.5: Cross-Prioritization	13–15
Step 2: Additional Learning Outcomes	**30–60**
Step 2.1: Additional Learning Outcomes from COACH	10–20
Step 2.2: Additional Learning Outcomes from General Education	20–40
Step 3: General Supports	**10–15**
Step 4: Annual Goals	**Time varies widely**
Step 5: Program-at-a-Glance	**10–15**
Step 6: Short-Term Objectives	**Time varies widely**

WHO PARTICIPATES IN COACH?

Different team members participate in different steps of COACH. Because each situation is unique, rather than providing definitive rules on who participates in the various steps of COACH, the team must understand the purpose and outcome of each step in COACH and make an individual determination about who needs to be involved in the various steps. The entire team should be aware of the plan so they can have opportunities to be involved when it is appropriate.

There is one notable exception to this individualization of participants: The Family Interview must include the family! Occasionally we are asked if the professionals can complete the Family Interview themselves. Our answer is "No." Without the family you cannot have a family interview. Professionals who are unable to get parent involvement in COACH might be able to use some concepts and ideas from COACH, but without family involvement it simply is not COACH. Readers should be aware that we are using the terms *family* and *parents* broadly to refer to the adults who live with and care for the child.

Although the full team should be aware of the Family Interview processes and outcomes, the interview itself is designed to be a more intimate activity, involving the facilitator, the special educator, the classroom teacher, and the parent(s). The family should make an individual determination about the presence and participation of the student during the Family Interview. When students participate in COACH, particularly young adults (ages 17–21), it is important to clarify who holds the decision-making authority for selecting the priorities, the student or the parents. A COACH Family Interview would not be the first time a parent and his or her teenager/young adult disagreed about the best course of action. As a rule of thumb, we suggest that students with disabilities be extended the same rights and responsibilities offered to their peers without disabilities. Typically this means that students assume increasing control as they get older. By the time students are 17 or 18 years old, the same age when their peers would be graduating from high school, they should be given as much control of priority selection as is possible and culturally acceptable to their family—such decisions will necessarily be individual ones.

It is often helpful for the general education teacher and a small group of core team members who are new to the student to observe the Family Interview because it provides a rich opportunity for team members to hear the perspectives of the family in ways that are difficult to capture on paper. Increasing the number of people at the Family Interview should be discussed with the family to ensure that they are comfortable with the situation and not overwhelmed or intimidated.

Steps 2 (Additional Learning Outcomes), 3 (General Supports), and 4 (Annual Goals) can be completed by a designated subgroup of team members (e.g., the group participating in the Family Interview). Although these steps do not require the presence of all team members at the same time, they *do* require people with knowledge of the student and knowledge of the school curriculum in various subject areas. For example, at the elementary school level the additional learning outcomes could be completed by the special educator, general educator, and parent. At the middle school and high school levels, where there are many teachers, a group meeting or a series of mini-meetings between the special educator and general educator can be scheduled. Selection of general supports may benefit from the presence of related services staff. Regardless of who the team designates to complete the various steps of COACH, the facilitator is responsible for sharing the information and decisions generated through the use of COACH with all team members for their feedback. Although this may be done by face-to-face meetings (large or small groups), it can also be accomplished through phone or correspondence (mail, fax, e-mail).

The Program-at-a-Glance (Step 5) can be prepared by an individual and therefore does not require the team to meet. Short-term objectives (Step 6) can be completed by designated subteams determined after making related services decisions. For example, when considering the priority learning outcome, "Makes choices using eye gaze when presented with two options," the team agreed that this goal required support from the occupational therapist and speech-language pathologist. Therefore, these staff members would join with the core team members to formulate the short-term objectives. Different configurations of team members would be used to develop short-term objectives for other annual goals.

When using Part B (Strategies and Processes to Implement a COACH-Generated Educational Program), it is desirable to have a full team meeting to initially use Step 7 (Organizing and Informing the Instructional Planning Team). Part of the task of the team would be to decide what subgroups of team members need to be involved in the ongoing use of Steps 8 (scheduling), 9 (lesson planning), and 10 (evaluation).

WHERE AND WHEN SHOULD COACH BE COMPLETED?

The place and time to complete the various steps of COACH should be individually negotiated with the family to maximize their opportunity for participation. Therefore, COACH steps can be completed at any convenient time and mutually agreed-upon location. When conducting the Family Interview, the two most common locations are the family's home and the school. School personnel should be open to other locations that match a family's preference (e.g., a community center).

WHEN DURING THE SCHOOL YEAR SHOULD COACH BE COMPLETED?

COACH is intended to be used to develop a student's IEP; therefore, it should be initiated prior to the IEP meeting date. COACH has been used successfully during the intake process for new students regardless of the time of year. For those students already in the school system, a number of schools have found it beneficial to complete Part A (Determining a Student's Educational Program) in the spring in preparation for the coming school year. Part B (Strategies and Processes to Implement a COACH-Generated Educational Program) can then be used in the fall and throughout the school year. However, COACH can be used with any IEP development process a school may use.

Teams should estimate the amount of time it will take them to complete Part A of COACH and begin scheduling times to complete the steps so they are finished by the scheduled IEP meeting date. For example, the team might initiate COACH activities 2 or 3 weeks prior to the scheduled IEP meeting date. IEPs developed using COACH usually result in a brief IEP meeting because team members have been involved in preparatory activities and are familiar with the components to be included in the IEP. In such cases the IEP meeting is used to review and summarize the components of the educational program that have been generated using Part A of COACH.

SHOULD COACH BE COMPLETED EVERY YEAR?

How frequently a team uses COACH varies, but here are some general guidelines for its use. The first time a team uses COACH to plan an IEP or transition for a student, we suggest you complete all of Parts A and B. The next time Part A (Determining a Student's Educational Program) is used for that same student (e.g., the following year), the team decides if Part A needs to be 1) done again in its entirety, 2) done again partially or in a modified format, or 3) verified but not done again at that time. These choices depend on the extent of change that has occurred or is expected in the student's circumstances or level of functioning that would likely result in changes in valued life outcomes, priority learning outcomes, additional learning outcomes, and general supports.

If significant change has occurred, the team might decide to use all of Part A again. In some cases, it is unnecessary to repeat every aspect of Part A each year because certain aspects, such as the valued life outcomes and general supports, may not have changed significantly. In these cases the team may decide to simply verify last year's valued life outcomes and general supports, noting minor adjustments, and then complete Steps 1.2–1.5, 2.1, and 2.2 in their entirety to determine updated priorities and additional learning outcomes, respectively. Updated information can be used to update IEP goals and objectives (Steps 4 and 6) and can then be summarized on the Program-at-a-Glance (Step 5).

In any case, new team members should become oriented to the team's use of COACH, and the team should make an individualized decision about the subsequent use of Part A after its initial use. This subsequent use should remain consistent with the principles forming the basis of COACH (see Section I). We recommend that teams complete Part A of COACH for their students at least once every 3 years or to coincide with significant transitions, such as from preschool to kindergarten or from middle school to high school.

Part B of COACH (Strategies for Processes to Implement a COACH-Generated Educational Program) includes a series of steps that are more likely to be repeated on an ongoing basis regardless of whether Part A has been completely or partially done again. Organizing and informing the team (Step 7), scheduling (Step 8), planning and adapting instruction (Step 9), and evaluating the impact of educational experiences (Step 10) rely on the information generated in Part A but should be completed each year and on an ongoing basis to ensure an appropriate and quality educational program.

Section III

DESCRIPTION AND DIRECTIONS

COACH is a planning tool designed to identify the contents of an individualized education program (Part A) and strategies for implementing such a program in general education settings and activities (Part B). The purpose of this section is to 1) describe the purpose and rationale for each part and step of COACH and 2) provide directions for each step.

Reminder!

COACH is a flexible tool. It is specifically intended to help teams develop and implement individualized education programs in general education and other integrated settings. Your team is encouraged to modify COACH to match the unique circumstances of your situation. However, you are cautioned that favorable results are more likely to occur when modifications you make to the process are consistent with the principles on which COACH is based. See Giangreco (1996a) for examples of adaptations that are incongruent with the underlying principles of COACH.

Throughout this section of the manual we have provided extended *descriptions* about each step of COACH, followed by *directions* stated as briefly and explicitly as possible. For each step of COACH, the directions include four distinct types of information; each is accompanied by a symbol throughout the text:

 Purpose

 Materials

 Instructions

 Helpful Hints

The directions for completing COACH are illustrated using the example of Joshua Green. Two additional examples, one for a kindergarten student with multiple disabilities and the other for a high school student with moderate disabilities, appear in Appendices C and D, respectively.

**DESCRIPTION OF
JOSHUA GREEN**

Joshua is an 8-year-old boy who lives with his father, step-mother, and younger sister. He loves being with other people, especially children. He shows his enthusiasm for interactions through his expressive facial and eye movements. He likes eating pizza, spaghetti, fruit, and frozen yogurt. Most of his foods need to be cut into small pieces and fed to him. It is unclear exactly how much Josh understands because he currently does not have a formalized communication system; his family feels strongly that he understands more than he is currently able to communicate. He communicates primarily through facial expressions, vocalizing, crying, and laughing. His team is exploring additional communication alternatives for him.

Josh moves from place to place by having others push him in his wheelchair. He likes being in places where there is a lot of activity. Josh has limited use of his arms and needs at least partial assistance with most activities of daily living. He enjoys music, looking at books, roughhousing, going outside, and his pet dog, Buster. He is an avid football fan, especially of the Buffalo Bills. Josh attends a Grade 3 class in his neighborhood school. He rides to school on the bus with his sister and the other children in his neighborhood. Josh's individualized education program is supported by a special educator, classroom assistant, physical therapist, occupational therapist, and speech-language pathologist.

Part A

DETERMINING A STUDENT'S EDUCATIONAL PROGRAM

DESCRIPTION

Part A, Determining a Student's Educational Program, consists of six steps designed to assist teams in determining the content of a student's educational program—the "what" (rather than the how) of the educational program. Determining the educational program is vital in providing a quality education because a team must know where they are headed if they have any hope of getting there. Too often students' educational programs are devoid of direction and substance that lead the students toward valued life outcomes. The steps in Part A are designed to help teams clarify their vision for the student and document it in explicit terms. A listing and diagram of the Parts of COACH are provided in Figures 3 and 4, respectively, and in the blank COACH forms (Appendix B) as well.

Part A: Determining a Student's Educational Program

Preparation Checklist

Step 1:   Family Interview

   Purpose: to determine family-selected learning priorities for the student through a series of questions asked by an interviewer

Step 2:   Additional Learning Outcomes

   Purpose: to determine learning outcomes beyond family priorities

Step 3:   General Supports

   Purpose: to determine what supports need to be provided *to or for* the student

Step 4:   Annual Goals

   Purpose: to ensure the family's priorities are reflected as IEP goals

Step 5:   Program-at-a-Glance

   Purpose: to provide a concise summary of the educational program

****

Determine Least Restrictive Educational Placement and Related Services

****

Step 6:   Short-Term Objectives

   Purpose: to develop short-term objectives to achieve annual goals

****

Finalize IEP Document

****

Part B: Strategies and Processes to Implement a COACH-Generated Educational Program

Step 7:   Organizing and Informing the Instructional Planning Team

   Purpose: to organize team functioning and ensure IEP implementation

Step 8:   Scheduling for the Student with Disabilities in the Classroom

   Purpose: to develop a schedule of activities that meets student needs

Step 9:   Planning and Adapting Instruction

   Purpose: to develop and implement instructional plans that address student needs and participation in class activities even when IEP goals differ from those of classmates'

Step 10:   Evaluating the Impact of Educational Experiences

   Purpose: to evaluate educational plans to determine their impact on learning outcomes and valued life outcomes

Figure 3.   The parts and steps of COACH.

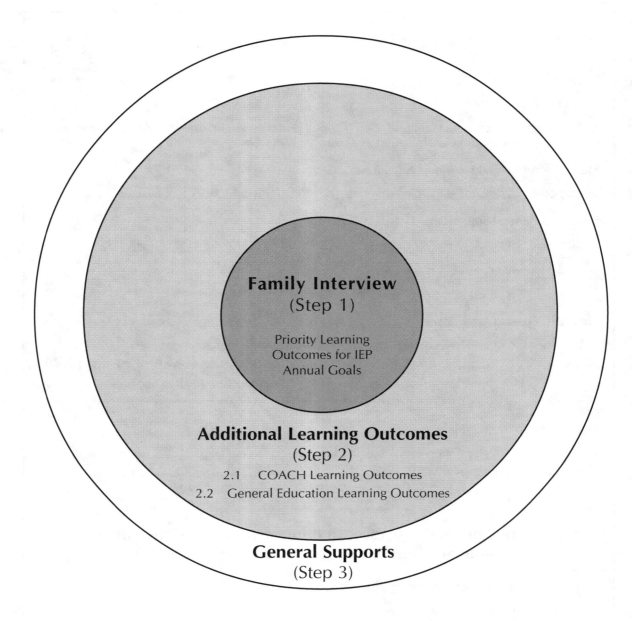

2.1 COACH Learning Outcomes

Communication	Home
Socialization	School
Personal Management	Community
Leisure/Recreation	Vocational
Selected Academics	Other

2.2 General Education Learning Outcomes

Reading/Language Arts	Foreign Language
Math/Science	Community Service
History/Social Studies	Home Economics
Arts/Music	Industrial Arts
Technology/Computer	Vocational
Physical/Health Education	Reasoning/Problem Solving

Figure 4.   COACH Part A: Determining a Student's Educational Program.

DIRECTIONS

PART A: DETERMINING A STUDENT'S EDUCATIONAL PROGRAM

! Purpose

Part A is designed to assist the team in identifying the content of the student's educational program, including the following components:

1. Priority learning outcomes (Step 1: Family Interview)
2. A broader set of learning outcomes beyond the top priorities (Step 2: Additional Learning Outcomes)
3. Supports that need to be provided to or for the student (Step 3: General Supports)
4. Ways to restate priorities as IEP goals (Step 4: Annual Goals)
5. A brief summary of the educational program (Step 5: Program-at-a-Glance)
6. Ways to develop short-term objectives for each annual goal (Step 6: Short-Term Objectives)

 **Materials**

- COACH manual
- Photocopy of Appendix A (Questions and Answers for Parents About COACH)
- Photocopy of Appendix B (Blank COACH Forms)
- Pencil and eraser

 **Instructions**

1. Identify a student for whom COACH is an appropriate educational planning tool.
2. Make sure all team members are sufficiently oriented to COACH (e.g., read manual, observe competent model of COACH, attend training).
3. Make a team decision about whether to use COACH for this student.

4. Decide how COACH fits into broader planning efforts for the student (e.g., IEP planning, transition planning).
5. Complete preparatory steps.
6. At one or more meetings complete:
Step 1 (Family Interview)
Step 2 (Additional Learning Outcomes)
Step 3 (General Supports)
7. Complete Step 4 (Annual Goals).
8. Complete Step 5 (Program-at-a-Glance).
9. Make placement and related services decisions.
10. Complete Step 6 (Short-Term Objectives).

Specific directions for each step are presented in upcoming sections.

 **Helpful Hints**

1. *Nothing can replace preparation* and practice. Taking the time to learn about COACH is a crucial first step. Practicing and getting feedback to refine your skills is invaluable.
2. Consider COACH one educational planning tool among a number of possibilities. Have other tools or approaches at your disposal so you can choose the one that best suits each situation.
3. It is crucial to complete all six steps in COACH (Part A). Stopping after the Family Interview results in an incomplete educational program.
4. Remember that Part A exclusively addresses *what* will be taught, not where or how.
5. Each family is unique. As your team considers the use of COACH, be sure to individualize its use to account for the cultural practices of each family.
6. Remember that first-time facilitators of COACH often exceed time estimates for completing COACH. Keep the time and the purpose in mind to help you stay on course. If participants start discussing the "wheres" and "hows" of the student's program, remind them that the purpose of COACH Part A is to deal with the "whats," which must be determined first.
7. Remember that completing COACH Part A is a beginning rather than an ending. Completing COACH should not culminate in the completed forms being filed away. On the contrary, completion of Part A should a) lead to transferring information from COACH onto appropriate places on the IEP or Transition Plan, b) assist in determining related services, c) lead to the sharing of the Program-at-a-Glance with all team members, and d) set the stage for ongoing educational planning and learning.

8. The activities in Part A may be completed in a variety of ways, such as in one meeting or in two or three shorter meetings. The activities may be completed by the entire team (especially if it is a small group) or by designated subteams.

PREPARATION
CHECKLIST

DESCRIPTION

The Preparation Checklist is a series of 10 preparatory steps designed to facilitate a productive use of COACH and to ensure accountability for completion. The checklist includes some logistical steps pertaining to the Family Interview (e.g., arranging time and place, preparing forms) as well as knowledge and awareness that will facilitate use of all parts of COACH. Our research on COACH indicates that some people attempt to use COACH without understanding its underlying principles or directions (Giangreco, Edelman, et al., 1995). Not surprisingly, this is likely to result in less favorable outcomes. Understanding its underlying principles is essential because, although COACH includes explicit directions for use, it is purposely not a standardized process. COACH is enhanced by skillful individualization of the process. This requires a foundational understanding of its underlying principles to ensure that modifications are consistent with, and not contradictory to, those guiding principles (Giangreco, 1996a). Consumers are encouraged to share Appendix A (Questions and Answers for Parents About COACH), as well as the entire COACH manual, with all team members to help familiarize them with COACH.

DIRECTIONS

PREPARATION CHECKLIST

! Purpose

The Preparation Checklist is designed to enhance the likelihood that your team will get the most out of using COACH by emphasizing a series of foundational ideas and tasks. By being informed and prepared, you can focus on assisting the family and other team members to participate in COACH. The following activities are designed to be completed in the days or weeks prior to initiating the Family Interview and other parts of COACH.

📖 Instructions

Follow the 10 steps on the Preparation Checklist (see Joshua's Preparation Checklist on p. 55).

★ Helpful Hints

1. If the family's primary language is other than English, plan ahead for translation or interpreter services.
2. In situations in which family members have difficulty reading, some of the background information from COACH (e.g., Appendix A: Questions and Answers for Parents About COACH) can be audiotaped in the family's native language, or you may wish to schedule a telephone conversation or meeting to discuss possible participation in COACH.
3. Remember, the whole team does not need to be present during the Family Interview. Typically, the number of people at the Family Interview ranges from two to four; often one or two family members and one or two professionals (e.g., special educator, regular class teacher, related services provider) are present.
4. Agreeing to participate in COACH means that individual professionals will *not* retain separate goals but rather will work together as a team to identify quality educational program components that are designed to improve the student's individually selected valued life outcomes.

Preparation Checklist

The following are important steps to take in preparation for using COACH. In the first column write the initials of the person responsible to ensure completion, and in the second column list the date completed.

	Who?	Date
1. Ensure all team members are sufficiently oriented to the purpose of COACH and directions for using it. (See Appendix A, Questions and Answers for Parents About COACH.)	SL	4/97
2. Ensure all team members agree to use COACH to plan the student's educational program.	Team	4/97
3. Ensure all team members agree to accept and act upon the educational priorities identified by the family during the Family Interview.	Team	4/97
4. Involve the family in determining who will facilitate the Family Interview. List names on the Planning Team Information form.	SL	4/97
5. Involve the family in determining when and where the Family Interview will be conducted. List information on the Planning Team Information form.	SL	4/97
6. Involve the family in determining who needs to be present at the Family Interview. (Not all team members need to be present. Typically, the Family Interview is a small group of 2–4 people.)	SL	5/97
7. Identify by whom, when, and how Steps 2–6 will be facilitated.	Team	5/97
8. Ensure all needed forms are ready for use in advance of the Family Interview. List names on the Planning Team Information form.	SL	5/97
9. Ensure the person who facilitates the Family Interview is familiar with the directions.	SL	5/97
10. Complete the COACH Cover Page, this Checklist, and the Planning Team Information form in advance of the Family Interview.	SL	5/97

Choosing Outcomes and Accommodations for Children • © 1998 by Michael F. Giangreco •
Baltimore: Paul H. Brookes Publishing Co.

Step 1

FAMILY INTERVIEW

Step 1

DESCRIPTION

The Family Interview is the initial step in Part A. The Family Interview is designed to assist families in selecting a small set of what they believe to be the most important learning outcomes for their child to pursue during the school year. The Family Interview also provides excellent opportunities for professionals to learn about the student and family. Each of the substeps of the Family Interview is described briefly in the following sections, with particular emphasis on their purpose and unique features.

Planning Team Information

As one aspect of preparation, the team uses the Planning Team Information form, which lists 1) basic demographic information about the student (e.g., name, date of birth); 2) facilitators of the various steps in Part A; 3) participants in COACH activities; and 4) team membership. This page does not list any diagnostic, assessment, or categorical disability-related information because such information is not relevant to completing COACH. COACH will draw out descriptive information about a student's educational needs without the use of disability labels.

Introducing the Family Interview

Introducing the Family Interview is designed to orient participants to what will happen during the Family Interview. This orientation should be more of a reminder to participants, not an initial orientation to COACH—that should have occurred in preparation for the meeting.

Step 1.1:   Valued Life Outcomes

Step 1.1 sets a context for the rest of COACH. COACH has modified the environmental/ecological approach (L. Brown et al., 1979; L. Brown, Nietupski, & Hamre-Nietupski, 1976) by referencing the selection of learning outcomes to the current and desired future status of valued life outcomes (e.g., having meaningful relationships, being safe and healthy, having meaningful activities and places to do them).

After reviewing the list of valued life outcomes, parents are asked a series of questions to gather information about the current and desired future status of valued life outcomes for their child. For each valued life outcome area, the family is asked, "Are you interested in answering questions on this topic?" This is done to respect the cultural and individual differences among families and give them the opportunity to simply decline answering without requiring an explanation. *Questions pertaining to valued life outcomes purposely have been written in a broad manner so families can attach their own meanings to the questions.* At the end of Step 1.1, the family is asked to rank the valued life outcomes to indicate which are of greatest concern to them this year. This convergent step provides valuable information to school personnel that can assist them in planning an educational

Step 1.2: Selection of Curriculum Areas to Be Explored During the Family Interview

program that is appropriate and responsive to the needs identified by the family.

Step 1.2 offers families the opportunity to consider a wide range of potential curriculum areas and then make a decision about which areas should be explored in greater depth. This is done by sharing lists of learning outcomes from nine different curriculum areas with parents and having them choose from one of three options. First, families may choose to explore a particular curricular area (e.g., communication) and the corresponding list of learning outcomes during the Family Interview. Families will do this if they believe the listing includes potential priorities for their child this year. The second option is to wait to review a particular curriculum area until Step 2.1 of COACH (Additional Learning Outcomes from COACH), rather than during the Family Interview. The curriculum areas selected to review in Step 2.1 are usually lower priorities than those to be explored in the Family Interview, but this does not imply that they are unimportant. A third option is to "Skip for Now." Making this selection usually indicates one of four things: 1) the student is already doing well enough on the listed outcome areas that they are presently not of great concern; 2) the contents of the listed outcome areas overlap significantly with general education curriculum that will be addressed in the classroom (e.g., selected academics); 3) the listed learning outcomes are significantly beyond the student's current functioning level; or 4) the listed learning outcomes are not immediately important but may be so when the child is older (e.g., community and vocational skills).

By considering all the possible curriculum areas in COACH and then narrowing the selection to be explored in more depth during the Family Interview, teams can use their time more efficiently and focus their energies. Although it is most common for families to select four or five areas to be explored during the Family Interview, there are no upper or lower limitations on the number of areas that can be selected. Obviously, the number of areas selected will have an impact on the amount of time it takes to complete the Family Interview.

It is important for the facilitator to communicate that the purpose of Step 1.2 is to consider all nine curriculum areas but then to *select a subset* to be explored during the Family Interview. Some parents are reluctant to eliminate any curriculum areas from the Family Interview out of concern that some areas may "fall through the cracks." The facilitator can minimize this problem by having done a good job of explaining Step 2.1 (Additional Learning Outcomes from COACH) during the introduction to the Family Interview. When parents realize they will have an opportunity to revisit a curriculum area during Step 2.1, they are often more comfortable using that option. Conversely, if they are not familiar with Step 2.1, they may request that every area be reviewed during the Family Interview in an effort to be comprehensive. This usually slows the process and presents barriers to its ultimate aim: having the family converge on their highest priority learning outcomes for this year. By the time Step 1.2 has been completed, the set of potential priorities has been narrowed to a subset of curriculum areas to be explored during the Family Interview.

Step 1.3: Learning Outcomes Lists

In Step 1.3, lists of learning outcomes are provided in each of nine curriculum areas divided into two broad categories. *Cross-environmental* curriculum areas include lists of learning outcomes that typically cross many environments, including communication, socialization, personal management, leisure/recreation, and selected academics. Learning outcomes within these listings (e.g., making requests, following instructions, commenting, offering assistance to others, drinking/eating, reading) are used across many settings, such as home, school, work, and a variety of community settings.

Motor (i.e., gross and fine), cognition, and sensory skills are three areas that cross environments yet are not separate COACH listings. These three areas represent subskills embedded in all learning outcomes listed in COACH. Subskills are ultimately useful only when they are used in the context of functional learning outcomes. For example, the motor skill of grasping and the cognitive skill of means–ends only become useful when they are combined to produce a meaningful outcome, such as feeding oneself, playing with a toy, or using a vending machine to get a drink. The purposeful omission of motor, cognitive, and sensory skills as separate listings does not diminish their importance. On the contrary, users of COACH are challenged to consider how these skills might be combined and incorporated into functional learning outcomes and how those outcomes may contribute to valued life outcomes.

Environment-specific curriculum areas list learning outcomes typically used in specific environments, including home, school, the community, and vocational settings. For example, preparing breakfast, doing household chores, and bathing are typically done at home. Participating in small-group instruction and managing school-related belongings usually are done in school. Crossing intersections and making purchases usually are done in the community. Interacting appropriately with co-workers and using a time clock/sign-in primarily are done at work. A blank "Other" form is also available to add any curriculum areas and learning outcomes that are potential priorities but do not logically fit into one of the COACH listings.

Cross-environmental and environment-specific lists of learning outcomes are *designed to extend or supplement learning outcomes included in the general education curriculum, not replace them.* Therefore, more extensive academic listings are not included in Step 1.3 of COACH, because curriculum areas such as math, language arts, social studies, science, art, music, and physical education are already included in the general education curriculum; these areas are considered in COACH planning during Step 2.2 (Additional Learning Outcomes from General Education).

The learning outcomes listed in Step 1.3 are observable, functional behaviors carefully selected based on field testing over many years. Blank spaces are available so items uniquely applicable for a particular student can be added. Learning outcomes purposely have been worded in broad terms so they may be interpreted differently by different families. These broadly stated learning outcomes are made up of clusters of skills that, when grouped together, allow a person to participate, at least partially, in typical settings and with people who do not have disabilities. We have attempted to reduce the use of professional jargon in this version of COACH, but that does not mean jargon is completely absent. Therefore, listed learning outcomes also include examples of alternative statements. For example, in the Communication Learning Outcomes listing, item 4, "Summons Others," is followed by "(e.g., has a way to call others to him or her)." An effective facilitator of COACH will individualize the language of the learning outcomes to match each situation.

If a learning outcome is ultimately selected as a priority, the meaning attached to it will be clarified when the priority is translated into an annual goal (Step 4) and short-term objectives (Step 6). This broad, interpretive approach assists families with the process of sorting and selecting priorities by avoiding the review of hundreds or even thousands of variations and subskills. For example, some behavioral checklists include more than 50 subskills pertaining to dressing; COACH includes one, "Dresses/Undresses." In using the more extensive listing, a consumer could assess or consider all 50 items yet still not have identified which are priorities. It is conceivable that none of the dressing items will be priorities for a particular student, or that only a few are important; therefore, reviewing the entire subset represents a significant waste of time (assuming your purpose is to develop an individualized education program). Using COACH, if dressing is not a priority concern, you will either not address it at all; or if Personal Management is not selected in

Step 1.2, you will spend only the time needed to address it as a single item. Conversely, if dressing ends up being a priority concern, it will be identified and can later be clarified and explored in more detail as needed.

In Step 1.3 the family is presented with each learning outcome and asked how their child currently does with that particular learning outcome using the following scoring key: *E*, Early/Emerging Skill; *P*, Partial Skill; or *S*, Skillful. These scoring codes are purposely written in a positive way to encourage all participants to think about what the student *can do*, rather than what he or she cannot do. Occasionally people ask, "Shouldn't there be a score for 'No Skill'?" Our response is that, if the student is alive and not in a coma, he or she has some prerequisite behaviors for everything. Not only does it serve little useful purpose to indicate a child has "no skill," it also can create an extremely negative experience for families, particularly those whose children have very profound or multiple disabilities. Imagine what it might be like to repeat 50 times, "My child has no skill" or, worse yet, if the scale were numeric, to repeat "zero" many times over. In our estimation, no one benefits by designating a child's skill as zero or nonexistent.

This scoring system is meant to provide a gross indication of functioning level as perceived by the family and may not necessarily be consistent with the opinions of other team members. This scoring approach frequently leads to parents providing additional descriptive information about their child and may prompt follow-up questions by the facilitator. Although this information can be very informative, be aware that extended discussion on every item will interfere with the purpose of COACH—selection of priority learning outcomes. Rather than spending a great deal of time discussing items that are unlikely to be priorities, COACH suggests first identifying the priorities; then more in-depth discussions and planning can occur focused on those priorities.

Another aspect of Step 1.3 is that, for each scored learning outcome, a second question is posed: *"Does the learning outcome need work this year?"* This is one of the unique features that distinguishes COACH from many other checklists of functional skills. Regardless of various scoring approaches, most tests, assessments, and checklists infer assumptions based on the score. Typically a low score presumes that the student needs work, while a high score often presumes that a student does not need work. We think these are inappropriate presumptions to make. In COACH, the score and whether the item needs work this year are related to but independent of each other. The fact that a learning outcome has the lowest rating in COACH (i.e., Early/Emerging) does not necessarily mean that it needs work this year. It simply may be a low priority, may be too far beyond the student's current level to be appropriate this year, may not be a preference of the student, or may be focusing too much on perceived weaknesses rather than on student strengths. Traditional approaches place a great deal of emphasis on identifying what students do poorly and then selecting those perceived deficiencies as learning priorities; COACH encourages consumers to consider a variety of criteria in selecting priorities and not to automatically make something a learning priority just because it has a low score.

Conversely, the fact that a learning outcome has a high score does not necessarily mean that it does not need work this year. So in COACH, a learning outcome can be scored at any of the three levels and the decision as to whether or not it needs work this year can be made independently. By the time Step 1.3 has been completed, the set of potential priorities has been further narrowed to only those reviewed items that were marked "Yes" (needs work this year).

Step 1.4: Prioritization

Step 1.4 is designed to have the family consider which of the learning outcomes are their top priorities within each listing reviewed. This step provides additional convergence by narrowing each list from all those learning outcomes that need work this year to those that are priorities. The family is asked to rank a maximum of the top five priorities. Families are encouraged to consider a variety of criteria in determining their priorities, such as the strengths and interests of their child, the immediacy of the need, the frequency of use, the practicality, the future use, and the potential impact on valued life outcomes. It is not unusual to find situations in which fewer than five priorities are identified within a learning outcome listing.

Step 1.5: Cross-Prioritization

Step 1.5 provides an opportunity for the family to select and rank overall priority learning outcomes for their child. This is accomplished by considering the priorities they have selected within the curriculum areas they have reviewed and ranked in the previous parts of the Family Interview. Using the same criteria as in Step 1.4 (e.g., strength/interest of the student, frequency of use, immediacy of need), the family ranks a maximum of their top eight overall priorities. What results is an individualized set of priority learning outcomes. Cross-prioritization provides another opportunity to reconsider each priority in relation to the other possibilities. It is not uncommon for an item that was ranked as a second or third priority to move up in the overall ranking. This phenomenon lends credibility to the fact that, when presented with multiple opportunities, at a slightly different time, and with different sets of choices, people will make different decisions. When using COACH, each step provides another chance to reconsider the potential priorities so that, by the time the cross-prioritization is completed, both the family and the other team members can feel confident that the selections truly represent important priorities for the student.

Learning outcomes in COACH are purposely stated broadly, so they can be widely interpreted by families. Therefore, it is important for the facilitator and other team members to be sure they understand the intent behind the selection of each priority. This is done by reviewing each ranked priority and having the facilitator offer his or her understanding of the meaning behind the family's selection by writing abbreviations corresponding to one or more valued life outcomes. For example, if the priority was "Initiates Social Interactions," the facilitator might say, "My understanding is that you selected that priority because you are interested in your child establishing more friendships with classmates (Valued Life Outcome 3—Having Meaningful Relationships). Is that accurate?" Then the parents would have the opportunity to verify the accuracy of the facilitator's statement, clarify it, or restate it. In most cases we find that facilitators do understand the meaning behind the family's priority selections. This aspect of Step 1.5 sends a clear and important message to the family that the facilitator has been listening intently to them and wants to understand their perspectives. Occasionally, the facilitator has misunderstood the meaning behind the selection of a priority; this substep provides the opportunity to clarify the meaning and also sends another important message to the family—that the facilitator recognizes that communication is sometimes misunderstood and that he or she is open to clarification.

Finally, the fact that a family selects a learning outcome as an overall priority does not necessarily mean that it needs to be documented on the IEP as an annual goal and short-term objectives. Some overall priorities—often most of them—do end up as IEP goals and objectives. Other overall priorities end up being part of the student's additional learning outcomes, or a home responsibility. For example, a family selects "Participates in Small Groups" as a priority for their child, recognizes that this is an ongoing part of classroom routine, and therefore feels comfortable listing this learning outcome on the Additional Learning Outcomes from COACH (Step 2.1) list. Even though the item is not listed as an IEP goal, it still provides the school team with important information about the family's perspectives—that is, that they value having their child work in groups with other children rather than being isolated one to one with a teaching assistant. In a different example, a parent identifies "Brushes/Flosses Teeth" as a priority because of ongoing dental health concerns for the child. Although this is a priority for the family, and they do want the child to brush after lunch at school, they do not wish this to be a focus of their child's instruction while in school and prefer to take the responsibility for this at home. By the end of the Family Interview the family will have selected a small set of discipline-free, priority learning outcomes that will be restated as IEP goals and objectives.

DIRECTIONS

STEP 1: FAMILY INTERVIEW

 Purpose

Step 1 is designed to enable the family to select a small number of discipline-free, high-priority learning outcomes for the student for the upcoming school year.

 **Instructions**

Complete Steps 1.1 through 1.5. Directions for substeps follow.

 **Helpful Hints**

1. Be yourself by adding your own personal style and warmth to the way you ask questions and verify your understanding of the family's comments.
2. Maintain a steady pace, and request short answers to keep the process moving forward without being rushed.
3. Respect families' personal preferences and cultural traditions regarding issues such as formality of greetings and interactions, seating, eye contact, use of language, partaking of food, and visiting before or after attending to work-related tasks.
4. Write on COACH forms in pencil to allow for changes.
5. *DO NOT* ask parents to fill out COACH forms by themselves. COACH is *not* designed to be used as a written questionnaire to be filled out by the family in isolation; its value is in the interaction between the family and the person conducting the interview.
6. It is crucial to complete all of Part A, culminating with the Program-at-a-Glance, as a summary of the educational program components.
7. Give the family members an opportunity to see what is being written on the forms or tell them what is being written.
8. You can make clarifying notes on the forms for use later in designing goals, objectives, and instruction.
9. It is important for the team to decide how COACH will fit into an overall planning process for the student. Be-

cause COACH is not a comprehensive assessment, other assessment and planning strategies are appropriately used in conjunction with COACH.

10. COACH is a planning tool that is sequential and systematic in its approach. Some families may prefer to use a less formalized approach to participating in educational planning. Once the family is oriented to COACH, respect their decision to use or not use COACH. COACH can be available as one of several options to solicit family involvement in educational planning.

11. Because COACH purposely is not standardized and you are encouraged to adapt it, the danger exists that adaptations will be incongruent with the underlying principles on which COACH is based—typically, this will lead to negative outcomes. As a team, be sure your adaptations match the underlying principles of COACH.

12. Because of the wide variation in the configuration of families, it is crucial to clarify the appropriate family participants from the outset. This can be a sensitive or challenging issue for some families in situations in which the student's parents are divorced or if the child is living with a foster family. In cases of divorce, many noncustodial parents remain closely involved with their children and participate in educational planning. Even in cases in which one parent has primary physical custody of a child, the noncustodial parent may have joint legal custody with the ex-spouse. This legal custody often gives the noncustodial parent rights, among which is frequently joint decision-making power regarding issues such as health and education. In the case of foster families, it would be advisable to coordinate planning with the agency responsible for the foster placement to clarify what decisions are appropriately made by the foster parents, the biological parents, and the agency. Although there is no best way to handle these situations because of the abundance of variations, we can say with some confidence that, if these issues are addressed at the outset, the process, outcomes, and aftermath are more likely to proceed smoothly.

DIRECTIONS

PLANNING TEAM INFORMATION

! Purpose

The Planning Team Information form is designed to provide the student's name, date of birth, educational placement, team membership, and person(s) facilitating the various steps of COACH.

 **Instructions**

1. Prior to the Family Interview, complete the background information about the student (i.e., name, date of birth, educational placement).
2. Prior to the Family Interview, list the dates and facilitators for the various steps in COACH.
3. Prior to the Family Interview, list the names of the team members and their relationship(s) to the student.
4. After the Family Interview, indicate the date on which Steps 1–4 were reviewed with each team member.

Joshua's Planning Team Information form is shown on page 70.

★ Helpful Hints

1. Have the information on the Planning Team Information form completed *before* the Family Interview.
2. Make sure the general educators are included as team members.
3. Make sure family members are included.
4. Be conscious of team size, and try to keep it manageable.

Planning Team Information

Student's name: _Joshua Green_   Date of birth: _2-24-89_

Educational placement(s): _Grade 3 with supports_

Family Interview (Step 1)

     Date: _June 3, 1997_   Interviewer: _Susan Lomax_

     Person(s) being interviewed: _Karen & James Green_

Additional Learning Outcomes (Step 2)

     Date: _June 3, 1997_   Facilitator: _Helena Sanchez_

General Supports (Step 3)

     Date: _June 3, 1997_   Facilitator: _Helena Sanchez_

Annual Goals (Step 4)

     Date: _June 6, 1997_   Facilitator: _Susan Lomax_

Program-at-a-Glance (Step 5)

     Date: _June 6, 1997_   Facilitator: _Susan Lomax_

Short-Term Objectives (Step 6)

     Date: _June 12, 1997_   Facilitator: _Susan Lomax_

Team Membership

Name of Team Member	Relationship to Student	Date Steps 1–4 Reviewed
Karen Green	Mother	June 8, 1997
James Green	Father	June 8, 1997
Helena Sanchez	Grade 3 Teacher	June 8, 1997
Susan Lomax	Special Educator	June 8, 1997
Lucy Rogan	Speech-Lang. Pathologist	June 8, 1997
Max Baker	Physical Therapist	June 10, 1997
Angela Jefferson	Occupational Therapist	June 10, 1997
Carey Scott	Classroom Assistant	June 8, 1997

Choosing Outcomes and Accommodations for Children • © 1998 by Michael F. Giangreco •
Baltimore: Paul H. Brookes Publishing Co.

DIRECTIONS

INTRODUCING THE FAMILY INTERVIEW

 Purpose

Introducing the Family Interview is intended to review basic information about the purpose, content, activities, time lines, and outcomes of the Family Interview with participants.

 Instructions

1. As participants gather for the Family Interview at the scheduled time and place, the person conducting the interview should ask the family members how they would like to be seated so they can participate and feel comfortable. Arrangements may vary based on personal preferences, cultural traditions, or both.
2. Review Introducing the Family Interview (see p. 72 and Appendix B).

 **Helpful Hints**

1. When introducing the Family Interview, it is helpful to use the diagrams found in the manual and completed example forms.
2. It is helpful to show participants a sample Program-at-a-Glance so they can visualize what they will end up with after the meeting.
3. Because basic information about COACH would have been shared with the family and other team members during the process of deciding to use COACH, this introduction need only be a brief review.
4. Remember, this step should take only about 5 minutes.

Introducing the Family Interview

Directions: The following headings include sample statements to be shared with participants. *The information must be individualized to match each situation.*

Purpose of the Family Interview

"The purpose of this interview is to identify the top learning priorities for [student's name] that you feel would improve his/her life. The team recognizes the importance of your role in making these decisions."

Content Addressed in the Family Interview

"COACH includes a variety of learning outcomes, many of which typically are not included in the general education curriculum. The learning outcomes in COACH are designed to add to or extend those in the general education curriculum. That is one reason why it is so important to go beyond the priorities you will select today and explore additional learning outcomes from the general education curriculum using Step 2."

Interview Activities and Timelines

"It will take about 1 hour to complete the Family Interview, a bit longer if two or more family members are participating. In the Family Interview you will be asked to consider many possible learning outcomes and to zero in on those you feel are most important to work on **this year**. You will be asked these questions at a steady pace and will be asked to give brief answers. Throughout the interview, please feel free to not answer any questions you don't want to. The overall priority learning outcomes you select will become the focus of ongoing planning by the team."

Outcomes of the Family Interview

"At the end of the Family Interview you will select a small set of the most important learning outcomes for [student's name] to improve his/her life. We will also reach an agreement about which priorities need to be included as IEP goals."

Next Steps

"After the Family Interview is completed, your selections will be shared with the team members who are not here today. The overall priorities you selected to be on the IEP will be restated as annual goals and objectives. Although the Family Interview is an important first step in determining the contents of [student's name] educational program, it will not be complete until a broader set of learning outcomes and general supports has been identified using the rest of COACH."

Choosing Outcomes and Accommodations for Children • © 1998 by Michael F. Giangreco •
Baltimore: Paul H. Brookes Publishing Co.

DIRECTIONS

STEP 1.1: VALUED LIFE OUTCOMES

! Purpose

Step 1.1 is designed to 1) assist the family in clarifying valued life outcomes for the student that address his or her interests, strengths, and/or needs; 2) provide information about the current and future status of valued life outcomes for the student from the family's perspective; 3) assist in determining which valued life outcomes the family feels are most important to emphasize this school year; and 4) help set a context for educational planning using COACH.

Instructions

1. Review the following list of valued life outcomes:
   a. Being safe and healthy
   b. Having a home, now and in the future
   c. Having meaningful relationships
   d. Having choice and control that matches one's age and culture
   e. Participating in meaningful activities in various places
2. Explain that these valued life outcomes have been identified by other families as important markers of a "good life." Acknowledge that these valued life outcomes have different meanings for different people, and that the family should discuss only the areas they feel comfortable talking about or feel are important to discuss at this time.
3. For each valued life outcome, *circle YES or NO* in the appropriate place on the form in response to the question, "Are you (family member) interested in answering questions on this topic?"
4. If the family member answers no, move to the next valued life outcome. If the family member answers yes, *ask the listed questions and record the responses.* Repeat for each of the five valued life outcomes.
5. Tell the family member being interviewed to "Please rank the valued life outcomes (where 1 is the most important) to help the team understand which ones you

feel are most important for [student's name] this year." *Record the rankings* (1 through 5) at the end of the form.

6. Encourage the family member being interviewed to think about the information generated regarding valued life outcomes throughout the remainder of COACH planning.

Joshua's Valued Life Outcomes forms are shown on pages 75–79.

Step 1.1
Valued Life Outcomes

Directions: Review the purpose of this section and the list of Valued Life Outcomes with participants prior to asking questions. All the Valued Life Outcomes are meant to facilitate student independence, interdependence with others, and pursuit of personal growth by expanding access, creating new opportunities, developing individual abilities, and providing ways to contribute to one's community. Terms that are presented in bold are abbreviations for use in Steps 1.5, 10.1, and 10.2.

Being **Safe** and **Healthy**

Having a **Home**, Now and in the Future

Having Meaningful **Relationships**

Having **Choice** and Control that Match One's Age and Culture

Participating in Meaningful **Activities** in Various Places

Being Safe and Healthy

Question: "Are you (family member) interested in answering questions on this topic?"

Circle (YES) or NO

1. What, if anything, would you like to see change in [student's name] current health or safety that would help him/her to have a better or more enjoyable life? _Concern raised about eating and drinking, aspirating food may be cause of recurrent respiratory infections, and difficulty getting enough fluids causes constipation_

Having a Home, Now and in the Future

Question: "Are you (family member) interested in answering questions on this topic?"

Circle (YES) or NO

2. If everything goes as you hope, do you anticipate that [student's name] will continue to live where he or she does throughout the school years?

   Circle (YES) or NO   Where is that? _at home with his family_

   If NO, where would be a desirable place? _____

3. Would you like to talk about where a desirable place would be for [student's name] to live as an adult? Feel free to answer "No" if you think that decision is too far in the future to discuss at this time.

   Circle YES or (NO)   If YES, where? _____

4. Is there any place you would not like to have [student's name] live in the future? _avoid any institution or large facilities (e.g., nursing homes, large group homes)_

Having Meaningful Relationships

Question: "Are you (family member) interested in
answering questions on this topic?"

Circle (YES) or NO

5. With whom does [student's name] have relationships and friendships? With whom
does [student's name] like to spend time? _immediate family; cousins Ty and_
Kendra; classmates (but only in school)

6. How, if at all, would you like [student's name] relationships to change or expand in
the near future? _Expand relationships in and out of school_

Having Choice and Control
that Match One's Age and Culture

Question: "Are you (family member) interested in
answering questions on this topic?"

Circle (YES) or NO

7. What kinds of choices and control does [student's name] have now that match his or
her age and family/community situation? _Josh currently has few choices; does_
choose between some toys shown to him

8. How, if at all, would you like to see [student's name] choices and control change or
expand in the near future? _Expand the kinds of things he gets to choose:_
food, toys, places, clothes, activities

Choosing Outcomes and Accommodations for Children • © 1998 by Michael F. Giangreco •
Baltimore: Paul H. Brookes Publishing Co.

Participating in Meaningful Activities in Various Places

Question: "Are you (family member) interested in answering questions on this topic?"

Circle (YES) or NO

9. What kinds of activities does [student's name] currently do that he or she likes or values? Where does he or she spend time? _Playground (swing & slide);_ _roughhousing on the floor; playing with his dog at home; watching_ _softball games at the park_

10. How, if at all, would you like to see these activities and places change or expand in the near future? _He follows the family routine, which is quite active. Parents_ _would like to see activities expand, particularly those he could do on his_ _own and with peers rather than adults_

11. *Usually, you ask this question only if the student is 13 years old or older.* Have you given any thought to what kinds of activities [student's name] might do or places he or she might go as a young adult? For example, in the future how might [student's name] spend his or her time that is now spent in school (e.g., competitive work, supported work, volunteering, continuing education)? _N/A_

Ranking Valued Life Outcomes to Emphasize this Year

Directions: Ask the person being interviewed, "Please rank the Valued Life Outcomes (where 1 is the most important) to help the team understand which ones you feel are most important for [student's name] this year." Terms that are presented in bold are abbreviations for use in Steps 1.5, 10.1, and 10.2.

Rank

_4_   Being **Safe** and **Healthy**

_5_   Having a **Home**, Now and in the Future

_1_   Having Meaningful **Relationships**

_2_   Having **Choice** and Control that Match One's Age and Culture

_3_   Participating in Meaningful **Activities** in Various Places

*** Relationship to Next Steps ***

This information about the student's Valued Life Outcomes will set the context for the selection of individualized learning outcomes and general supports.

Helpful Hints

1. If family members indicate they do not wish to answer questions about a particular valued life outcome, it is important that the interviewer simply acknowledge that choice in a nonjudgmental manner and move on to the next area. The interviewer should not inquire regarding the reasons for the choice or pressure the family member to answer.

2. When asking questions, you are encouraged to word them in ways that make sense in the situation and ask follow-up or clarifying questions.

3. If necessary, remind the family that you are seeking brief responses to get a general idea of the current status of the valued life outcome and their hopes for the future. In part you can facilitate this by moving on to the next area once you have a sense of the family's perspective.

4. When ranking the valued life outcomes at the end of Step 1.1, do not have family members spend excessive amounts of time distinguishing between rankings they feel are very close. For example, if they are having difficulty deciding between two valued life outcomes as the number one ranking, they can simply both be number one. It is important to recognize that the purpose of the ranking is a convergent activity designed to provide a general sense of how the family views the relative importance of the valued life outcomes *this year.*

5. Try to summarize the essence of what the family members are saying and record it. Read it back to them for validation.

6. Remember, this step should take approximately 10–15 minutes to complete.

DIRECTIONS

STEP 1.2: SELECTING CURRICULUM AREAS TO EXPLORE DURING THE FAMILY INTERVIEW

! Purpose

Step 1.2 is intended to familiarize participants with each of the learning outcomes lists in COACH and then to select which lists they would like to review in the next steps of the Family Interview.

📖 Instructions

1. Introduce this step by explaining "I am going to show you the nine learning outcomes lists. As I show you each one I will ask you to make a choice from three options. For each learning outcomes list you can choose to discuss the listed items in
   a. *Step 1 (Family Interview)* if you feel the list includes potential priorities for *this year*; or
   b. *Step 2.1 (Additional Learning Outcomes from COACH)* if you feel the list includes learning outcomes that might be part of the student's educational program but are either part of the general education program or are lower priorities at this point in time; or
   c. *Skip for now* because you do not think this is a vital area to emphasize this year. This may be because the student is doing well in this area, because the area represents learning outcomes that may be more important in the future but are not currently, because the learning outcomes are too difficult, or because the learning outcomes will be addressed through general supports."
2. Remind the family that the purpose of this step is to narrow the number of curriculum areas that are to be considered further. Although no set number of learning outcomes lists is required, most families pick four or five to review during Step 1.2.

3. Show the family the Communication Learning Outcomes list, quickly review the list with them and ask them which of the three options they would like to choose. *Mark the selected box.*

4. *Repeat the process* for the remaining eight learning outcomes lists BEFORE beginning any work on Step 1.3.

5. Offer the Other Learning Outcomes list as an opportunity to include other curriculum areas in the Family Interview.

Step 1.2 on Joshua's Communication Learning Outcomes list is shown on page 83 (see portion of form highlighted in gray).

 **Helpful Hints**

1. Remind the family that their task is to select a subset of areas to be included in the next steps of the Family Interview.

2. Your preparation, particularly in explaining additional learning outcomes, will be important in completing this step. Some parents who do not have a clear understanding of Step 2.1 (Additional Learning Outcomes from COACH) or who have no scheduled time to address additional learning outcomes have told us they fear some things will "fall between the cracks" and be lost if they do not include everything in the Family Interview. This concern can be addressed by thoroughly preparing for and completing Part A.

3. It may be appropriate at times to review a single item or small subset of items from a listing. For example, a parent may review the Personal Management Learning Outcomes list and say, "There is only one item on here that I'm concerned about, 'Mobile Within and Between Rooms of a Building.'" In such cases you might just review that one item during the next steps of the Family Interview and not the rest.

4. An effective facilitator will demonstrate his or her knowledge of COACH content by applying it in situations in which it can assist the family in making a decision. For example, a facilitator might say, "As you consider socialization as a possible area to select, be aware that this listing includes many skills designed to facilitate positive social interactions. I know this is important to you because you identified 'Having Meaningful Relationships' as a highly ranked valued life outcome in Step 1.1."

5. Remember, this step takes approximately 5–10 minutes to complete.

Communication

Step 1.2

Mark only one box to indicate if the family wants to discuss this set of learning outcomes in:
Step 1 (Family Interview; priority this year?) ☒; Step 2 (Additional Learning Outcomes) ☐; Skip for Now ☐

Currently, in what ways does the student communicate?

Expressively: _____

Receptively: _____

#	Learning Outcomes	Step 1.3 Circle Score	Needs Work?	Step 1.4 Rank up to 5 Priorities
1	**Expresses Continuation or "More"** (e.g., makes sounds or movement when desired interaction stops to indicate he or she would like eating, playing, etc., to continue)	E P S	N Y	
2	**Makes Choices When Given Options**	E P S	N Y	
3	**Makes Requests** (e.g., for objects, food, interactions, activities, assistance)	E P S	N Y	
4	**Summons Others** (e.g., has a way to call others to him or her)	E P S	N Y	
5	**Expresses Rejection/Refusal** (e.g., indicates when he or she wants something to stop or does not want something to begin)	E P S	N Y	
6	**Expresses Greetings and Farewells**	E P S	N Y	
7	**Follows Instructions** (e.g., one step, multistep)	E P S	N Y	
8	**Sustains Communication with Others** (e.g., takes turns, attends, stays on topic, perseveres)	E P S	N Y	
9	**Initiates Communication with Others**	E P S	N Y	
10	**Responds to Questions** (e.g., if asked a question, he or she attempts to answer)	E P S	N Y	
11	**Comments/Describes** (e.g., expands vocabulary for events, objects, interactions, feelings)	E P S	N Y	
12	**Asks Questions of Others**	E P S	N Y	
		E P S	N Y	

Comments:

Scoring Key (use scores for Step 1.3 alone or in combination):
  E = Early/Emerging Skill (1% – 25%) **P** = Partial Skill (25% – 80%) **S** = Skillful (80% – 100%)

Choosing Outcomes and Accommodations for Children • © 1998 by Michael F. Giangreco •
Baltimore: Paul H. Brookes Publishing Co.

DIRECTIONS

STEP 1.3: LEARNING OUTCOMES LISTINGS, AND STEP 1.4: PRIORITIZATION

! Purpose

Steps 1.3 and 1.4 are designed to 1) gather general information about the student's current level of functioning as perceived by the family, 2) determine whether or not the family thinks the student needs work on each learning outcome *this year*, and 3) rank a maximum of five top priorities within each area.

📖 Instructions

1. Only complete Steps 1.3 and 1.4 for Learning Outcomes lists that have been selected in Step 1.2.
2. For each listed learning outcome, ask, "How would you describe your child's level of functioning given these three scoring options: 1) early/emerging skill, 2) partial skill, and 3) skillful?" Listen to the response, ask for clarification as needed, verify the response, and *record the level of functioning by circling the appropriate letter* (i.e., E, P, or S, respectively).
3. BEFORE proceeding to score the next learning outcome, move to the next column ("Needs Work?") and ask, "Do you think your child needs work on this learning outcome *this year?*" *Record the response by circling either N (no) or Y (yes) under "Needs Work?"*
4. *Repeat the sequence* of determining the *score* and whether the learning outcome *needs work* for each item listed within a single learning outcomes list (e.g., Socialization). Arrows on Joshua's sample form for Step 1.3 (see p. 86) depict the correct sequence.
5. *Add unique items in the blank spaces* provided.
6. *Record comments* in the space provided.
7. *After completing both parts of Step 1.3* within an area (e.g., Communication), but *before leaving the page, have the family rank a maximum of five top priorities* (Step

1.4), by selecting among the subset of learning outcomes that were marked Y ("yes, needs work this year") (see Joshua's sample form on p. 87). When having the parents rank their priorities, introduce criteria such as the usefulness of the learning outcome now and in the future, immediacy of need, frequency of use, and whether it builds on the strengths and interests of the student.

8. Repeat the aforementioned process for each of the learning outcomes lists selected in Step 1.2.

Communication

Step 1.2

Mark only one box to indicate if the family wants to discuss this set of learning outcomes in:
Step 1 (Family Interview; priority this year?) ☒ ; Step 2 (Additional Learning Outcomes) ☐ ; Skip for Now ☐

Currently, in what ways does the student communicate?

Expressively: _facial expressions, eye movements, vocalizations_

Receptively: _speech_

#	Learning Outcomes	Step 1.3 Circle Score	Needs Work?	Step 1.4 Rank up to 5 Priorities
1	**Expresses Continuation or "More"** (e.g., makes sounds or movement when desired interaction stops to indicate he or she would like eating, playing, etc., to continue)	E P Ⓢ	Ⓝ Y	
2	**Makes Choices When Given Options**	E Ⓟ S	N Ⓨ	
3	**Makes Requests** (e.g., for objects, food, interactions, activities, assistance)	Ⓔ P S	N Ⓨ	
4	**Summons Others** (e.g., has a way to call others to him or her)	Ⓔ P S	N Ⓨ	
5	**Expresses Rejection/Refusal** (e.g., indicates when he or she wants something to stop or does not want something to begin)	E P Ⓢ	Ⓝ Y	
6	**Expresses Greetings and Farewells**	E Ⓟ S	N Ⓨ	
7	**Follows Instructions** (e.g., one step, multistep)	Ⓔ P S	N Ⓨ	
8	**Sustains Communication with Others** (e.g., takes turns, attends, stays on topic, perseveres)	E Ⓟ S	N Ⓨ	
9	**Initiates Communication with Others**	Ⓔ P S	Ⓝ Y	
10	**Responds to Questions** (e.g., if asked a question, he or she attempts to answer)	Ⓔ P S	N Ⓨ	
11	**Comments/Describes** (e.g., expands vocabulary for events, objects, interactions, feelings)	Ⓔ P S	Ⓝ Y	
12	**Asks Questions of Others**	Ⓔ P S	Ⓝ Y	
		E P S	N Y	

Comments: ③ _Needs communication system to make requests_
⑦ _Instructions must be those he can physically do_
⑧ _Yes/no using eye & head movement_

Scoring Key (use scores for Step 1.3 alone or in combination):
   E = Early/Emerging Skill (1% – 25%)   **P** = Partial Skill (25% – 80%)   **S** = Skillful (80% – 100%)

Choosing Outcomes and Accommodations for Children • © 1998 by Michael F. Giangreco •
Baltimore: Paul H. Brookes Publishing Co.

Communication

Step 1.2

Mark only one box to indicate if the family wants to discuss this set of learning outcomes in:
Step 1 (Family Interview; priority this year?) ☒ ; Step 2 (Additional Learning Outcomes) ☐ ; Skip for Now ☐

Currently, in what ways does the student communicate?

Expressively: *facial expressions, eye movements, vocalizations*

Receptively: *speech*

#	Learning Outcomes	Step 1.3 Circle Score	Needs Work?	Step 1.4 Rank up to 5 Priorities
1	Expresses Continuation or "More" (e.g., makes sounds or movement when desired interaction stops to indicate he or she would like eating, playing, etc., to continue)	E P (S)	(N) Y	
2	Makes Choices When Given Options	E (P) S	N (Y)	1
3	Makes Requests (e.g., for objects, food, interactions, activities, assistance)	(E) P S	N (Y)	3
4	Summons Others (e.g., has a way to call others to him or her)	(E) P S	N (Y)	
5	Expresses Rejection/Refusal (e.g., indicates when he or she wants something to stop or does not want something to begin)	E P (S)	(N) Y	
6	Expresses Greetings and Farewells	E (P) S	N (Y)	4
7	Follows Instructions (e.g., one step, multistep)	(E) P S	N (Y)	
8	Sustains Communication with Others (e.g., takes turns, attends, stays on topic, perseveres)	E (P) S	N (Y)	5
9	Initiates Communication with Others	(E) P S	(N) Y	
10	Responds to Questions (e.g., if asked a question, he or she attempts to answer)	(E) P S	N (Y)	2
11	Comments/Describes (e.g., expands vocabulary for events, objects, interactions, feelings)	(E) P S	(N) Y	
12	Asks Questions of Others	(E) P S	(N) Y	
		E P S	N Y	

Comments: (3) *Needs communication system to make requests*
(7) *Instructions must be those he can physically do*
(8) *Yes/no using eye & head movement*

Scoring Key (use scores for Step 1.3 alone or in combination):
E = Early/Emerging Skill (1% – 25%) **P** = Partial Skill (25% – 80%) **S** = Skillful (80% – 100%)

Choosing Outcomes and Accommodations for Children • © 1998 by Michael F. Giangreco •
Baltimore: Paul H. Brookes Publishing Co.

Helpful Hints

1. Facilitators will benefit from familiarity with the lists of learning outcomes and their potential relationship to valued life outcomes.

2. Individualize the wording of items to match the situation.

3. Use your knowledge of the student to avoid asking unnecessary questions.

4. The process moves along more smoothly when family members are provided with the three discrete scoring choices from which to choose, rather than being asked open-ended questions.

5. During Step 1.3, family members frequently offer valuable information that should be recorded in the "Comments" space provided at the bottom of each learning outcomes list.

6. Throughout the Family Interview you will have to make judgments on how much supporting information to listen to and when to politely redirect the family to the interview questions. Family members obviously have a wealth of information to share with other team members, so we encourage you to listen carefully but also be cognizant of the task (COACH) you mutually agreed to complete within a specified amount of time.

7. Do not spend extra time having family members make distinctions between scores when they feel the student is between two scores or when the parents disagree. In such cases, encourage the scoring to reflect that ambivalence by using combination scores such as E/P or P/S.

8. It is OK to have fewer than five priorities within a curriculum area.

9. Typically, do not waste time ranking more than five priorities within each area because a maximum of five move on to the next level of selection. In cases when parents select a small number of learning outcomes lists to discuss in Step 1.2, such as Communication and Socialization, the number rankings might be extended by one or two (e.g., seven priorities).

10. Occasionally, when families select areas about which they may be less familiar, such as the School Learning Outcomes list, parents often find themselves requesting input from the teacher or special educator regarding the student's current level of functioning. This can be a helpful and appropriate dialogue.

11. Always remember that it is the parents, not the professionals, who are selecting the priorities for the student during the Family Interview.

12. Remember, Step 1.3 should take approximately 15–25 minutes and Step 1.4 another 12–15 minutes.

DIRECTIONS

STEP 1.5: CROSS-PRIORITIZATION

! **Purpose**

Step 1.5 is designed to 1) determine a maximum of eight top overall priorities from among those selected in each curriculum area reviewed in Step 1.3; 2) clarify which valued life outcomes are being sought by the selection of each overall priority; 3) identify the context in which each priority learning outcome will be learned; and 4) clarify whether each priority will be listed as an IEP goal, as an additional learning outcome, or as primarily a home responsibility.

Instructions

1. Have the participants take a short break. This will give the facilitator an opportunity to *transfer the priorities from Step 1.4 to the first page of the form for Step 1.5* in their ranked order.
2. When the group reconvenes, ask the family to rank a maximum of their top eight priorities, considering criteria similar to those they used when they prioritized during Step 1.3. *Record these priorities on the second page of the form for Step 1.5.*
3. Once the top eight overall priorities have been identified, have the family verify the list by asking something like, "As you look at this list of overall priorities, do you feel comfortable that these represent the most important things you'd like your child to learn this year?"
4. Verify which valued life outcomes were sought by the selection of each learning outcome and *record abbreviations corresponding to the valued life outcomes* in the spaces provided. This verification is initiated by the facilitator using active listening techniques. For example, a facilitator might say, "I'd like to make sure I am understanding your selection of 'Drinks and Eats' as a priority. My understanding is that you selected this because you are concerned that Joshua is not getting enough food

and liquids—it's a health concern. Am I understanding you correctly?" "Am I understanding correctly that you want Joshua to improve his ability to sustain communication and interactions better because it will increase his chances to establish meaningful relationships with his peers?" The family then has the opportunity to verify or clarify the meaning behind their selections.

5. As clarification is sought regarding priority learning outcomes, *additional information may be added to priorities* to help clarify their meaning. In Joshua's COACH, the priority, "Responds to Questions" was followed by ("Yes/No") indicating the type of questions. The priority, "Offers Assistance to Others" was followed by ("through classroom/school jobs") to clarify the context in which the student would offer assistance and "Engages in Individual Active Leisure" was followed by ("learns to use switch"). These priorities will be further clarified and refined in Step 4 (Annual Goals), Step 6 (Short-Term Objectives), and Step 9 (Planning and Adapting Instruction).

6. For each overall priority, *list the context* (where, under what circumstances) *within which the student will be expected to learn*, such as within general education activities, with peers, or in the community.

7. For each overall priority, *check one of the three boxes provided to indicate whether the family would like to have the priority written as an IEP goal, or included in the student's program less formally* as an additional learning outcome, or whether *the priority will remain primarily a home responsibility.*

8. The facilitator concludes the Family Interview by thanking people for their participation, and by explaining the next steps in COACH and the relationship of the Family Interview to the rest of COACH.

Joshua's Cross-Prioritization form is shown on pages 92 and 93.

 **Helpful Hints**

1. Sometimes during cross-prioritization, learning outcomes are switched in order of ranking; this is not only acceptable, it is desirable because it demonstrates that, when given another opportunity, people refine and adjust their selections. Let parents know it is OK to move things around in this fashion.

2. Cross-prioritization can be facilitated by stating the priorities aloud with pauses for responding. For example, a facilitator might say, "What would be your top priority? Would it be [then read off a few of the top priorities from

the various areas]?" Conversely, some parents prefer silence while they formulate their thoughts. Facilitators should try to be sensitive to the participants' styles of interaction.

3. You can help the family visually keep track of which items have been selected by putting checkmarks next to them.

4. When the family is having difficulty selecting the top priority, it can be helpful to say, "If you are having difficulty picking the top priority, could you tell which are the top three or four because their exact order isn't crucial?" Conversely, you can ask, "Are there any items that can be eliminated from the list?"

5. Always remember that it is the family, not the professionals, who are selecting the priorities for the student during the Family Interview.

6. Remember, Step 1.5 should take approximately 13–15 minutes to complete.

Step 1.5: Cross-Prioritization

Directions: Transfer priorities, in their ranked order, from each list of learning outcomes (Step 1.4) reviewed with the family.

#	Communication	Socialization	Personal Management	Leisure/ Recreation	Selected Academics
1	Makes Choices	Offers Assistance ….	Drinks & Eats	Individual Active Leisure	Additional Learning Outcomes (ALO)
2	Responds to Questions	Sustains Social Interactions	Gives Self-ID	Active Leisure with Others	
3	Makes Requests	Responds to the Presence of Others			
4	Expresses Greetings				
5	Sustains Communication				

#	Home	School	Community	Vocational	Other
1				Does Classroom Job	
2	Skip for now	ALO	Skip for now	Does School Job with Peers	
3					
4					
5					

Directions: Referring to the above listings, use the next page (Step 1.5 continued) to have the family member(s) being interviewed:
1. Rank a maximum of the top eight overall priorities, explicitly clarifying the wording to reflect what the student will be expected to learn. Review the overall priority selections to ensure that they accurately reflect student priorities.
2. Verify the reasoning behind the family's selection and record abbreviations corresponding to the valued life outcome(s).
3. Determine the proposed context in which learning of each priority will occur (e.g., classroom, community worksite, cafeteria with peers).
4. Indicate how each priority will be addressed as an IEP annual goal, an additional learning outcome, or primarily as a home responsibility (check only one of the three boxes for each ranked priority).

Choosing Outcomes and Accommodations for Children • © 1998 by Michael F. Giangreco • Baltimore: Paul H. Brookes Publishing Co.

Step 1.5. (continued)

Rank	1) Overall Priority Learning Outcomes (word priorities to explicitly clarify what the student will be expected to learn)	2) Write the Abbreviation of Valued Life Outcome(s)	3) List the Context for Learning	4) Check (✔) Only One Box for Each Priority		
				IEP Goal	Additional Learning Outcomes	Home
1	Makes Choices Given Options (yes/no)	Choice; Activities	general education activities	✔		
2	Responds to Questions (yes/no with eye gaze)	Relationships; Choice; Activities	general education activities	✔		
3	Drinks & Eats (chews, swallows)	Safe/Healthy	home & school			✔
4	Sustains Communication/Interactions	Relationships	with peers & adults		✔	
5	Offers Assistance to Others (through classroom/school jobs)	Relationships; Activities	general education activities	✔		
6	Makes Requests	Choice; Activities	general education activities	✔		
7	Engages in Individual Active Leisure (learns to use head switch)	Choice; Activities	school & home	✔		
8	Engages in Active Leisure with Peers	Relationships; Choice; Activities	school & home		✔	

Directions: The interviewer explains the next steps and the relationship of the Family Interview to the rest of COACH.

Choosing Outcomes and Accommodations for Children • © 1998 by Michael F. Giangreco • Baltimore: Paul H. Brookes Publishing Co.

Step 2

ADDITIONAL LEARNING OUTCOMES

DESCRIPTION

After completing the Family Interview, team members complete Step 2: Additional Learning Outcomes. The presence of this step recognizes that the selection of priorities may be too narrow and that students need and deserve a broad-based curriculum. Determining the additional learning outcomes requires a subset of team members who know the student and who have knowledge of the general education curriculum. The Additional Learning Outcomes step is divided into two substeps, Additional Learning Outcomes from COACH (Step 2.1) and Additional Learning Outcomes from General Education (Step 2.2). Both sets of information can be attached to the IEP as an addendum to document team decisions about the student's educational program but need not conform to any particular format, thus providing teams with flexible ways to document their decisions.

Step 2.1: Additional Learning Outcomes from COACH

Step 2.1 ensures that important selections made during the Family Interview but not slated for inclusion as IEP goals, as well as learning outcome areas that were tabled in Step 1.2 (Selection of Curriculum Areas to Be Explored During the Family Interview), are revisited. This is a safety-valve step so that items from COACH do not accidentally fall through the cracks.

Step 2.2: Additional Learning Outcomes from General Education

Step 2.2 ensures that students with disabilities are provided with the same opportunities as their classmates to pursue a broad-based educational program and to be exposed to a variety of educational content (e.g., language arts, math, science, social studies, art, music, health, physical education). The set of general education learning outcomes selected for the student should be individualized and be at an appropriate level. Far too often students with disabilities are excluded from general education class activities because they are functioning at a different level from their classmates. In addition, many times there is a lack of agreement among team members about the curricular expectations for the child in various subject areas. Step 2.2 draws on the earlier discussion of multilevel curriculum and curriculum overlapping by asking team members to consider the student's type of participation in general education classes (i.e., same, multilevel, curriculum overlapping; refer to pp. 11–12). When Step 2.2 is completed, team members are in agreement about what the student will be expected to learn from the general education curriculum. Documenting examples of learning outcomes provides a starting point for teachers and recognizes that they must be afforded the opportunity to get to know the student.

Step 2

DIRECTIONS

STEP 2: ADDITIONAL LEARNING OUTCOMES

 Purpose

Step 2 is designed to identify learning outcomes beyond the priorities selected during the Family Interview. Selection of additional learning outcomes that are individually determined is intended to ensure the student has access to a broad range of learning opportunities and his or her program is not artificially narrow, as could be the case if only a small set of priorities were identified.

 Instructions

1. Complete Step 2.1 (Additional Learning Outcomes from COACH).
2. Complete Step 2.2 (Additional Learning Outcomes from General Education).

 **Helpful Hints**

1. Selection of additional learning outcomes partially addresses the content of a student's educational program but does not suggest where the student will receive instruction or how the instruction will occur. Sometimes people confuse these points and draw inferences that may not be accurate. For example, if a student has no identified learning outcomes in science, this does not mean that she will not be included in science class or activities. She could be included through curriculum overlapping.
2. This step is not meant to document every conceivable learning outcome that a student might be exposed to; rather, it is designed to identify and *document critical learning outcomes that will be targeted for instruction*. Therefore, it is vital to select a quantity of learning outcomes that the team agrees can be reasonably pursued during a school year. Historically, users of COACH have tended to identify more learning outcomes than they can reasonably address in a year.

3. Team members have expressed concern that, if learning outcomes are not documented as IEP annual goals and short-term objectives, they will not be addressed and accountability will suffer. This can be avoided by attaching the additional learning outcomes to the IEP as an addendum. Remember, the IEP has minimum requirements but does allow your team to include information that extends beyond those minimum standards—attaching additional learning outcomes represents one means of doing so.

Step 2

DIRECTIONS

STEP 2.1: ADDITIONAL LEARNING OUTCOMES FROM COACH

! Purpose

Step 2.1 is designed to ensure that learning outcomes and learning outcome areas in COACH that were not selected as priorities for inclusion on the IEP as annual goals or were not considered within the Family Interview (during Step 1.2) are reviewed for consideration as additional learning outcomes from COACH. This step is intended to provide opportunities for participation to all team members.

Instructions

1. As a team, decide who will participate in determining the additional learning outcomes from COACH. We recommend that a core group including the parent(s), general class teacher, and special educator determine the additional learning outcomes. Other team members may be invited to participate as determined by the team.

2. Refer to the overall priority learning outcomes listed in Step 1.5. For those priorities that were checked as "Additional Learning Outcomes" in column 4, *check the space in Step 2.1 corresponding to those priorities.*

3. Refer to the listing of priorities by curriculum area shown in Step 1.5 (under the heading "Cross-Prioritization"). Consider if any of those items not already included in the IEP should be listed as additional learning outcomes. *Check the spaces in Step 2.1 corresponding to those priorities.*

4. Refer to learning outcomes listings that were marked "Step 2 (Additional Learning Outcomes)" in Step 1.2 (Selection of Curriculum Areas to Be Explored During the Family Interview). Review those lists to determine if any of those items should be *targeted for instruction this year. Check the spaces in Step 2.1 corresponding to those learning outcomes.*

5. Throughout the school year these additional learning outcomes should be reviewed to add new items as initial learning outcomes are achieved.

Joshua's Additional Learning Outcomes from COACH form is shown on pages 102 and 103.

 **Helpful Hints**

1. Remember to alternate the use of divergent and convergent thinking as your team makes decisions about additional learning outcomes. This will encourage the team to consider a broad set of learning outcomes, then select a smaller set to work on this year.
2. If certain team members are unable to attend the meeting to determine the additional learning outcomes, their input can be obtained prior to the meeting and the outcomes shared with them.
3. Remember that there may be some overlap between the learning outcomes listed in COACH and the general education curriculum. This is most likely to occur when the team is considering preschool, kindergarten, and primary grade general education curriculum and selected academics. Be aware of these potential overlaps so you can avoid duplicating items in Step 2.1 (Additional Learning Outcomes from COACH) and Step 2.2 (Additional Learning Outcomes from General Education).

Step 2.1

Step 2.1
Additional Learning
Outcomes from COACH

Directions: Consider the learning outcomes on this list and select a subset to be targeted for instruction as Additional Learning Outcomes. These pages may be included as an addendum to the IEP.

Participants: _Karen Green, Susan Lomax, Helena Sanchez_

COMMUNICATION

___ 1. Expresses continuation or "more"
___ 2. Makes choices when given options
___ 3. Makes requests
✓ 4. Summons others
___ 5. Expresses rejection/refusal
✓ 6. Expresses greetings and farewells
✓ 7. Follows instructions
✓ 8. Sustains communication with others
___ 9. Initiates communication with others
___ 10. Responds to questions
___ 11. Comments/describes
___ 12. Asks questions of others
___ _____
___ _____
___ _____

SOCIALIZATION

✓ 13. Responds to the presence and interactions of others
___ 14. Initiates social interactions
✓ 15. Sustains social interactions
___ 16. Terminates social interactions
___ 17. Distinguishes and interacts differently with familiar people, acquaintances, and strangers
___ 18. Maintains socially acceptable behavior when alone and with others
___ 19. Accepts assistance from others
___ 20. Offers assistance to others

___ 21. Makes transitions between routine activities
___ 22. Adjusts to unexpected changes in routine
___ 23. Shares with others
___ 24. Advocates for self
___ _____
___ _____
___ _____

PERSONAL MANAGEMENT

___ 25. Drinks and eats
___ 26. Eats with hands/fingers
___ 27. Eats with utensils
___ 28. Dresses/undresses
___ 29. Cares for bowel and bladder needs
___ 30. Cares for hands and face
___ 31. Combs/brushes hair
✓ 32. Gives self-identification information
___ 33. Responds to emergency alarm
___ 34. Manages personal belongings
___ 35. Mobile within and between rooms of a building
___ 36. Recognizes and avoids potentially dangerous situations
___ _____
___ _____
___ _____

LEISURE/RECREATION

___ 37. Engages in individual, passive leisure activities
___ 38. Engages in individual, active leisure activities

___ 39. Engages in passive leisure activities with others
✓ 40. Engages in active leisure with others
___ _____
___ _____

SELECTED ACADEMICS

___ 41. Reacts to objects, activities, and/or interactions by displaying some observable change in behavior
✓ 42. Directs and sustains attention to activity
✓ 43. Explores surroundings
✓ 44. Differentiates/discriminates between various things
✓ 45. Imitates skills used in daily life
___ 46. Uses objects for intended purposes
✓ 47. Identifies symbols
___ 48. Reads to get information and/or follow instructions
___ 49. Uses writing tools to form letters and words
___ 50. Composes phrases and sentences
___ 51. Counts with correspondence
___ 52. Calculates
___ 53. Uses clock
___ 54. Uses calendar
✓ 55. Uses computer
___ _____
___ _____
___ _____

(continued)

Choosing Outcomes and Accommodations for Children • © 1998 by Michael F. Giangreco •
Baltimore: Paul H. Brookes Publishing Co.

HOME

___ 56. Brushes/flosses teeth
___ 57. Selects appropriate clothing to wear
___ 58. Cares for personal hygiene needs
___ 59. Picks up after self
___ 60. Prepares food
___ 61. Does household chores
___ 62. Cares for clothing
___ 63. Uses telephone
___ _____
___ _____
___ _____
___ _____

SCHOOL

___ 64. Travels to and from school safely
✓ 65. Participates in small groups
✓ 66. Participates in large groups
✓ 67. Works at a task independently
___ 68. Manages school-related belongings
___ 69. Follows school rules/ routines
___ 70. Uses school facilities
___ 71. Makes purchases in school
___ 72. Participates in extra-curricular activities
___ _____
___ _____
___ _____
___ _____

COMMUNITY

___ 73. Travels safely in the community
___ 74. Uses restaurants
___ 75. Uses recreational facilities
___ 76. Makes purchases of merchandise or services
___ 77. Uses vending machines
___ 78. Uses banking facilities
___ 79. Travels by public transportation
___ 80. Uses pay phone
___ _____
___ _____
___ _____
___ _____

VOCATIONAL

___ 81. Does classroom and/or home job(s)
___ 82. Does job(s) at school, beyond the classroom, with peers without disabilities

For Students at Community Worksites

___ 83. Travels to and from worksite
___ 84. Uses time clock or check-in procedure
___ 85. Interacts appropriately with co-workers, customers, and supervisors
___ 86. Follows worksite rules for safety, conduct, and appearance
___ 87. Works independently at a task
___ 88. Works with others
___ 89. Follows schedule of work activities
___ 90. Uses worksite breaktime facilities
___ 91. Applies for job(s)
___ _____
___ _____
___ _____

OTHER:

___ _____
___ _____
___ _____
___ _____
___ _____
___ _____
___ _____
___ _____
___ _____
___ _____
___ _____
___ _____
___ _____
___ _____
___ _____
___ _____
___ _____
___ _____
___ _____
___ _____

OTHER:

___ _____
___ _____
___ _____
___ _____
___ _____
___ _____
___ _____
___ _____
___ _____
___ _____
___ _____

OTHER:

___ _____
___ _____
___ _____
___ _____
___ _____
___ _____
___ _____
___ _____
___ _____
___ _____
___ _____
___ _____
___ _____
___ _____
___ _____
___ _____
___ _____
___ _____
___ _____
___ _____

Choosing Outcomes and Accommodations for Children • © 1998 by Michael F. Giangreco •
Baltimore: Paul H. Brookes Publishing Co.

DIRECTIONS

STEP 2.2: ADDITIONAL LEARNING OUTCOMES FROM GENERAL EDUCATION

! Purpose

Step 2.2 is designed to ensure that learning outcomes and learning outcome areas from the general education curriculum are considered for all students, including those with disabilities. As mentioned previously, the learning outcomes listed in COACH are designed to extend or augment the general education curriculum; they are not meant to replace it. This step encourages the team to consider a broad range of learning outcomes for the student in areas such as language arts, math, science, social studies, art, music, physical education, technology, and foreign languages. In addition, this step is designed to assist team members in developing shared expectations for the type of participation students with disabilities will have in general education. This step is intended to provide opportunities for participation to all team members.

📖 Instructions

1. *Complete the background information* at the top of Step 2.2 (e.g., name, participants).
2. Review the list of curriculum areas and *put a checkmark in the box to the left of all those that are typically part of the general education curriculum* at the grade placement for which your team is planning.

For each checked curriculum area

3. Ask the classroom teacher to describe the basic content of the curriculum area at that grade level (e.g., units, major topics). *Record this in the space provided* after the curriculum area (e.g., math [computation, fractions, time, money, problem solving]).
4. Based on the team members' knowledge of the student and knowledge of the general education curriculum con-

tent, have the team consider whether the student should pursue learning outcomes within each curriculum area. *Record this by circling one of the three options listed under Primary Type* on the form for Step 2.2:

a. Circle *S* for "Same" if the student is expected to pursue the same grade-level learning outcomes as his or her classmates without disabilities (even though the student may require specialized instruction or adaptations).

b. Circle *ML* for "Multilevel" if the student should pursue learning outcomes within the curriculum area being considered (e.g., math), but at a different level (e.g., different math content; same content with fewer learning outcomes).

c. Circle *N/CO* for "None/Curriculum Overlapping" if the student will NOT be expected to pursue any learning outcomes within the curriculum area being considered (e.g., science, social studies).

The term *Curriculum Overlapping* is added to the "None" code to remind team members that this substep addresses ONLY the consideration of learning outcomes, NOT the location of learning (e.g., classes, school activities). For example, even though a student may have no learning outcomes in science, he or she may attend science class and participate using curriculum overlapping. Decisions about attendance in specific classes or participation in other school activities are made later in the COACH process using the Scheduling Matrix (Step 8.1) and the Student Schedule (Step 8.2). For additional information, see the Key on the Step 2.2 form and further explanations on pages 11–12.

5. If ML (multilevel) has been circled in any curriculum area, discuss whether the adapted subject matter will be the *same or different* and circle the decision. For example, in math Joshua's participation is multilevel because team members believe that he should have math learning outcomes, but the adapted subject matter is different from that of most of his classmates (see Joshua's Additional Learning Outcomes from General Education form on pp. 106 and 107). While his classmates are working on topics such as computation, fractions, and time, Joshua is learning to distinguish shapes and count with correspondence. While in art class, although Joshua's participation is adapted, the subject matter is the same (using various tactile to media to draw, paint, and complete seasonal art projects).

6. In the space provided to list the "Individual's Learning Outcomes," *record some initial, representative examples of the kind of learning outcomes being sought* for the student. This noncomprehensive listing is de-

Step 2.2: Additional Learning Outcomes from General Education

Directions: 1) Check all curriculum areas taught in the grade being planned for; 2) beside curriculum areas, clarify subject content; 3) circle the type of participation (**same**, **multilevel**, **none/curriculum overlapping**); 4) if multilevel, indicate if adapted subject content is the same or different by circling your response; and 5) record examples of the student's learning outcomes.

Student Name: *Josh Green*   **The Grade Placement Being Planned for Is:** *Grade 3*   **Date of Meeting:** *June 3, 1997*

Participants: *Karen Green, Susan Lomax, Helena Sanchez*

✓	General Education Curriculum Areas: Class Content	Primary Type?			If Multilevel, Is the Adapted Subject Matter?	
✓	**Reading/Language Arts/Humanities:** *Reading, writing, listening* Individual's Learning Outcomes: *sustains communication, listens to stories, recognizes photos/drawings/symbols*	S	(ML)	N/CO	Same	(Different)
✓	**Math:** *Computation, fractions, time, money, problem solving* Individual's Learning Outcomes: *distinguishes shapes, counts with correspondence*	S	(ML)	N/CO	Same	(Different)
✓	**Science:** *Life science (plants, insects, animals)* Individual's Learning Outcomes: –	S	ML	(N/CO)	Same	Different
✓	**History/Social Studies:** *State history* Individual's Learning Outcomes:	S	ML	(N/CO)	Same	Different
✓	**Arts (Visual)/Performing):** *Drawing, painting, seasonal projects* Individual's Learning Outcomes: *uses various art media*	S	(ML)	N/CO	(Same)	Different
✓	**Music (Vocal)/Instrumental):** *Choral singing, rhythm, reads music* Individual's Learning Outcomes: *cultural aspects of music, uses tape player to play rhythms, plays music using switch to keyboard*	S	(ML)	N/CO	(Same)	Different
✓	**Technology/Computer Literacy:** *Software applications, keyboarding* Individual's Learning Outcomes: *uses single-response software to play educational games*	S	(ML)	N/CO	Same	(Different)
✓	**Physical Education:** *Group games & sports, fitness* Individual's Learning Outcomes: *participates in group games and activities*	S	(ML)	N/CO	(Same)	Different

Choosing Outcomes and Accommodations for Children • © 1998 by Michael F. Giangreco • Baltimore: Paul H. Brookes Publishing Co.

Step 2.2. (continued)

✓	General Education Curriculum Areas: Class Content	Primary Type?			If Multilevel, Is the Adapted Subject Matter?	
✓	Health Education: *Nutrition, safety, feelings, wellness* Individual's Learning Outcomes: *expresses emotions, describes physical states (tired, hungry)*	S	(ML)	N/CO	Same	(Different)
	Foreign Language: Individual's Learning Outcomes:	S	ML	N/CO	Same	Different
	Community Service/Social Responsibility: Individual's Learning Outcomes:	S	ML	N/CO	Same	Different
	Home Economics: Individual's Learning Outcomes:	S	ML	N/CO	Same	Different
	Industrial Arts: Individual's Learning Outcomes:	S	ML	N/CO	Same	Different
	Vocational: Individual's Learning Outcomes:	S	ML	N/CO	Same	Different
	Reasoning and Problem Solving: Individual's Learning Outcomes:	S	ML	N/CO	Same	Different
	Other: Individual's Learning Outcomes:	S	ML	N/CO	Same	Different

Codes: **S** = Same (same learning outcomes as others); **ML** = Multilevel (learning outcomes in the same curriculum area at a different level, such as content, quantity, performance criteria); **N/CO** = None/Curriculum Overlapping (there are no learning outcomes identified for instruction in these curriculum areas, but the student participates in class activities by working on learning outcomes from different curriculum areas).

Choosing Outcomes and Accommodations for Children • Michael F. Giangreco • © 1998 by Michael F. Giangreco • Baltimore: Paul H. Brookes Publishing Co.

signed to give teachers a starting point and an opportunity to learn more about the student.

7. Throughout the school year these additional learning outcomes should be reviewed to add new items as initial learning outcomes are achieved.

 **Helpful Hints**

1. In cases in which there are several general education teachers, such as in high school, the team can have a large group meeting or a series of mini-meetings with each general educator.

2. Consider whether any curriculum areas are state or district requirements (e.g., physical education, health education).

3. Although you are attempting to select additional learning outcomes at an appropriate level of difficulty for the student, be sure you are providing opportunities for your students to surprise you by exceeding your expectations. These learning outcomes are provided to guide a student's learning, never to limit his or her opportunities.

4. Although it was stated previously, it is worth repeating that you want to select a quantity of additional learning outcomes your team feels they can reasonably address given the number of hours in the school day. Try to balance your optimism with realism.

5. When narrowing the focus of course content at the high school level, consider student preferences.

Step 3

GENERAL SUPPORTS

DESCRIPTION

COACH also provides a method for identifying and documenting General Supports that *need to be provided to or for a student* to allow access to or participation in the educational program. Unlike learning outcomes, which seek observable change in student behavior, general supports identify what other people need to do to assist the student. General supports are broad based and often are cross-situational, rather than highly specific to a particular lesson. What are referred to in COACH as "General Supports" are known by various other labels on IEP forms around the United States (e.g., "Accommodations," "Management Needs"). General supports typically fall into five categories:

1. *Personal needs* (e.g., feeding, dressing, giving medication)
2. *Physical needs* (e.g., therapeutic positioning, managing specialized equipment, environmental modifications)
3. *Teaching others about the student* (e.g., teaching classmates a student's augmentative/alternative communication system, teaching staff health/emergency procedures, teaching staff positive behavioral supports and crisis intervention protocols)
4. *Sensory needs* (e.g., providing books in braille, providing access to large-print materials, maintaining charged batteries in a hearing aid)
5. *Providing access and opportunities* (e.g., arranging community vocational experiences, providing literacy materials in a student's native language, providing access to general education class activities)

General supports may be provided by teachers, related services staff, teaching assistants, family members, and others. Peers may appropriately provide some general supports. For example, a small group of students who were in class with the student with disabilities the previous school year can explain to their new classmates how the student with disabilities communicates and how they might interpret some of his or her unique sounds and movements (e.g., an "ahhh" sound with eyes up means "yes" or an affirmation). Caution should be exercised when involving peers in assisting with the provision of general supports to ensure that such involvement is considered mutually beneficial, appropriate, and respectful.

Some general supports can be appropriately addressed within the general education classroom if doing so is considered status neutral or, preferably, status enhancing. In other words, the provision of general supports in typical settings should have a neutral or positive impact on how other people perceive the student with disabilities. Conversely, some general supports should be provided in private (e.g., dressing, toileting). These private places need not be exclusively for students with disabilities but should be places available for the same purposes for students who do not have disabilities (e.g., a lavatory that has been made accessible). It is critical not to subject students with disabilities to status-diminishing experiences. In other words, we should not do things to or for students that might cause personal embarrassment or lack of personal dignity, or otherwise cause them to be perceived negatively—this should be true for any student, whether he or she has a disability label or not. By the time the team has completed Step 3, they will have selected a set of general supports that need to be provided to or for the student to facilitate access and participation in school.

DIRECTIONS

STEP 3: GENERAL SUPPORTS

! Purpose

Step 3 is designed to determine and document general supports that are necessary for the student to access and participate in his or her individualized education program. General supports clarify what others need to do to or for the student.

Instructions

1. Determine which team members will complete this step. Although the core group of the parent(s), general education teacher(s), and special educator can usually complete this step, input from related services personnel (e.g., speech-language pathologist, physical therapist, occupational therapist) can be very helpful. Your team should decide what makes the most sense for you in each case.

For each category (e.g., Personal Needs, Physical Needs)

2. Consider each item on the list and *check those items that need to be provided* to or for the student.
3. *Add unique items in the spaces provided.*

Joshua's General Supports form is shown on pages 114 and 115.

Helpful Hints

1. Remember that these are meant to be cross-situational, *general* supports. They are not meant to be specific instructional supports and accommodations. Those are addressed in Step 9 (Planning and Adapting Instruction).
2. Although IEPs vary by locality, most have a space for general supports. The language used may be different, but the meaning is the same. Some synonyms we have seen are "Adaptations," "Accommodations," and "Management Needs."

Step 3
General Supports

Directions: Check those items to be included in the student's educational program as "General Supports" (those supports or accommodations provided to or for the student). Space has been provided under each item to allow for clarifying or specifying information individually pertinent to the student. *General Supports are not a comprehensive list of specific instructional supports.* These pages may be included as an addendum to the IEP or the information may be transferred to the IEP in an appropriate section.

Participants: _Susan Lomax, Karen Green_
Helena Sanchez, Max Baker

PERSONAL NEEDS

✓ 1. Needs to be fed food and drinks

✓ 2. Needs to be dressed

✓ 3. Needs assistance with bowel and bladder management

✓ 4. Needs assistance with personal hygiene

___ 5. Needs to be given medication

___ 6. Needs suctioning and/or postural drainage

Other Personal Needs:

___ _____

___ _____

___ _____

PHYSICAL NEEDS

✓ 7. Needs to be physically repositioned at regular intervals

✓ 8. Needs to have environmental barriers modified to allow access

✓ 9. Needs to have physical equipment managed (e.g., wheelchair, braces, orthotics)

✓ 10. Needs specialized transportation accommodations

✓ 11. Needs to be moved and positioned in specialized ways

✓ 12. Needs to be physically moved from place to place

Other Physical Needs:

___ _____

___ _____

___ _____

___ _____

___ _____

TEACHING OTHERS ABOUT THE STUDENT

✓ 13. Teach staff and classmates about the student's augmentative communication system and other communicative behaviors

✓ 14. Teach staff and students how to communicate with the student

___ 15. Teach staff seizure management procedures

___ 16. Teach staff emergency procedures (e.g., medical, evacuation)

___ 17. Teach staff preventive behavior management procedures

___ 18. Teach staff behavioral crisis intervention procedures

Other Needs Related to Teaching Others About the Student:

___ _____

___ _____

___ _____

___ _____

_____

(continued)

Choosing Outcomes and Accommodations for Children • © 1998 by Michael F. Giangreco •
Baltimore: Paul H. Brookes Publishing Co.

Step 3. (*continued*)

SENSORY NEEDS

___ 19. Needs to have hearing aids monitored (e.g., batteries, settings)

___ 20. Needs to have people use FM unit/auditory trainer

___ 21. Needs people to manually communicate (e.g., American Sign Language, common gestures)

___ 22. Needs to have glasses managed (e.g., adjusted, cleaned)

___ 23. Needs tactile materials

___ 24. Needs enlarged materials

___ 25. Needs materials in braille

___ 26. Needs to be positioned to accommodate sensory needs (e.g., specified distance from source)

___ 27. Needs environmental modifications to accommodate for sensory needs (e.g., lighting, location, background, volume, color)

Other Sensory Needs:

___ _____

___ _____

___ _____

___ _____

___ _____

___ _____

___ _____

PROVIDING ACCESS AND OPPORTUNITIES

✓ 28. Provide access to general education classes and activities

✓ 29. Needs to have instructional accommodations to general education activities and materials prepared in advance to facilitate multilevel instruction and/or curriculum overlapping

___ 30. Provide access to community-based experiences with people without disabilities

___ 31. Provide access to vocational experiences with people without disabilities

___ 32. Provide access to co-curricular activities with people without disabilities

___ 33. Provide access to materials in the student's native language

___ 34. Provide access to materials and activities associated with the student's cultural background as well as other cultures

___ 35. Provide access to nonaversive approaches to dealing with challenging behaviors

Other Needs Related to Providing Access and Opportunities:

___ _____

___ _____

___ _____

OTHER GENERAL SUPPORTS (not listed elsewhere)

___ 36. Needs time limits extended or waived

___ 37. Needs classnotes recorded in any form

___ 38. Needs alternative testing modifications

Other General Supports:

___ _____

___ _____

___ _____

___ _____

___ _____

___ _____

___ _____

___ _____

___ _____

___ _____

Step 3

Step 4

ANNUAL GOALS

DESCRIPTION

Some of the overall priority learning outcomes selected during the Family Interview were designated for inclusion as IEP goals. These priorities are restated from their current form to annual goal statements (Step 4) for the IEP.

Step 4, Annual Goals, provides a process for developing annual goals that include an *observable behavior* that is believed to be *attainable within a year* and the *contexts* in which the proposed behavior will be used (e.g., school, home, community, with peers who do not have disabilities, with co-workers in the breakroom at a jobsite). By establishing the actual context in which the student is expected to function, team members are encouraged to plan for instruction in natural environments. Including context within IEP annual goal statements can also provide documentation and justification for both transportation and access to general education classes, community worksites, and other places frequented by people without disabilities.

If IEP goals are designed to serve as a road map of the educational program—where the student is headed—then these goals must be stated in such a way as to offer direction to the team who will implement the plan. For example, *stating the mode of responding* (e.g., speaking, pointing, eye gaze, writing, drawing) helps add clarity to an annual goal because it adds to the observable aspect of the priority. This becomes particularly important when IEPs span parts of two different school years, correspond with placement or staff changes, or both. When these types of changes occur and IEP goals are not clearly written, the danger exists that the intention behind the goal selection may be misunderstood. For example, if a goal was written, "In community stores, Tommy will improve his ability to make purchases," one might assume that the focus of this goal was the acquisition of core skills associated with purchasing (e.g., locating merchandise and paying for it). Although such core skills may be the intention for one student, other students with the same goal may have a different focus related to purchasing. For example, one student may need to learn problem-solving strategies for what to do when he cannot find an item; another may need to expand her repertoire of purchasing to extend beyond prepackaged items to include fresh produce, bulk, or deli purchases, each of which require additional skills. By clarifying the intent of the annual goal, direction is provided for further refinement through the development of short-term objectives (Step 6).

Annual goals generated using COACH are designed to provide a relevant, individualized focus to a student's education and avoid some of the common problems historically associated with IEPs (Giangreco, Dennis, et al., 1994). Here are some of these common problems with potential solutions:

Step 4

- **Problem 1:** *Goals that are vague and use very broad categories of behavior* (e.g., "Jose will improve communication"). What communication skills are being referred to? This goal does not tell us.
  COACH Alternative 1: *Individualized learning outcomes* (e.g., "Jose will initiate the use of 15 new manual signs during first-grade activities")

- **Problem 2:** *Rhetoric without substance* (e.g., "Gina will enlarge her circle of friends"). What will Gina learn to help her enlarge her circle of friends? This goal does not tell us.
  COACH Alternative 2: *Family-selected priorities based on valued life outcomes* (e.g., "Gina will initiate and maintain social interactions [e.g., greetings, conversation] with classmates during co-curricular activities")

- **Problem 3:** *IEPs that are unnecessarily long, which renders them less usable, makes it difficult to fulfill the promises they imply, and makes it difficult to figure out which goals are the priorities.*
  COACH Alternative 3: *Development of a Program-at-a-Glance, which is short and useful and distinguishes priority learning outcomes from additional learning outcomes*

- **Problem 4:** *Goals that are written as behaviors for the staff rather than for the students* (e.g., "Mary Ann's hearing aids will be checked daily by the speech-language pathologist").
  COACH Alternative 4: *Goals for students that are distinguished from general supports provided by staff* (e.g., "A teacher assistant, taught by a speech-language pathologist, will check Mary Ann's hearing aids daily" is written in the IEP as a general support)

- **Problem 5:** *Goals that are discipline referenced and jargon filled* (e.g., "Darren will improve articulation of bilabial sounds in speech therapy").
  COACH Alternative 5: *Goals that are discipline free* (e.g., "Darren will increase the intelligibility of his speech in one-to-one conversation with his parents, siblings, classmates, and teachers")

All of these examples provide clarification about *what* will be learned and *where* it will be learned, but they do not specify *how* instruction will occur.

DIRECTIONS

STEP 4: ANNUAL GOALS

! **Purpose**

Step 4 is designed to translate priority learning outcomes selected during the Family Interview (Step 1.5) into annual goal statements for the IEP.

Instructions

1. In the space labeled "Priority Learning Outcome," *list the priority to be included on the IEP* from Step 1.5 (Cross-Prioritization).

2. *Describe the student's current level of functioning related to the priority learning outcome.*

3. In the space labeled "Behavior," *list an observable behavior that will be sought* as an annual goal. To increase clarity, *add a response mode* to the behavior if it is not already clear. For example, how will Josh "Make choices when given options"? Observable response modes might include speaking, pointing, eye gaze, or others. *Include other clarifying information* that will assist in clearly stating the goal. For example, "Responds to Questions" could be clarified by rephrasing the goal as "In a variety of settings (e.g., home, school, community), Josh will respond to yes/no questions using head/eye movements (Up = Yes, Down = No)."

4. In the space labeled "Context," *list any contextual variables that are crucial to the clarity of the goal;* some goals need this more than others. When attainment of the goal depends on access to the context, contextual variables can be crucial. For example, this most frequently occurs when the behavior must be exhibited 1) in a particular location (e.g., at a worksite, on the playground); 2) during a particular activity (e.g., while eating lunch, while participating in whole-class instruction); or 3) with particular people (e.g., peers without disabilities).

5. In the space labeled "Team Member Suggestions," *list input received from team members* that would help clarify or add to the context or behavior.
6. In the space labeled "Annual Goal," *combine the information and ideas that have been collected to state the annual goal* in a way that includes a context and a behavior that the team agrees is attainable within a year.
7. The completed Annual Goals form can then be shared with team members face to face or by telephone, fax, or e-mail to verify its contents and make any final adjustments before the goals are transferred to the IEP document.

For example, the following are Joshua's Annual Goals (two of his Annual Goals forms are shown on pp. 124 and 125):

- In class and school activities (e.g., class, recess, lunch), Josh will make choices using eye gaze when given two options.
- In a variety of settings (e.g., home, school, community), Josh will respond to yes/no questions using head/eye movements (Up = Yes , Down = No).
- In a variety of settings (e.g., home, school, community), Josh will make requests for food, people, places, and activities using eye gaze and a photo communication board.
- During classroom and school jobs done with classmates, Josh will offer assistance to others.
- In a variety of settings, Josh will engage in individual active leisure by activating devices (e.g., tape player, toys, appliances) using an adapted switch.

Helpful Hints

1. Clarify among the team members who will assume or share responsibility for developing the annual goals based on the selected priorities.
2. Remember when writing the student's annual goals that they are meant to provide a general road map for your instruction. Your team may encounter detours along the way or decide that you wish to change your route; therefore, we suggest you do a good job with the goals but at the same time do not spend too much time on details that are likely to change. These initial goals represent your collective "best guess"; they are not written in stone and should not constrain your instruction.
3. It is always helpful to get feedback and ideas from team members. This can be accomplished by routing the Annual Goals form, with at least the behaviors listed, to team members.

4. As suggested previously, in COACH we favor IEPs that list a small set of top-priority learning outcomes that are discipline free. Problems have arisen when professional staff generate priorities using the Family Interview in COACH and then either 1) do not translate those priorities to IEP goals or 2) do so and then include additional annual goals representing their individual priorities based on the orientation of their various disciplines. Try to avoid these problems by using the Additional Learning Outcomes (Steps 2.1 and 2.2), the General Supports (Step 3), and VISTA (*Vermont Interdependent Services Team Approach*) (Giangreco, 1996c) to help clarify additional learning outcomes and the roles of related services personnel.

Step 4

Step 4:   Annual Goals

Priority Learning Outcome (from Step 1.5): _Responds to questions (yes/no)_

Current Level of Functioning Related to the Priority Learning Outcome: _Josh has the ability to move his eyes up and down and his head to some extent. He responds to yes/no questions with eye/head movement about 20% of the time._

Behavior: _Moves eyes/head up to indicate yes; down to indicate no._

Context: _Across settings_

Team Member Suggestions: _Give homework assignments to use yes/no; head positioned at midline_

Annual Goal: _In a variety of settings (e.g., home, school, community), Josh will respond to yes/no questions using head/eye movements (up = yes, down = no)._

Step 6:   Short-Term Objectives

Clarify the intent/focus of Annual Goal to be reflected in the objectives (check those that apply or determine others):

_____ Decreasing prompts/cues	_____ Increasing response to natural cues
_____ Desensitizing/increasing tolerance	_____ Accepting assistance from others
_____ Acquiring core skills	_____ Initiation of behavior
_____ Preparation for the activity	_____ Quality of performance
_____ Appropriateness of tempo or rate	_____ Extending or reducing duration
_____ Self-monitoring	_____ Problem solving
_____ Termination of the behavior	_____ Assisting others with the behavior
_____ Safety aspects	_____ Expansion of repertoire
_____ Communication aspects	_____ Social behaviors aspects and manners
_____ Indication of choice or preference	_____ Retention over time
_____ Generalization across settings	_____ Generalization across people
_____ Generalization across materials	_____ Generalization across cues

	Conditions	Behavior	Criteria
1			
2			
3			

Choosing Outcomes and Accommodations for Children • © 1998 by Michael F. Giangreco •
Baltimore: Paul H. Brookes Publishing Co.

Step 4: Annual Goals

Priority Learning Outcome (from Step 1.5): _Engages in individual active leisure_

Current Level of Functioning Related to the Priority Learning Outcome: _Josh can move his head side to side but often gets stuck turned to his right. He can initiate use of a head switch, but it takes over a minute and lasts 2-3 seconds._

Behavior: _Engages in active individual leisure by turning on a switch_

Context: _Across a variety of settings_

Team Member Suggestions: _Music, toys, page turner, computer, small appliances; ensure safety with use of electrical devices._

Annual Goal: _In a variety of settings, Josh will engage in individual active leisure by activating devices (e.g., tape player, toys, appliances) using an adapted switch._

Step 6: Short-Term Objectives

Clarify the intent/focus of Annual Goal to be reflected in the objectives (check those that apply or determine others):

_____ Decreasing prompts/cues	_____ Increasing response to natural cues
_____ Desensitizing/increasing tolerance	_____ Accepting assistance from others
_____ Acquiring core skills	_____ Initiation of behavior
_____ Preparation for the activity	_____ Quality of performance
_____ Appropriateness of tempo or rate	_____ Extending or reducing duration
_____ Self-monitoring	_____ Problem solving
_____ Termination of the behavior	_____ Assisting others with the behavior
_____ Safety aspects	_____ Expansion of repertoire
_____ Communication aspects	_____ Social behaviors aspects and manners
_____ Indication of choice or preference	_____ Retention over time
_____ Generalization across settings	_____ Generalization across people
_____ Generalization across materials	_____ Generalization across cues

	Conditions	Behavior	Criteria
1			
2			
3			

Step 4

Step 5

PROGRAM-AT-A-GLANCE

DESCRIPTION

Many teachers find IEP documents too cumbersome to be useful for everyday planning. The Program-at-a-Glance keeps critical information about a student's curricular and support needs available "at-a-glance" throughout the school day. Therefore it should be kept in a handy spot for quick access. The Program-at-a-Glance typically is a concise summary of the educational program components presented in an abbreviated format, including 1) annual goals (from Step 4) based on family-selected priorities (from Step 1.5); 2) additional learning outcomes (from Steps 2.1 and 2.2); and 3) the general supports (from Step 3).

The Program-at-a-Glance offers a concise format to document and communicate a student's educational program components. It is a useful summary to share with classroom teachers, special area teachers (e.g., art, music, physical education, library), related services personnel (e.g., speech-language pathologists, physical therapists, occupational therapists), and teaching assistants.

The components of the Program-at-a-Glance are also essential in determining educationally relevant and necessary related services for students. The order of presentation (e.g., general supports, priority learning outcomes, additional learning outcomes) may vary depending on how the Program-at-a-Glance will be used and what makes sense to the team members. For example, some people like to list the annual goals first to signify their importance. Others prefer to list general supports first to facilitate related services decision making. Research on related services decision making indicates that considering general supports first is helpful because often they affect multiple priorities and additional learning outcomes (Giangreco, Edelman, Luiselli, & MacFarland, in press-b). Variations of the Program-at-a-Glance are included in this section as well as Appendices C and D. We believe that the Program-at-a-Glance should be organized in whatever way works best for your team.

Step 5

DIRECTIONS

STEP 5: PROGRAM-AT-A-GLANCE

! Purpose

Step 5 is designed to summarize the student's educational program components on one or two pages so it can be used as a handy way to communicate student needs to a variety of school staff (e.g., classroom teachers, related services personnel, instructional assistants, special area teachers) and assist in determining an appropriate educational placement and educationally necessary related services.

Instructions

1. *Write the student's name and the date* in the spaces provided at the top of the form.
2. *Transfer the student's educational program components* from the various parts of COACH to the Program-at-a-Glance *using whatever sequence makes most sense to your team.* Include
   a. The checked items from Step 3 (General Supports) listed by categories (e.g., Personal Needs, Physical Needs, Sensory Needs)
   b. The top priorities/IEP annual goals based on Step 4 (Annual Goals)
   c. The checked items from Step 2.1 (Additional Learning Outcomes from COACH) and the "Individual's Learning Outcomes" from Step 2.2 (Additional Learning Outcomes from General Education), listed by curriculum areas
3. *Number the Program-at-a-Glance entries* to provide easier reference for team members as they use the document.

Joshua's Program-at-a-Glance is shown on pages 132 and 133.

 **Helpful Hints**

1. Some teams find it advantageous to reorganize Program-at-a-Glance entries so that related items are grouped together. For example, if three different communication goals were identified as priority learning outcomes but were ranked 1, 3, and 7 in Step 1.5, the corresponding annual goals could be grouped together on the Program-at-a-Glance to assist in communicating related needs to staff and to assist in related services decision making. Similarly, in the "Additional Learning Outcomes" section of the Program-at-a-Glance, communication learning outcomes from COACH could be grouped together with language arts learning outcomes from general education; this will reduce redundancy.

2. Some people find it easier to simply enter the Program-at-a-Glance onto a computer disk, rather than using the forms provided in the manual. This way it can be easily updated when necessary without having to rewrite the entire document.

3. It is important to have the Program-at-a-Glance readily available to staff working with the student while also maintaining confidentiality.

Step 5

Step 5
Program-at-a-Glance

Student's Name: *Joshua Green*   Date: *June 6, 1997*

General Supports
List Educational Program Components

1. *PERSONAL NEEDS: Needs to be: (a) fed food and drinks, (b) dressed, (c) given assistance with bowel and bladder management, (d) given assistance with personal hygiene*

2. *PHYSICAL NEEDS: Needs: (a) repositioning at regular intervals, (b) environmental barriers modified to allow access, (c) equipment managed, (d) specialized transportation, (e) movement/positioning in specialized ways, (f) moved from place to place*

3. *TEACHING OTHERS ABOUT THE STUDENT: (a) staff and students need to learn about Joshua's augmentative communication systems, other communicative behaviors; (b) how to communicate with Joshua*

4. *PROVIDING ACCESS AND OPPORTUNITIES: (a) provide access to general education classes and activities, (b) provide instructional accommodations to general education classes/activities and materials prepared in advance for multilevel instruction & curriculum overlapping*

Annual Goals
(from Family-Selected Priority Learning Outcomes)

5. *Makes choices using eye gaze when given two options*

6. *Responds to yes/no questions using eye gaze and head movements (Up = Yes, Down = No)*

7. *Makes requests for food, people, places, and activities using a photo communication board and eye gaze*

8. *During classroom and school jobs done with classmates, Josh will offer assistance to others*

9. *Engages in individual active leisure by activating devices (e.g., toys, tape player, page turner, computer, small appliances) using an adapted switch*

Choosing Outcomes and Accommodations for Children • © 1998 by Michael F. Giangreco •
Baltimore: Paul H. Brookes Publishing Co.

Step 5. (*continued*)

10. *COMMUNICATION/LANGUAGE ARTS:* (a) summons others; (b) expresses greetings/farewells; (c) follows instructions; (d) sustains communication; (e) listens to stories/looks at books; (f) recognizes photos, drawings, symbols

11. *SOCIALIZATION/HEALTH:* (a) responds to the presence and interactions of others, (b) sustains social interactions, (c) expresses emotions, (d) describes physical states (e.g., tired, hungry, discomfort)

12. *LEISURE/RECREATION/PHYSICAL EDUCATION:* (a) engages in active leisure with others, (b) participates in group games and activities

13. *COMPUTER:* uses single-response software to play educational games

14. *PERSONAL MANAGEMENT:* gives self-identification information

15. *SCHOOL:* (a) participates in small and large groups, (b) works independently at a task at a nonfrustrational level

16. *SELECTED ACADEMICS/MATH:* (a) directs and sustains attention to activity; (b) explores surroundings, differentiates/discriminates between various things; (c) imitates skills used in daily life; (d) identifies symbols; (e) distinguishes shapes; (f) counts with correspondence

17. *ART/MUSIC:* (a) uses various art media, (b) plays rhythms and music using tape player, (c) plays music using adapted switch to keyboard

Educational Placement and Related Services

After your team has completed the Program-at-a-Glance, you have the information you will need to make some other important decisions that will be documented on the IEP.

Educational Placement

Once you have the educational program information contained in your Program-at-a-Glance, you are ready to ask the question: *"Where is the least restrictive educational placement where the student can pursue his or her educational program given supplemental supports and services?"* You should always begin by considering the neighborhood school and general education classes the student would attend if he or she did not have a disability.

Related Services

In order to make educationally relevant and necessary related services decisions, your team must know the student's educational program components (summarized in the Program-at-a-Glance) and the educational placement. By determining related services at this juncture, the team can determine which related services providers need to be involved in developing particular short-term objectives and subsequent instructional planning. Although related services providers who are already part of the team may be involved earlier in the planning process, their prior involvement is not required because the selection of priorities is family centered, and IEP goals and additional learning outcomes are meant to be discipline free. Given the larger caseload sizes of many related services staff, it is often impractical to have them participate extensively prior to this point in the process. Clearly, in some cases related services staff may have essential input earlier in the process, and your team should decide when and how they need to be involved.

Step 6

SHORT-TERM OBJECTIVES

DESCRIPTION

Step 6, Short-Term Objectives, provides a process by which to break down an annual goal into a sequence of smaller parts. This step is designed to offer additional clarity to the priorities that have been restated as annual goals. This is accomplished by first describing the student's current level of functioning related to the annual goal so that objectives can be set at an appropriate level of difficulty. Next, a listing is provided to clarify the intent of the objectives that includes options (e.g., increasing tolerance, acquiring core skills, tempo/rate, generalization, quality, duration) (Brown, Evans, Weed, & Owen, 1987; Guess & Helmstetter, 1986).

Although short-term objectives may be written in a variety of ways, one of the widely accepted formats is to include three distinct components: 1) conditions, 2) behavior, and 3) criteria (Snell & Brown, 1993). *Conditions* under which the behavior will occur should be included. These conditions are crucial in order for the student to engage in the behavior. These conditions frequently refer to specific *cues* (e.g., "Show me what you want," "Turn on the switch"); special *equipment or materials* (e.g., heavy ruled writing paper, spoon with a built-up handle, time card, plate secured with a suction cup); and/or *contexts* (e.g., in class, on the playground during recess, at work, upon arrival). Conditions may be stated in a variety of combinations. *It is not necessary to include every condition, but rather only those that are unique and crucial in order for the student to pursue the objective.* Also, it is important to remember that, ultimately, it is desirable for students to respond to natural cues in natural contexts (Ford & Mirenda, 1984). Therefore, *assistive (non–naturally occurring) conditions should be used conservatively,* and plans should be made to fade such conditions when possible.

A *behavior displayed by the learner* is the central feature of any objective. The behavior must be *observable and measurable.* Sometimes people inappropriately write IEP goals and objectives about what they, as teachers or related services personnel, are going to do for the student rather than what the student will be able to do as a result of instruction. Avoid terms like *understand* or *know.* Instead, write a behavior you can observe that may be an indicator that the student "knows" or "understands" (e.g., points, says, writes, washes, counts, purchases).

The objective should also include *criteria.* Selection of the type of criteria is based on how they match the behavior. For example, if you want a student to increase the number of times he or she initiates appropriate greetings with other people, you might take a frequency count to determine how many times the student initiates or determine a percentage comparing the number of initiations with the number of opportunities the student had during a specified time period. Types of criteria may include, but are not limited to, *frequency, percent, rate, quality, duration,* and *latency.* It is good practice for the objective to include a second component that indicates how stable the behavior must be before you feel comfortable reporting that the objective has been met (e.g., 4 of 5 consecutive school days over a 2-week period). Sobsey and Ludlow (1984) provide helpful guidelines for setting instructional criteria.

Short-term objectives should assist in the educational process. Like any tool, they can be used or misused. Some people fear that developing quantifiable objectives may trivialize what a student needs to learn or restrict the staff's creativity in planning or implementation. This need not be the case. Objectives can be trivial, boring, and confining or relevant, interesting, and creative depending on how the team approaches the challenge. Under the best circumstances, objectives can be used as a map of the path to be taken to reach an identified destination (annual goal). Like any travel plans, you may start out on one path and later change that path to match new information you have gained. Because most schools are in session for approximately 40 weeks, it is suggested that three or four objectives be written for each goal, spaced over intervals of approximately 10–12 weeks or to coincide with the school's marking periods. Like most things related to education, objectives are never perfect and are often in a state of change. Therefore, although setting objectives is a valuable activity, it is important not to get bogged down with excessive details because the objectives probably will need readjustment at a later date. The initial set of short-term objectives is your team's "best guess" at the time given current information.

DIRECTIONS

STEP 6: SHORT-TERM OBJECTIVES

! Purpose

Step 6 is designed to develop a series of short-term objectives for each annual goal that provide smaller steps leading toward the attainment of the annual goal.

Instructions

1. Refer to the Annual Goals form (Step 4), which includes Step 6 on the form.
2. *Clarify the intent/focus of the annual goal* to be reflected in the objectives *by checking those items that apply.* In other words, ask yourself, "What aspect of the behavior is the focus of the goal (e.g., acquiring core skills, generalization across people, tempo/rate, quality of performance)?"
3. Using the grid at the bottom of the Short-Term Objectives worksheet (row 1, left and middle columns), 1) *list any crucial conditions* that must be present for the student to learn the behavior, and 2) *list a behavior* that includes the information identified when clarifying the intent.
4. To *write the measurable criteria,* ask yourself, "How far might we expect the student to progress from his or her current level of functioning given 10–15 weeks of instruction?" The criteria also should *include a measure of stability* (e.g., 4 of 5 days for 2 consecutive weeks).
5. The combination of the three components (i.e., conditions, behavior, criteria) form an initial short-term objective.
6. *Write additional short-term objectives by changing one or more of the three components* (i.e., conditions, behavior, criteria). In some cases the conditions and behavior remain constant and the criteria increase. In other cases, the conditions (e.g., fading of prompts) change while the behavior remains constant and the criteria may or may not change. In still other cases, the behavior changes (e.g., learning new sets of words) while the con-

ditions and criteria remain constant. Any combination of the short-term objectives can change to create an individualized program for the student.

Short-Term Objectives forms for two of Joshua's annual goals are shown on pages 141 and 142.

 **Helpful Hints**

1. List only crucial conditions that are cross-situational. There will be an opportunity to describe more situation-specific conditions in Step 9 (Planning and Adapting Instruction).
2. Undoubtedly, you will find it helpful to seek input from various team members about what makes the most sense as you develop short-term objectives.

Finalizing the IEP Document

After your team has completed Part A of COACH, the team is prepared to finalize the IEP document. Because quality IEP planning is a process that includes a series of interrelated steps, by the time the team completes Part A of COACH, the IEP meeting typically involves only minor adjustments to the work that has been completed in advance with the family and other team members. There should not be surprises at the IEP meeting.

Step 4: Annual Goals

Priority Learning Outcome (from Step 1.5): _Responds to questions (yes/no)_

Current Level of Functioning Related to the Priority Learning Outcome: _Josh has the ability to move his eyes up and down and his head to some extent. He responds to yes/no questions with eye/head movement about 20% of the time._

Behavior: _Moves eyes/head up to indicate yes; down to indicate no._

Context: _Across settings_

Team Member Suggestions: _Give homework assignments to use yes/no; head positioned at midline_

Annual Goal: _In a variety of settings (e.g., home, school, community), Josh will respond to yes/no questions using head/eye movements (up = yes, down = no)._

Step 6: Short-Term Objectives

Clarify the intent/focus of Annual Goal to be reflected in the objectives (check those that apply or determine others):

_____ Decreasing prompts/cues	_____ Increasing response to natural cues
_____ Desensitizing/increasing tolerance	_____ Accepting assistance from others
✓ Acquiring core skills	_____ Initiation of behavior
_____ Preparation for the activity	_____ Quality of performance
_____ Appropriateness of tempo or rate	_____ Extending or reducing duration
_____ Self-monitoring	_____ Problem solving
_____ Termination of the behavior	_____ Assisting others with the behavior
_____ Safety aspects	_____ Expansion of repertoire
✓ Communication aspects	_____ Social behaviors aspects and manners
_____ Indication of choice or preference	_____ Retention over time
_____ Generalization across settings	_____ Generalization across people
_____ Generalization across materials	_____ Generalization across cues

	Conditions	Behavior	Criteria
1	When seated properly with head at midline, shown a photo and asked yes/no questions from communication board categories (food, people, places, activities)	Josh will answer using a combination of head and eye movements (up = yes, down = no)	regarding 10 questions with at least 75% correct for 3 consecutive sessions
2	As above	As above	regarding a second set of 15 questions with at least 75% correct for 3 consecutive sessions
3	As above	As above	regarding a third set of 20 questions with at least 75% correct for 3 consecutive sessions

Choosing Outcomes and Accommodations for Children • © 1998 by Michael F. Giangreco •
Baltimore: Paul H. Brookes Publishing Co.

Step 4: Annual Goals

Priority Learning Outcome (from Step 1.5): _Engages in individual active leisure_

Current Level of Functioning Related to the Priority Learning Outcome: _Josh can move his head side to side but often gets stuck turned to his right. He can initiate use of a head switch, but it takes over a minute and lasts 2-3 seconds._

Behavior: _Engages in active individual leisure by turning on a switch_

Context: _Across a variety of settings_

Team Member Suggestions: _Music, toys, page turner, computer, small appliances; ensure safety with use of electrical devices._

Annual Goal: _In a variety of settings, Josh will engage in individual active leisure by activating devices (e.g., tape player, toys, appliances) using an adapted switch._

Step 6: Short-Term Objectives

Clarify the intent/focus of Annual Goal to be reflected in the objectives (check those that apply or determine others):

- _____ Decreasing prompts/cues
- _____ Desensitizing/increasing tolerance
- ✓ Acquiring core skills
- _____ Preparation for the activity
- _____ Appropriateness of tempo or rate
- _____ Self-monitoring
- _____ Termination of the behavior
- _____ Safety aspects
- _____ Communication aspects
- _____ Indication of choice or preference
- _____ Generalization across settings
- _____ Generalization across materials

- _____ Increasing response to natural cues
- _____ Accepting assistance from others
- ✓ Initiation of behavior
- _____ Quality of performance
- ✓ (Extending) or reducing duration
- _____ Problem solving
- _____ Assisting others with the behavior
- _____ Expansion of repertoire
- _____ Social behaviors aspects and manners
- _____ Retention over time
- _____ Generalization across people
- _____ Generalization across cues

	Conditions	Behavior	Criteria
1	Given access to a head switch that turns on a variety of devices (e.g., toys, tape player, page turner)	Josh will initiate activation of the switch by moving his head to midline within 20 seconds of being asked	and will keep the switch on for at least 20 seconds for 4 of 5 sessions over 3 consecutive days
2	Same as above	As above within 10 seconds of being asked	As above for at least 60 seconds
3	Same as above	Same as above	As above for at least 2 minutes

Choosing Outcomes and Accommodations for Children • © 1998 by Michael F. Giangreco •
Baltimore: Paul H. Brookes Publishing Co.

142

Part B

STRATEGIES AND PROCESSES TO IMPLEMENT A COACH-GENERATED EDUCATIONAL PROGRAM

DESCRIPTION

Part B, Strategies and Processes to Implement a COACH-Generated Educational Program, focuses on *how* teams can effectively implement the educational program components generated in Part A. This is accomplished through a series of four steps designed to 1) organize and inform the instructional planning team (Steps 7.1–7.3); 2) develop a schedule for the student's participation in general education activities (Steps 8.1 and 8.2); 3) plan and adapt lessons to be implemented (Step 9); and 4) evaluate the impact of the educational program (Steps 10.1 and 10.2). A distinguishing feature of all the steps in Part B is that they are cyclical and ongoing throughout the school year. Although they are presented in a sequence, they are all interrelated and their use will overlap.

DIRECTIONS

PART B: STRATEGIES AND PROCESSES TO IMPLEMENT A COACH-GENERATED EDUCATIONAL PROGRAM

 Purpose

Part B of COACH is intended to provide a set of strategies and processes that will assist team members to implement a COACH-generated educational program. This is accomplished by organizing and informing the instructional planning team (Step 7), scheduling for the student with disabilities in the classroom (Step 8), planning and adapting instruction (Step 9), and evaluating the impact of educational experiences (Step 10).

 Materials

- COACH manual
- Photocopy of Appendix B (Blank COACH Forms)
- Pencil and eraser

 Instructions

Complete Steps 7, 8, 9, and 10. Specific directions for each step are presented in upcoming sections.

 Helpful Hints

1. Remember that Part B of COACH takes the planning that was done in Part A and turns it into reality on a day-to-day basis.
2. Steps included in Part B are intended to be used on an ongoing, cyclical basis.

Step 7

ORGANIZING AND INFORMING THE INSTRUCTIONAL PLANNING TEAM

DESCRIPTION

The effectiveness of the instructional planning team is a critical factor in facilitating a successful educational experience for a student with special educational needs in a general education classroom. The purpose of the instructional planning team is to enable team members to work together to plan and implement quality educational experiences for the students they teach. Although a team should be established before using Part A of COACH, it is not uncommon for IEP development and implementation to span parts of 2 school years. Throughout the course of the year the focus of the instructional planning team shifts from IEP development to more refined instructional planning and implementation. During this process, team membership may change, and with it the need to revisit a variety of issues regarding 1) team functioning and expectations (Step 7.1), 2) knowledge of the student (Step 7.2), and 3) knowledge of the general education program (Step 7.3).

Step 7.1: Reorganize the Team and Clarify Expectations

Step 7.1 addresses some of the most important teamwork tasks and common problems encountered by teams, such as identifying members' relationship to the team (e.g., core member, extended member); establishing meeting schedules and guidelines; and developing mechanisms for ongoing communication among team members. In addition, Step 7.1 provides reminders to clarify a variety of issues that, if left unclarified, will likely lead to a breakdown in team functioning and subsequently interfere with the student receiving an appropriate education. We suggest you clarify the following issues as well as others you identify:

- Who will be the service coordinator?
- Who will really teach the student?
- Who will train, plan for, and supervise paraprofessional staff?
- Who will make or adapt instructional materials?
- Who will maintain/care for specialized equipment?

Clarifying these and other instruction-related issues will assist team functioning by helping you establish an agreed-upon set of shared expectations.

Step 7.2: Become Familiar with the Student

Step 7.2 may seem too obvious to mention, but you might be surprised how common it is for some team members to proceed with their work without knowing some of the most basic information about the student. It is critical that all team members become familiar with the student's educational program components generated using Part A of COACH and summarized in the Program-at-a-Glance (Step 5). This establishes the shared student goals that are foundational to effective teamwork. In addition, team members should share student-

Step 7

specific information such as strengths, interests, motivations, preferred learning styles, and instructional approaches known to be effective. Although team members can gain knowledge of the student by reviewing documents, talking with staff who know the student, and meeting with the family, nothing can replace the invaluable knowledge you will gain by simply spending time with the student and other class members during naturally occurring class activities as well as less formal times (e.g., arrival, lunch, recess).

Step 7.3: Become Familiar with the General Education Program

Step 7.3 encourages team members to become familiar with the general education program and settings. None of us works in a vacuum, so we have to learn the context of the school and classroom and strive to ensure that our efforts on behalf of a student with disabilities match that context. To be most effective, team members need to have a working knowledge of basic information such as classroom schedules, typical routines, physical arrangement, curriculum content, teaching arrangements, and teacher expectations.

Team members providing support to the classroom teacher should provide support that reflects what the team has agreed the student needs (from the Program-at-a-Glance) within the context of what the teacher needs to provide a successful learning environment for the entire class (Giangreco, 1996d; Giangreco, Edelman, Dennis, Prelock, & Cloninger, 1997).

DIRECTIONS

STEP 7: ORGANIZING AND INFORMING THE INSTRUCTIONAL PLANNING TEAM

 **Purpose**

The purpose of Step 7 is to 1) reorganize the team and clarify expectations (Step 7.1); 2) become familiar with the student (Step 7.2); and 3) become familiar with the general education program (Step 7.3).

 **Instructions**

1. Complete Step 7.1 (Reorganize the Team and Clarify Expectations) (see listings for all substeps on Joshua's Step 7 form on p. 152).
2. Complete Step 7.2 (Become Familiar with the Student).
3. Complete Step 7.3 (Become Familiar with the General Education Program).

 **Helpful Hints**

1. We suggest you use a combination of face-to-face interactions and other forms of communication (e.g., mail, telephone, fax, e-mail) to complete Steps 7.1–7.3 initially and on an ongoing basis.
2. Continually addressing the issues raised in Step 7 will help you develop a shared framework as a team.
3. We suggest you keep team meeting agendas and minutes in a notebook that is available to all team members. The team meeting minutes can document your group's decisions.

Step 7:   Organizing and Informing the Instructional Planning Team

Directions: Write date(s) when each item is completed. Team meeting minutes can be used to document team decisions and actions pertaining to the items.

	Date Done

Step 7.1   Reorganize the Team and Clarify Expectations

1. Clarify any changes in team membership and people's relationship to the team (e.g., core, extended, situational resource). — *8/97*

2. Establish a team meeting schedule and guidelines (e.g., who needs to attend, dates and time, agenda, rotating roles). — *8/97*

3. Develop a way to exchange information and ideas among team members about upcoming classroom instructional activities to facilitate lesson planning, instruction, and evaluation. — *8/97*

4. Clarify who will assume service coordination responsibilities (e.g., information sharing among team members, coordinating paperwork requirements, scheduling, contacting parents). — *8/97*

5. Clarify who will design and implement the student's instruction. — *8/97*

6. Clarify who will train, plan for, and supervise paraprofessionals. — *8/97*

7. Clarify who will make and/or adapt instructional materials. — *8/97*

8. Clarify who will maintain/care for specialized equipment. — *8/97*

Step 7.2   Become Familiar with the Student

9. Ensure that all team members are familiar with the student's Program-at-a-Glance, Annual Goals, and related services. — *9/97*

10. Share information among team members about student-specific information (e.g., preferred learning styles, arrangements, motivations, instructional strategies, adaptations). — *9/97*

Step 7.3   Become Familiar with the General Education Program

11. Ensure that team members are knowledgeable about the general education program and settings (e.g., schedule, typical routines and activities, physical arrangements, curriculum content, class rules, teacher expectations). — *9/97*

12. Ask general class teachers what support they need from various team members, and how they wish to receive support. — *9/97*

Choosing Outcomes and Accommodations for Children   •   © 1998 by Michael F. Giangreco   •
Baltimore: Paul H. Brookes Publishing Co.

Step 8

SCHEDULING FOR THE STUDENT WITH DISABILITIES IN THE CLASSROOM

DESCRIPTION

All too often, team members expend significant effort developing an individualized education program that is not necessarily reflected in the daily schedule of activities for a student (Giangreco, Dennis, et al., 1994). Students may even be welcomed and included in general education activities, but they may not be pursuing the individualized learning outcomes that were selected as their priorities (Giangreco, Cloninger, et al., 1994). Step 8 (Scheduling for the Student with Disabilities in the Classroom) provides the team with a means to ensure that the student's IEP goals and objectives are incorporated into his or her daily class schedule using a Scheduling Matrix (Step 8.1) to develop an individualized Student Schedule (Step 8.2).

Step 8.1:
Scheduling Matrix

Step 8.1 is designed to address the aforementioned problems by explicitly comparing a student's priority learning outcomes and additional learning outcomes to a listing of class activities (e.g., arrival routine, opening routine, language arts, science, physical education). The scheduling matrix is a divergent activity in which team members consider the possibilities for working on a student's learning outcomes within the various class activities. This process is aided by the information gathered in Step 2.2 (Additional Learning Outcomes from General Education), which documents the nature of a student's participation in general class (e.g., multilevel; curriculum overlapping). Of course, the Scheduling Matrix can be used effectively only when team members are familiar with both the student and the general education program (Step 7).

Step 8.2:
Student Schedule

Step 8.2 is a convergent activity in which decisions are made about the possibilities generated using the Scheduling Matrix (Step 8.1). Deciding which learning outcomes will be addressed in which daily classes or activities requires team members to consider and balance a variety of issues:

- Are there sufficient opportunities for the student to work on identified learning priorities?
- Are there sufficient opportunities that pertain to the student's identified additional learning outcomes?
- Does the student's schedule follow the class routine as much as possible?
- Are learning outcomes and general supports addressed at the most naturally occurring times?
- Does the student have the same opportunities for breaks as students without disabilities so he or she has time to just be a kid?

The answers to these and other questions that arise as a result of scheduling may lead your team to rethink the range of the additional learning outcomes in the student's program as well as how instruction occurs.

The Student Schedule provides a space to list educational program components that should be addressed across all classes and activities. For example, for one student the team decides that using a rubber stamp to write his name, greeting others, participating in groups, and making choices are learning outcomes that will be addressed across all classes and activities. Other learning outcomes will be addressed during specific classes or activities. For example, using a computer will be worked on in language arts and computer class, while doing a classroom job will be addressed during the arrival and departure routines. When the schedule is completed, it provides increasing clarity to expectations for a student's participation throughout the school day. By looking at the schedule, a teacher or assistant would know what the instructional focus should be for a student when he or she is in math, language arts, or any other class. The physical education, art, and music teachers would have a clear understanding of their role with the child—of course, they should be involved in making such decisions. As the student progresses through the school year and as team members learn more about the student, the schedule should be adjusted accordingly.

DIRECTIONS

STEP 8: SCHEDULING FOR THE STUDENT WITH DISABILITIES IN THE CLASSROOM

! **Purpose**

Step 8 is intended to develop a schedule for the student with disabilities that addresses his or her individual needs as outlined in the Program-at-a-Glance within the context of general education classes and activities to the maximum extent appropriate.

📖 **Instructions**

1. Complete Step 8.1 (Scheduling Matrix).
2. Complete Step 8.2 (Student Schedule).

Specific directions for each step are presented in the upcoming subsections.

★ **Helpful Hints**

1. When exploring scheduling possibilities, keep in mind that a student may participate in general education class activities with classmates who do not have disabilities even if his or her learning outcomes are different from those of the rest of the class. This can be accomplished using multilevel curriculum and instruction, curriculum overlapping, or both (see Section I).
2. When scheduling, keep in mind the options available to students without disabilities in your school. For example, at the high school level students generally have more options for the types of courses they will take—use that flexibility to your student's advantage.
3. When scheduling, limit the number of students with disabilities participating in any single activity to a natural proportion with students who do not have disability labels. For example, in a whole-class activity of 25 students, you would expect to see about 3 students with disabili-

ties, and only 1 of those with severe disabilities. There is a danger that some schools or classes get targeted as the "inclusion classes" and end up with a disproportionately high number of students with disabilities—this scenario should be avoided.

DIRECTIONS

STEP 8.1: SCHEDULING MATRIX

! **Purpose**

Step 8.1 is designed to explore scheduling possibilities by comparing a student's educational program components to general class activities.

📖 Instructions

1. *List the student's name and grade* in the spaces provided.
2. Across the top of the matrix, *list general class activities or subjects* (e.g., arrival routine, circle time, language arts, math, social studies, industrial arts, library, lunch, recess, music, science).
3. Under each general class activity or subject, *list the typical amount of time devoted to that class or activity* when it occurs. This refers to the amount of time, not the time of day.
4. In the spaces provided on the left side of the matrix, *list abbreviations of each of the student's IEP annual goals* (e.g., "Makes Requests," "Makes Choices," "Offers Assistance to Others").
5. In the spaces provided on the left side of the matrix, *list the additional learning outcomes categories from the student's Program-at-a-Glance* (e.g., Communication/Language Arts; Socialization/Health; Selected Academics/Math). Specific learning outcomes can be found on the student's Program-at-a-Glance.
6. For each item listed under IEP Annual Goals and Additional Learning Outcomes categories, work horizontally across the page to *consider whether there are opportunities for the student to have learning experiences related to each entry. In the intersecting box, put a mark to indicate a possibility.* Use whatever marking system makes sense to you. Options include a) simple checkmarks, b) numbers corresponding to the Program-at-a-Glance, c) a designation regarding the type of participation (e.g., ML for multilevel; CO for curriculum overlapping); d) a designation indicating whether the

possibility is available currently (C) or could be with some adaptation (A); or e) any unique codes that you design to fit your own situation.

7. The information you generate in Step 8.1 is used to develop the actual schedule in Step 8.2.

Joshua's Scheduling Matrix is shown on page 161.

 **Helpful Hints**

1. Remember that using the Scheduling Matrix is a divergent step; therefore, explore possibilities of what is as well as what could be.

2. It is important to involve the classroom teachers in making decisions about what will be addressed in their respective classes. Your team has a head start on that with the information generated in Step 2.2 (Additional Learning Outcomes from General Education).

3. Sometimes when the matrix is completed, it highlights the fact that there is insufficient time available to work on certain learning outcomes. This might mean that new opportunities must be created so the student has sufficient learning opportunities. It may also mean that the number of additional learning outcomes may be too extensive and the team may need to reconsider the list. Alternatively, some of the additional learning outcomes may be considered consecutively, rather than addressing all of them simultaneously. For example, you could designate some of the additional learning outcomes for work during the first semester and others during the second semester.

Step 8.1: Scheduling Matrix

Directions: 1) List the IEP Annual Goals (Step 4), Additional Learning Outcomes categories (Steps 2.1 and 2.2), and class activities in the spaces provided. 2) Use the intersections of the learning outcomes and class activities to note instructional possibilities to assist in scheduling.

Note: General Supports will need to be considered when planning a schedule.

Student name: Joshua Green

Grade: 3

Class Activities

		Arrival	Lang. Arts	Math	Science	Social Studies	Phys. Ed.	Art	Music	Library	Recess	Lunch/Snack	Computer	Health	Depart
		20	75	45	40	40	35	35	35	35	20	20	35	35	10
IEP Annual Goals	Makes choices given options	✓	✓	✓	✓	✓	✓	✓	✓	✓	✓	✓	✓	✓	
	Responds to yes/no questions	✓	✓	✓	✓	✓	✓	✓	✓	✓	✓	✓	✓	✓	
	Makes requests	✓	✓	✓	✓	✓	✓	✓	✓	✓	✓	✓	✓	✓	
	Offers assistance to others	✓	✓	✓	✓	✓	✓	✓	✓	✓	✓	✓	✓	✓	
	Engages in individual leisure activities	✓	✓				✓	✓	✓	✓	✓	✓			
Additional Learning Outcomes Categories	Communication/Lang. Arts	✓	✓	✓	✓	✓	✓	✓	✓	✓	✓	✓	✓	✓	
	Socialization/Health	✓	✓	✓	✓	✓	✓	✓	✓	✓	✓	✓	✓	✓	
	Leisure/Rec./PE	✓				✓				✓					
	Computer											✓	✓		
	Personal Management		✓				✓								
	School	✓	✓	✓	✓	✓	✓	✓	✓	✓	✓	✓	✓	✓	
	Selected Academics/Math		✓	✓	✓			✓							
	Art/Music	✓						✓		✓					

Choosing Outcomes and Accommodations for Children • © 1998 by Michael F. Giangreco • Baltimore: Paul H. Brookes Publishing Co.

Step 8.1

161

DIRECTIONS
STEP 8.2: STUDENT SCHEDULE

! Purpose

Step 8.2 is used to develop a schedule that ensures the student with disabilities will have sufficient opportunities to work on priority learning outcomes and additional learning outcomes within general education classes and activities. The schedule should not constrain team member creativity or flexibility, but it should provide a focus so inclusion in general class activities directly addresses student needs. Given the wide variation in school and classroom scheduling, we have provided a mostly blank form so you can organize your schedule in whatever way makes the most sense to you.

Instructions

1. Consider whether there are any general supports that lend themselves to being addressed as an ongoing part of the daily schedule (see Helpful Hint 1). Consider whether they can be provided in conjunction with regularly scheduled class activities (e.g., fed at snack- and lunch time) or whether they must be scheduled based on time of day (e.g., clean intermittent catheterization scheduled upon arrival, midday, departure). *List these on the schedule in the appropriate places.* For those general supports that do not lend themselves to daily scheduling, information on how they will be addressed should be documented in team meeting minutes.

2. Consider whether there are any general supports, annual goals, or additional learning outcomes that should be addressed across all classes and activities. *List those in the appropriate places on the Student Schedule.*

3. For each general education class or activity listed on the Scheduling Matrix (Step 8.1), consider which annual goals, additional learning outcomes, and general supports will be addressed during those times (in addition to those already addressed across all classes/activities). *List these on the schedule in the appropriate places.* When mak-

ing these decisions, consider the amount of time devoted to the class or activity weekly. For example, presumably your team can address more in 75-minute language arts classes that occur daily than in a 35-minute art class that occurs once a week.

4. After completing the schedule, if any learning outcomes are not addressed, the team should verify when they will be addressed (e.g., second semester) or adjust the additional learning outcomes accordingly.

5. Distribute the schedule to the appropriate staff members.

Joshua's Student Schedule is shown on pages 164 and 165.

 **Helpful Hints**

1. Some general supports a) lend themselves to being addressed in the schedule on an ongoing basis (e.g., fed food and drinks, moved from place to place); b) happen initially but are not ongoing (e.g., teaching staff and peers about the student's communication); c) are primarily planning functions that occur at times when students are not present (e.g., instructional accommodations to general classes/activities and materials prepared in advance for multilevel instruction and curriculum overlapping); or d) do not relate to the daily classroom schedule (e.g., specialized transportation, environmental barriers modified to allow access).

2. People always ask if this approach includes opportunities for individual instruction. The answer is "Yes." This approach to scheduling is not meant to limit your options to meet a student's individual needs, but it does seek to avoid unnecessary separation from peers and typical class activities. Too often students with disabilities work individually with a paraprofessional or other special education staff member not because it is necessarily the most appropriate option, but rather because we have not fully explored the possibilities for addressing the student's needs within typical class activities.

3. As a team, make a conscious decision about whether part of the student's day should be unprogrammed. For example, although it is true that lunch and recess provide excellent opportunities to work on certain goals and objectives, consider giving the student a break the way other students without disabilities have a break. They may still be engaged in social learning through their peer interactions, even though it is not structured.

4. When determining a reasonable number of learning outcomes and general supports to address in a given class, consider the interrelationships among the learning outcomes. For example, a number of learning outcomes could be clustered within a single activity (e.g., participates in small group; responds to the presence and interactions of

Step 8.2
Student Schedule

for

Josh Green

(Student Name)

Directions: List classes/activities with corresponding Annual Goals, Additional Learning Outcomes, and General Supports.

Educational Program Components Addressed in All Classes

- *Makes choices given options (G)*
- *Responds to yes/no questions (G)*
- *Makes requests (G)*
- *Offers assistance to others (G)*
- *Expresses greetings/farewells (G)*
- *Recognizes photos, drawings, symbols (A)*
- *Responds to presence & interaction of others (A)*

- *Follows instructions (A)*
- *Participates in groups (A)*
- *Repositioned/specialized positioning (S)*
- *Moved from place to place (S)*

GENERAL CLASS OR ACTIVITY	*LEARNING OUTCOMES & GENERAL SUPPORTS*
ARRIVAL	• *Bathroom assistance (S)* • *Personal hygiene assistance (S)*
LANGUAGE ARTS	• *Summons others (A)* • *Listens to stories/looks at books (A)* • *Engages in active individual leisure (G)* • *Expresses emotions/physical states (A)* • *Works independently at task (A)* • *Identifies symbols (A)* • *Explores surroundings, differentiates/discriminates between things (A)*
MATH	• *Identifies symbols (A)* • *Distinguishes shapes (A)* • *Counts with correspondence (A)*

Key: **G** = Annual **Goal**   **A** = **Additional** Learning Outcomes   **S** = General **Supports**

(continued)

Choosing Outcomes and Accommodations for Children   •   © 1998 by Michael F. Giangreco   •
Baltimore: Paul H. Brookes Publishing Co.

SNACK
- Fed food and drinks (S)
- Bathroom assistance (S)

SCIENCE
- Explores, differentiates, discriminates between things (A)

SOCIAL STUDIES
- Gives self-identification info (A)
- Listens to stories, looks at books (A)

PHYSICAL EDUCATION
- Engages in active leisure with others (A)
- Participates in group games and activities (A)

ART
- Uses various art media (A)

MUSIC
- Plays rhythms on tape player (A)
- Plays music on keyboard with switch (A)

LIBRARY
- Listens to stories/looks at books (A)
- Summons others (A)

RECESS
- Engages in active leisure with others

LUNCH
- Fed food and drinks (S)
- Bathroom assistance (S)
- Personal hygiene assistance (S)

COMPUTER
- Uses single-response software to play educational games (A)

HEALTH
- Expresses emotions/physical states (A)

DEPARTURE
- Bathroom assistance (S)
- Personal hygiene assistance (S)

Key: **G** = Annual **Goal**   **A** = **Additional** Learning Outcomes   **S** = General **Supports**

Choosing Outcomes and Accommodations for Children   •   © 1998 by Michael F. Giangreco   •
Baltimore: Paul H. Brookes Publishing Co.

others; greets others; directs and sustains attention to activity; responds to yes/no questions). Also, not every learning outcome necessarily will be addressed in every class period; rather, these are the set of learning outcomes to be addressed at some time during these listed classes.

5. Even though a form is available to develop the student's schedule, those of you who have access to a computer may find it to be an alternative that will save time as you make adjustments in the schedule.

6. Scheduling may include community-based instruction such as vocational experiences for older high school students.

7. We suggest that you code your schedule entries to help team members remember the status of the educational program components (i.e., *G* = Annual Goal, *A* = Additional Learning Outcome, *S* = General Support).

Step 9

PLANNING AND ADAPTING INSTRUCTION

DESCRIPTION

At this point in the planning process, you have reached the stage of specific lesson planning and adaptation. Although a complete discussion of instructional planning is beyond the scope of this manual, there are a few basic points we would like to share with you to help you get the most out of COACH. Consider these questions:

- What is the lesson for the whole class or small group?
- What are the learning outcomes for the student?
- What materials do you need?
- What will you do, as a teacher, to teach the lesson?
- What do you expect the student to do (how will he or she respond)?
- What will you do if the student responds correctly?
- What will you do if the student responds incorrectly?
- How will you document the student's progress?

To facilitate inclusion of students with varying characteristics in shared educational activities, we must consider a range of potential adaptations, such as adjusting the expectations; changing the instructional format (e.g., small cooperative groups rather than lecture); providing an alternative way of responding (e.g., pointing rather than speaking); extending the time to complete a task; adapting materials; or providing access to peers for competent modeling.

Obviously, there are many more complete resources pertaining to instructional methods and approaches (e.g., Alberto & Troutman, 1995; Gardener et al., 1994; Johnson, Johnson, & Holubec, 1986; Snell, 1993; Stainback & Stainback, 1996; Thousand, Villa, & Nevin, 1994). We encourage you to obtain these and other resources to assist you in your instructional planning because *one of the single most pressing concerns regarding inclusive education is the lack of adequate instruction* that occurs for students with disabilities in general education classes. We do not believe this is a rationale to return to the former practice of placing students in special classes. Rather, recognition of the need for better instruction means that we must adapt instructional practices known to be effective and apply them in new ways.

One of the most exciting aspects of this challenge is the creativity required by team members and the class to invent these new ways of making instruction relevant and motivating. We have found that using the Osborn-Parnes Creative Problem-Solving (CPS) process (Parnes, 1988) (see p. 25) and variations of it (Giangreco, 1993) have proved to be extremely effective in inventing ways to include diverse groups of students who have different learning outcomes in shared educational experiences. A summary of how to apply CPS to curriculum overlapping challenges is available in Giangreco, Cloninger, et al. (1994). We know that passive

Step 9

instruction (e.g., lecture) presents limitations to teaching diverse groups. Conversely, if the instruction is active and participatory, the possibilities for adapting the curriculum and instruction are vast. By engaging in lesson planning on an ongoing basis, you can ensure that including students with disabilities in general education classes means more than "just being there"; it means students are truly part of the classroom community and are receiving an appropriate education.

DIRECTIONS

STEP 9: PLANNING AND ADAPTING INSTRUCTION

 Purpose

Step 9 is designed to develop and implement specific instructional plans to address short-term objectives in general class activities.

 **Instructions**

1. *List* a) *the student's name,* b) *who planned the lesson,* and c) *who will implement the plan* in the spaces provided on the form.
2. *List the class activity or lesson* (e.g., circle time, math class on fractions, science lab experiment on chemical reactions) in the space provided.
3. *List the short-term objective being addressed* for the student with disabilities in the space provided.
4. *List any materials needed for the lesson* in the space provided, including those for the whole class as well as specialized or individualized materials for the student with disabilities.
5. In the first column, *describe the sequence of what the teacher will do* (e.g., introduce the lesson, arrange materials, ask students questions, give students directions).
6. In the second column, *describe what you expect the student with a disability to do*—this should be described in observable terms so that it can be measured.
7. In the third column, *describe the consequences of correct and incorrect student responses.* In other words, note what will happen if the student responds correctly and what will happen if he or she does not (e.g., second try, errorless learning, prompted assistance, correction procedure).
8. In the fourth column, *describe how student progress will be measured and documented* (e.g., number/percentage

of correct responding, frequency count, duration of activity, permanent product such as writing or drawing, videotape).

A Planning and Adapting Instruction form for Joshua is shown on page 173.

 **Helpful Hints**

1. Step 9 is designed to provide your team with some very general prompts regarding instruction so you have a plan of what you will do and how you intend to do it. The vast aspects of planning instruction are beyond the scope of COACH, but a wealth of information is available on the topic, some of which is listed in Section II.

2. Although planning and adapting instruction has systematic components, this should not inhibit your creativity in planning interesting and motivating learning experiences.

3. We suggest that the planning for this step be completed by trained professional staff and that teachers implement most of the instruction. Too often the majority of planning and implementation for students with disabilities is relegated to undertrained, unsupervised paraprofessionals. Although these staff members may have great ideas, it is the teachers (general and special education) who have the primary responsibility for planning and implementing instruction.

4. You may find that a substantial amount of content from some of the lesson plans you develop can be applied to related situations. For example, if your team has developed an instructional procedure to teach choice making, you may find that the descriptions of the student's observable target behavior, consequences of correct and incorrect responding, and measurement of progress may remain rather consistent across various activities in which choice making is taught. This consistent part of the plan may be applied to various activities in which the materials and teacher behaviors may be different.

Step 9
Planning and Adapting Instruction

Student: _Josh Green_   Planned by: _Susan Lomax_   Implemented by: _Helena Sanchez and peers_

Class Activity/Lesson: _Social Studies – Teacher-made board game on the rainforest_

Short-Term Objective: _When asked yes/no questions, Josh will answer using eye/head movement (Obj. 1)_

Materials Needed: _Teacher-made board game; cards for each student with photos and questions (answers on reverse side); score cards and pencils for each student_

Describe the sequence of what the instructor will do	Describe what the student will do (in observable terms)	Describe the consequences of correct and incorrect student responses	Describe how student progress will be measured and documented
(1) Teacher introduces small-group game to four students, including Josh. Peers will ask questions of each other and keep track of correct answers. Teacher reviews game rules and floats among groups while students play. Cards have been prepared by teacher in advance to match student levels. (2) When it is Josh's turn, a peer shows him the card and asks him the question.	Josh will respond "yes" by moving his eyes/head up and "no" by moving his eyes/head down within 5 seconds of the question being asked.	If correct, peer tells him he was correct and moves his marker ahead on the board (number of spaces noted on the card). If incorrect: a) does not respond within 5 seconds – he is given a second chance. b) does not respond after second chance – he is told the answer and prompted to give the yes or no response. c) responds within 5 seconds but incorrectly – told it was a wrong answer and prompted to give correct response. d) responds correctly after second chance – told he's correct, moves 5 spaces ahead.	Each child has a score card with spaces 1–10. For each turn: 10 points/spaces for a correct response 5 points/spaces for a correct response on a second try 2 points/spaces for responding but being incorrect 0 points/spaces for not responding

Choosing Outcomes and Accommodations for Children • © 1998 by Michael F. Giangreco • Baltimore: Paul H. Brookes Publishing Co.

Step 9

Step 10

EVALUATING THE IMPACT OF EDUCATIONAL EXPERIENCES

DESCRIPTION

Often it is erroneously assumed that if students get good grades, that will translate into future educational, professional, and personal success. This is a dangerous assumption for any student, but particularly for those with disabilities. Although traditional forms of testing and evaluations may provide certain types of information, they won't predict the impact of your teaching on the student's post-school life. Unfortunately, far too many graduates with disabilities are plagued by unemployment, health problems, loneliness, or isolation—despite their glowing school progress reports.

We need to continually evaluate whether students are applying their achievements to real life, by looking at the effects on their physical and emotional health, personal growth, and positive social relationships; and their ability to communicate, advocate for themselves, make informed choices, contribute to the community, and increasingly access places and activities that are personally meaningful. The aim is to ensure that our teaching will really make a positive difference in our students' lives. (Giangreco, 1996d, p. 59)

Step 10, Evaluating the Impact of Educational Experiences, consists of two substeps, one that addresses the impact of learning outcomes (Step 10.1) and another that addresses the impact of general supports (Step 10.2). Each includes a short set of questions that team members ask each other to evaluate the activities and outcomes of the educational program as they relate to a student's corresponding valued life outcomes. The evaluation of impact process is meant to be used in conjunction with more standard evaluation approaches; it is not meant to replace them. It poses questions to the team designed to keep them focused on the valued life outcomes being sought for the student. The evaluation of impact process is designed to be used on an ongoing basis as part of the instructional cycle that includes planning, implementation, and evaluation.

The evaluation of impact process recognizes that *the status of valued life outcomes may be improved by the process and activities of working toward identified learning outcomes or general supports, even in the absence of significant student progress toward attaining educational outcomes.* The following examples illustrate some variations depicting potential relationships between student learning outcomes, general supports, and valued life outcomes. The examples also highlight how student learning outcomes, general supports, and valued life outcomes may be both independent and interdependent.

Step 10

**Example 1:
Learning Outcomes**

Emilio, a student with multiple disabilities, has a goal to "improve his eating skills" (e.g., chewing, swallowing, amount of food intake). Using COACH (Step 1.5), this goal was selected as a priority by Emilio's family because he has a very difficult time eating. He is frequently undernourished and underhydrated. Emilio's physician has told the family that, if his eating skills do not improve soon, he will need a gastrostomy tube for feeding. In addition, problems with swallowing occasionally result in the aspiration of food, leading to respiratory infections (e.g., pneumonia), some of which may be life threatening. As documented in COACH Step 1.5, the family indicated that they selected improvement in eating skills as a priority because it corresponds with the valued life outcome "Being Safe and Healthy."

Using the evaluation of impact process, Emilio's chewing, swallowing, and food intake skills would be evaluated based on his IEP goals and objectives related to eating. This aspect of the process is similar to any evaluation process, but the evaluation of impact process extends beyond this traditional approach of using objectives as the exclusive measure of success. If Emilio's eating skills improve (e.g., he attains his objectives), it is not enough to claim success or impact. The evaluation of impact process also asks the team to consider whether changes in student behavior (e.g., attaining IEP objectives) have resulted in the corresponding valued life outcome(s)—in this case, improved health for Emilio as determined by a decrease in aspiration-related illness, weight gain, and improved nutrition and vitality. Emilio's family is necessarily going to be important in considering whether the valued life outcome(s) have been fulfilled. In this example, the evaluation of impact process is used to examine the status of student achievement (eating skills) and is referenced to corresponding valued life outcomes (being healthy).

**Example 2:
Facilitating Valued
Life Outcomes
in the Absence of
Student Learning**

In another scenario, Amy's family selected having a way to "call others to her" (summoning) as a priority. Because Amy is not self-mobile in her wheelchair, she cannot approach other people on her own. When physically in a different location from people with whom she wishes to interact, Amy frequently will cry in an attempt to gain their attention or just sit passively waiting for someone to approach her. As a result, Amy's classmates spent very little time with her during social times (e.g., before school, lunch, recess), and, when they did, classroom staff reported that the nature of the interactions typically did not seem positive.

It was decided it would be desirable for Amy to have an alternate method to express herself that would be more socially acceptable than crying or waiting. "Calling others to her" was selected to pursue the valued life outcome "Having Meaningful Relationships." It was hoped that new skills in this area would result in greater frequency of contact between Amy and her classmates as well as enhance the nature of the contact.

The team developed an educational program (Step 9) to teach Amy how to use an augmentative communication device activated by a switch. The switch activated summoning messages recorded by Amy's classmates. Classmates participated in designing and decorating the box in which Amy's switch was mounted and were an integral part of the training on how to use the switch. Classmates' interactions with Amy in response to switch activation were natural reinforcers for Amy.

After several weeks of diligent work on teaching this summoning behavior, Amy had not made any noticeable gains. If the sole criterion for success had been Amy achieving her objectives related to summoning, it would have to be said that this experience was not successful to date. However, using the evaluation of impact process, the team asked an additional question about the status of the corresponding valued life outcome and learned that the frequency of contact between Amy and her classmates during social times (e.g., before school, lunch, recess) had increased and the nature of the contact had also improved. Considering changes in valued life outcomes fundamentally alters what constitutes success in an educational program. That is, although progress toward Amy's objective of summoning others was limited, progress on the valued life outcome of "Having Meaningful Relationships" was significant.

Example 3: General Supports

There are also occasions when a team may consciously decide they are not targeting certain skills for the student to acquire. Rather, they intend to facilitate identified valued life outcomes by providing general supports to the student's educational program in integrated settings. For example, they may establish a peer support network in an attempt to develop personal relationships, build ramps to allow access to new places, or provide different equipment or techniques to improve the student's health.

Providing general supports is not done to abandon skill development; skill development can be an important vehicle to a better life. At the same time, it is unreasonable to make skill development a prerequisite or the exclusive path to valued life outcomes. What could be the rationale for requiring behavior change exclusively on the part of an individual who experiences serious challenges to learning and adaptive behavior, while not simultaneously asking people without disabilities (presumably with less challenges to learning) to also make changes? This notion is particularly important as it relates to access to school environments. In the past, and still in some places today, students are asked to "earn" the right to be integrated by demonstrating skill development/behavior change (Kunc, 1992). As Kunc points out, students are more likely to pursue achievement-oriented outcomes if they are in a school that welcomes and accepts them regardless of their "skills." Students are able to pursue valued life outcomes and the benefits of general education placements given supports without necessarily demonstrating significant behavior change.

DIRECTIONS

STEP 10: EVALUATING THE IMPACT OF EDUCATIONAL EXPERIENCES

! Purpose

Step 10 is designed to evaluate instruction on annual goals, additional learning outcomes, and the provision of general supports to determine if they are having the desired impact on students and to make decisions about the need for change.

📖 Instructions

1. Complete Step 10.1 (Evaluation of Impact Process for Learning Outcomes) for each annual goal on the IEP and Additional Learning Outcomes categories from the Program-at-a-Glance at agreed-upon intervals.
2. Complete Step 10.2 (Evaluation of Impact Process for General Supports) for each general support category pertinent to the student at agreed-upon intervals.

Specific directions for each step are presented in the upcoming subsections.

★ Helpful Hint

1. The evaluation of impact process is not meant to replace quantitative measures of student progress or traditional forms of progress reporting (e.g., report cards, progress narratives). Rather, it is meant to augment these approaches and assist teams in focusing on whether and how the student's education is affecting valued life outcomes.

DIRECTIONS

STEP 10.1: EVALUATION OF IMPACT PROCESS FOR LEARNING OUTCOMES

! Purpose

Step 10.1 is designed to evaluate instruction on learning outcomes (e.g., annual goals, additional learning outcomes) to determine if they are having the desired impact on the student and to make decisions about the need for change.

📖 Instructions

1. Decide the frequency with which you plan to use the evaluation of impact process. We suggest that the questions be used informally to guide a team discussion whenever progress on a particular goal is being discussed. The evaluation of impact process can be formally completed at times that coincide with the school's marking periods.
2. *List the student's name, date* of the meeting, and *participating team members* in the spaces provided.
3. *List the annual goal or additional learning outcome being discussed* in the space provided. Usually an abbreviated format is sufficient.
4. *List the valued life outcome(s) being facilitated* through the listed learning outcome. This is meant to refocus team members on the purpose of their work.
5. *List the date that the learning outcome was last discussed and what has been done* to teach the student.
6. *List any student progress* regarding the learning outcome.
7. *List any changes in the valued life outcome(s).*
8. *List any changes agreed to by team members.*

Joshua's Evaluation of Impact Process for Learning Outcomes form is shown on page 184.

 **Helpful Hints**

1. Evaluation of Impact Process forms can be part of the student's portfolio.

2. When possible, questions from the evaluation of impact process can be directed to the student using individually appropriate communication strategies.

3. The Evaluation of Impact Process for Learning Outcomes is designed specifically to address the priority learning outcomes identified as IEP annual goals and can be applied to additional learning outcomes that have been identified for the student. As with priority learning outcomes, if the evaluation of impact process is used for additional learning outcomes or categories, it is meant to augment rather than replace existing forms of progress evaluation and reporting.

4. The family should be included in discussions regarding the Evaluation of Impact Process for Learning Outcomes.

5. The completed Evaluation of Impact Process for Learning Outcomes form should be made available to team members and used to establish accountability that needed changes are made.

Step 10.1
Evaluation of Impact Process
for Learning Outcomes

Directions: Answer the following questions to discuss student progress toward IEP Annual Goals or Additional Learning Outcomes categories.

Student name: _Josh Green_ Date of team meeting: _11/6/96_

Team members participating in discussion: _Karen Green, Susan Lomax, Helena Sanchez, Carey Scott_

---

1. **Annual Goal** or **Additional Learning Outcome(s)** being discussed: _Responds to yes/no questions_

2. **Valued Life Outcome(s)** being facilitated through the learning outcome(s): _Relationships/activities and places/choices and control_

---

3. When was the last time this learning outcome was discussed by the team? Date: _9/18/96_

4. What has been done to teach the student this learning outcome since it was last discussed? _Adaptations have been made in each class to work on yes/no responses with class activities._

5. What progress has the student made on the learning outcome? _Josh has increased correct responding from about 20% to 40% correct, but it seems to decrease as the day goes on (tired)._

6. What changes, if any, has the student experienced on the corresponding Valued Life Outcome(s)? _Classmates have begun to ask Josh more questions out of the context of lessons; he's having more peer-initiated opportunities during social times._

7. What changes, if any, need to be made in the educational program to enhance progress or facilitate the corresponding Valued Life Outcome(s)? _Talk to PT about ways to provide Josh with a resting position when he is not communicating, so he doesn't fade as much as the day goes on._

Choosing Outcomes and Accommodations for Children • © 1998 by Michael F. Giangreco •
Baltimore: Paul H. Brookes Publishing Co.

DIRECTIONS

STEP 10.2: EVALUATION OF IMPACT PROCESS FOR GENERAL SUPPORTS

! Purpose

Step 10.2 is designed to evaluate the provision of general supports to determine if they are having the desired impact on the student and to make decisions about the need for change.

Instructions

1. Decide the frequency with which you plan to use the evaluation of impact process. We suggest that the questions be used informally to guide a team discussion whenever progress on a particular general support category is being discussed. The Evaluation of Impact Process for General Supports can be formally completed at times that coincide with the school's marking periods.

2. *List the student's name, date* of the meeting, and *participating team members* in the spaces provided.

3. *List the general support category being discussed, as well as individual items,* in the space provided. Usually an abbreviated format is sufficient. Depending on the number of items in a category, you may need to use more than one page of the form.

4. *List the valued life outcome(s) being facilitated* through the listed general support category. This is meant to refocus team members on the purpose of their work.

5. *List the date that the general support category was last discussed and what has been done* since then.

6. *List the current status* regarding the general support category.

7. *List any changes in the valued life outcomes* the student has experienced as a result of having the general support provided.

8. *List any changes agreed to by team members.*

Joshua's Evaluation of Impact Process for General Supports form is shown on page 187.

 **Helpful Hints**

1. Evaluation of Impact Process for General Supports forms can be part of the student's portfolio.
2. When possible, questions from the Evaluation of Impact Process for General Supports can be directed to the student using individually appropriate communication strategies.
3. The family should be included in discussions regarding the Evaluation of Impact Process for General Supports.
4. The completed Evaluation of Impact Process for General Supports form should be made available to team members and used to establish accountability that needed changes are made.

Step 10.2
Evaluation of Impact Process
for General Supports

Directions: Answer the following questions to discuss the student's status regarding the identified General Supports category; use one page for each area.

Student name: _Josh Green_____ Date of team meeting: _11/6/96_____

Team members participating in discussion: ___Karen Green, Susan Lomax, Helena Sanchez, Carey Scott_

1. **General Supports** category being discussed: _Physical needs_____
   Items: _a) repositioning, b) environmental barriers (others on a different page)_

2. **Valued Life Outcome(s)** being facilitated through these general supports: _____
   a) health, b) access to places/activities/choices

3. When was the last time these general supports were discussed by the team?
   Date: _9/10/96_____

4. What has been done since then related to these general supports? _Staff have been trained in positioning; a booklet with Polaroids has been made; a ramp has been built to provide access in the library._

5. What is the current status of these general supports? _Original tasks completed_

6. What changes, if any, has the student experienced on the corresponding Valued Life Outcome(s) as a result of having these general supports provided? _Josh is being positioned in ways to maintain his health; he has access and choice to use parts of the library that weren't accessible before._

7. What changes, if any, need to be made in the educational program regarding these general supports to facilitate the corresponding Valued Life Outcome(s)? _Develop a plan to monitor positioning to ensure that it is happening at the appropriate intervals and happening properly._

Choosing Outcomes and Accommodations for Children   •   © 1998 by Michael F. Giangreco   •
Baltimore: Paul H. Brookes Publishing Co.

CONCLUSION

In closing, we wish to remind you that COACH, like any tool, must be used with care and skill to achieve optimal results. Such care and skill on your part will mean that you are constantly thinking about what you are doing rather than filling out forms in a rote manner. This means you must individualize what you do to match the situation; continually seek to improve your own skills; deepen your own understanding; and judge your collective success by the impact your team's actions have on the lives of your students, their families, and the broader community. We know through our experiences that many of you will find new and creative ways to use the ideas in COACH to improve on the work we offer to you; we applaud those efforts and hope you will share them with us.

The fact that COACH has been revised so many times over the past several years is a reflection that our field and our understanding of what constitutes exemplary practices is always changing and being refined. We offer you the ideas contained in this book as our current thinking at the time of writing and with the recognition that future change is inevitable and desirable. We hope that the ideas and skills you bring to using COACH will improve it beyond our current conceptualization of the process to match the needs in your community and the children you serve.

REFERENCES

Alberto, P., & Troutman, A.C. (1995). *Applied behavior analysis for teachers.* Columbus, OH: Charles E. Merrill.

Biklen, D., & Knoll, J. (1987). The disabled minority. In S. Taylor, D. Biklen, & J. Knoll (Eds.), *Community integration for people with severe disabilities* (pp. 3–21). New York: Teachers College Press.

Brown, F., Evans, I., Weed, K., & Owen, V. (1987). Delineating functional competencies: A component model. *Journal of The Association for Persons with Severe Handicaps, 12,* 117–124.

Brown, L., Branston, M.B., Hamre-Nietupski, S., Pumpian, I., Certo, N., & Gruenewald, L. (1979). A strategy for developing chronologically age-appropriate and functional curricular content for severely handicapped adolescents and young adults. *Journal of Special Education, 13,* 81–90.

Brown, L., Nietupski, J., & Hamre-Nietupski, S. (1976). The criterion of ultimate functioning and public school services for severely handicapped students. In M.A. Thomas (Ed.), *Hey, don't forget about me! Education's investment in the severely, profoundly, and multiply handicapped* (pp. 2–15). Reston, VA: Council for Exceptional Children.

Campbell, C., Campbell, S., Collicott, J., Perner, D., & Stone, J. (1988). Individualized instruction. *Education New Brunswick–Journal Education, 3,* 17–20.

Dennis, R.E., & Giangreco, M.F. (1996). Creating conversation: Reflections on cultural sensitivity in family interviewing. *Exceptional Children, 63*(1), 103–116.

Dennis, R.E., Williams, W., Giangreco, M.F., & Cloninger, C.J. (1993). Quality of life as a context for planning and evaluation of services for people with disabilities. *Exceptional Children, 59,* 499–512.

Donnellan, A. (1984). The criterion of the least dangerous assumption. *Behavioral Disorders, 9,* 141–150.

Downing, J.E. (1996). *Including students with severe and multiple disabilities in typical classrooms: Practical strategies for teachers.* Baltimore: Paul H. Brookes Publishing Co.

Dunn, W. (1991). Integrated related services. In L.H. Meyer, C.A. Peck, & L. Brown (Eds.), *Critical issues in the lives of people with severe disabilities* (pp. 353–377). Baltimore: Paul H. Brookes Publishing Co.

Edelman, S., Knutson, J., Osborn, D., & Giangreco, M.F. (1995). Heidi's inclusion in junior high: Transition and educational planning for a student with deaf-blindness. *Deaf-Blind Perspectives, 2*(3), 1–6.

Education for All Handicapped Children Act of 1975, PL 94–142, 20 U.S.C. §§ 1400 *et seq.*

England, J. (1994). *Related services in inclusive classrooms.* Detroit: Developmental Disabilities Institute, University Affiliated Program of Michigan, Wayne State University.

Falvey, M.A., Forest, M., Pearpoint, J., & Rosenberg, R.L. (1994). Building connections. In J.S. Thousand, R.A. Villa, & A.I. Nevin (Eds.), *Creativity and collaborative learning: A practical guide to empowering students and teachers* (pp. 347–368). Baltimore: Paul H. Brookes Publishing Co.

Ferguson, D.L., & Baumgart, D. (1991). Partial participation revisited. *Journal of The Association for Persons with Severe Handicaps, 16*(4), 218–228.

Ford, A., & Mirenda, P. (1984). Community instruction: A natural cues and corrections decision model. *Journal of The Association for Persons with Severe Handicaps, 9*, 79–87.

Gardener, R., III, Sainato, D., Cooper, J.O., Heron, T.E., Heward, W., Eshleman, J., & Grossi, T. (Eds.). (1994). *Behavior analysis in education: Focus on measurably superior instruction.* Pacific Grove, CA: Brooks/Cole.

Giangreco, M.F. (1993). Using creative problem solving methods to include students with severe disabilities in general education classroom activities. *Journal of Educational and Psychological Consultation, 4*(2), 113–135.

Giangreco, M.F. (1996a). Choosing options and accommodations for children (COACH): Curriculum planning for students with disabilities in general education classrooms. In S. Stainback & W. Stainback (Eds.), *Inclusion: A guide for educators* (pp. 237–254). Baltimore: Paul H. Brookes Publishing Co.

Giangreco, M.F. (1996b). "The stairs didn't go anywhere!" A self-advocate's reflections on specialized services and their impact on people with disabilities. *Physical Disabilities: Education and Related Services, 14*(2), 1–12.

Giangreco, M.F. (1996c). *Vermont interdependent services team approach (VISTA): A guide to coordinating educational support services.* Baltimore: Paul H. Brookes Publishing Co.

Giangreco, M.F. (1996d). What do I do now? Teacher's guide to including students with disabilities. *Educational Leadership, 53*(5), 56–59.

Giangreco, M.F., Baumgart, D., & Doyle, M.B. (1995). How inclusion can facilitate teaching and learning. *Intervention in School and Clinic, 30*(5), 273–278.

Giangreco, M.F., Cloninger, C.J., Dennis, R.E., & Edelman, S.W. (1993). National expert validation of COACH: Congruence with exemplary practice and suggestions for improvement. *Journal of The Association for Persons with Severe Handicaps, 18*(2), 109–120.

Giangreco, M.F., Cloninger, C.J., Dennis, R.E., & Edelman, S.W. (1994). Problem-solving methods to facilitate inclusive education. In J.S. Thousand, R.A. Villa, & A.I. Nevin (Eds.), *Creativity and collaborative learning: A practical guide to empowering students and teachers* (pp. 321–346). Baltimore: Paul H. Brookes Publishing Co.

Giangreco, M.F., Cloninger, C.J., & Iverson, V.S. (1993). *Choosing options and accommodations for children (COACH): A guide to planning inclusive education.* Baltimore: Paul H. Brookes Publishing Co.

Giangreco, M.F., Cloninger, C., Mueller, P., Yuan, S., & Ashworth, S. (1991). Perspectives of parents whose children have dual sensory impairments. *Journal of The Association for Persons with Severe Handicaps, 16*(1), 14–24.

Giangreco, M.F., Dennis, R., Edelman, S., & Cloninger, C. (1994). Dressing your IEPs for the general education climate: Analysis of IEP goals and objectives for students with multiple disabilities. *Remedial and Special Education, 15*(5), 288–296.

Giangreco, M.F., Edelman, S., & Dennis, R. (1991). Common professional practices that interfere with the integrated delivery of related services. *Remedial and Special Education, 12*, 16–24.

Giangreco, M.F., Edelman, S., Dennis, R., & Cloninger, C.J. (1995). Use and impact of COACH with students who are deaf-blind. *Journal of The Association for Persons with Severe Handicaps, 20*(2), 121–135.

Giangreco, M.F., Edelman, S.W., Dennis, R.E., Prelock, R.E., & Cloninger, C.J. (1997). Getting the most out of support services. In M.F. Giangreco (Ed.), *Quick-guide to inclusion: Ideas for educating students with disabilities* (pp. 85–111). Baltimore: Paul H. Brookes Publishing Co.

Giangreco, M.F., Edelman, S.W., Luiselli, T.E., & MacFarland, S.Z. (in press-a). Helping or hovering? Effects of instructional assistant proximity on students with disabilities. *Exceptional Children.*

Giangreco, M.F., Edelman, S.W., Luiselli, T.E., & MacFarland, S.Z. (in press-b). Reaching consensus about educationally necessary support services: A qualitative evaluation of VISTA. *Special Services in the Schools.*

Giangreco, M.F., & Meyer, L.H. (1988). Expanding service delivery options in regular schools and classrooms for students with severe disabilities. In J.L. Graden, J.E. Zins, & M.J. Curtis (Eds.), *Alternative educational delivery systems: Enhancing instructional options for all students* (pp. 241–267). Washington, DC: National Association of School Psychologists.

Giangreco, M.F., & Putnam, J.W. (1991). Supporting the education of students with severe disabilities in regular education environments. In L.H. Meyer, C.A. Peck, & L. Brown (Eds.), *Critical issues in the lives of people with severe disabilities* (pp. 245–270). Baltimore: Paul H. Brookes Publishing Co.

Giangreco, M.F., & Snell, M.E. (1996). Severe and multiple disabilities. In R. Turnbull & A. Turnbull (Eds.), *Improving the implementation of the Individuals with Disabilities Education Act: Making schools work for all of America's children* (pp. 97–132). Washington, DC: National Council on Disability.

Giangreco, M.F., Whiteford, T., Whiteford, L., & Doyle, M.B. (1997). *Planning for Andrew: A case study of COACH and VISTA use in an inclusive early childhood program.* Burlington: University of Vermont, University Affiliated Program of Vermont.

Guess, D., & Helmstetter, E. (1986). Skill cluster instruction and the individualized curriculum sequencing model. In R.H. Horner, L.H. Meyer, & H.D.B. Fredericks (Eds.), *Education of learners with severe handicaps: Exemplary service strategies* (pp. 221–248). Baltimore: Paul H. Brookes Publishing Co.

Harry, B. (1992). *Cultural diversity, families and the special education system: Communication and empowerment.* New York: Teachers College Press.

Individuals with Disabilities Education Act (IDEA) of 1990, PL 101-476, 20 U.S.C. §§ 1400 *et seq.*

Individuals with Disabilities Education Act Amendments of 1997, PL 105-17, 20 U.S.C. §§ 1400 *et seq.*

Johnson, D.W., Johnson, R.T., & Holubec, E.J. (1986). *Circles of learning: Cooperation in the classroom* (Rev. ed). Edina, MN: Interaction Book Company.

Kunc, N. (1992). The need to belong: Rediscovering Maslow's hierarchy of needs. In R.A. Villa, J.S. Thousand, W. Stainback, & S. Stainback (Eds.), *Restructuring for caring and effective education: An administrative guide to creating heterogeneous schools* (pp. 25–39). Baltimore: Paul H. Brookes Publishing Co.

Kunc, N. (1996 June). *Speech presented at the CARC annual meeting*. South Burlington, VT.

Laski, F.J. (1991). Achieving integration during the second revolution. In L.H. Meyer, C.A. Peck, & L. Brown (Eds.), *Critical issues in the lives of people with severe disabilities* (pp. 409–421). Baltimore: Paul H. Brookes Publishing Co.

Lipsky, D.K., & Gartner, A. (Eds.). (1989). *Beyond separate education: Quality education for all.* Baltimore: Paul H. Brookes Publishing Co.

Lynch, E.W., & Hanson, M.J. (Eds.). (1992). *Developing cross cultural competence: A guide for working with young children and their families.* Baltimore: Paul H. Brookes Publishing Co.

McEwen, I. (1995). *Occupational and physical therapy in educational environments* . Binghamton, NY: Haworth Press.

National Center for Inclusive Education and School Restructuring. (1995). *National study of inclusive education* (2nd Ed.). New York: Author.

Nisbet, J. (Ed.). (1992). *Natural supports in school, at work, and in the community for people with severe disabilities.* Baltimore: Paul H. Brookes Publishing Co.

Oberti v. Board of Education of the Borough of Clementon School District, 995 F.2d 1204 (3rd Cir. 1993).

Orelove, F.P., & Sobsey, D. (1996). *Educating children with multiple disabilities: A transdisciplinary approach* (3rd ed.). Baltimore: Paul H. Brookes Publishing Co.

Osborn, A. (1953). *Applied imagination: Principles and procedures of creative thinking.* New York: Charles Scribner's Sons.

Parnes, S.J. (1988). *Visionizing: State-of-the-art processes for encouraging innovative excellence.* East Aurora, NY: D.O.K. Publishing.

Parnes, S.J. (1992). *Source book for creative problem-solving: A fifty year digest of proven innovative processes.* Buffalo, NY: Creative Education Foundation Press.

Powell, T.H., & Gallagher, P.A. (1993). *Brothers & sisters—A special part of exceptional families* (2nd ed.). Baltimore: Paul H. Brookes Publishing Co.

Rainforth, B., & York-Barr, J. (1997). *Collaborative teams for students with severe disabilities: Integrating therapy and educational services* (2nd ed.). Baltimore: Paul H. Brookes Publishing Co.

Sacramento City Unified School District v. Rachel H., 14 F.3d. 1398 (9th Cir. 1994).

Snell, M.E. (Ed.). (1993). *Instruction of students with severe disabilities* (4th ed.). Columbus, OH: Charles E. Merrill.

Snell, M.E., & Brown, F. (1993). Instructional planning and implementation. In M.E. Snell (Ed.), *Instruction of students with se-*

vere disabilities (4th ed., pp. 99–151). Columbus, OH: Charles E. Merrill.

Sobsey, D., & Ludlow, B. (1984). Guidelines for setting instructional criteria. *Education and Treatment of Children, 7,* 157–165.

Speight, S., Myers, L., Cox, C., & Highlen, P. (1991). A redefinition of multicultural counseling. *Journal of Counseling and Development, 70,* 29–36.

Stainback, S., & Stainback, W. (Eds.). (1996). *Inclusion: A guide for educators.* Baltimore: Paul H. Brookes Publishing Co.

Taylor, S.J. (1988). Caught in the continuum: A critical analysis of the principle of the least restrictive environment. *Journal of The Association for Persons with Severe Handicaps, 13,* 41–53.

Thousand, J.S., & Villa, R.A. (1992). Collaborative teams: A powerful tool in school restructuring. In R.A. Villa, J.S. Thousand, W. Stainback, & S. Stainback (Eds.), *Restructuring for caring and effective education: An administrative guide to creating heterogeneous schools* (pp. 73–108). Baltimore: Paul H. Brookes Publishing Co.

Thousand, J.S., Villa, R.A., & Nevin, A.I. (Eds.). (1994). *Creativity and collaborative learning: A practical guide to empowering students and teachers.* Baltimore: Paul H. Brookes Publishing Co.

Turnbull, A., Turnbull R., Shank, M., & Leal, D. (1995). *Exceptional children: Exceptional lives.* Englewood Cliffs, NJ: Prentice Hall.

Villa, R., & Thousand, J. (1996). *Creating an inclusive school.* Alexandria, VA: Association for Supervision and Curriculum Development.

Wolfensberger, W. (1970). *The principle of normalization in human services.* Toronto, Ontario, Canada: National Institute on Mental Retardation.

York, J., Giangreco, M.F., Vandercook, T., & Macdonald, C. (1992). Integrating support personnel in the inclusive classroom. In S. Stainback & W. Stainback (Eds.), *Curriculum considerations in inclusive classrooms: Facilitating learning for all students* (pp. 101–116). Baltimore: Paul H. Brookes Publishing Co.

Appendix A

QUESTIONS
AND ANSWERS
FOR PARENTS
ABOUT COACH

Dear Parent:

Your child's educational team is interested in using a process called "COACH" to help them plan and implement a quality educational program for your child by involving your family in the planning process along with other team members. What follows are commonly asked questions about COACH and answers we hope will give you a good sense of what COACH is about.

Q1: What does COACH stand for?

A1:   *C*hoosing *O*utcomes and *A*ccommodations for *CH*ildren.

Q2: What is COACH?

A2:   COACH is a planning tool used by educational teams to develop individualized education programs (IEPs) for students with special educational needs. COACH is divided into two major parts, each having a series of steps.

Part A: Determining a Student's Educational Program
Step 1:   Family Interview (to determine family learning priorities for the student's educational program)
Step 2:   Additional Learning Outcomes (to determine learning outcomes in addition to the family priorities)
Step 3:   General Supports (to determine what needs to be done to or for the student)
Step 4:   Annual Goals (to ensure that the family's priorities are reflected in the IEP)
Step 5:   Program-at-a-Glance (a one- to two-page summary of the educational program—Part A, Steps 1, 2, 3, and 4)
Step 6:   Short-Term Objectives (to develop short-term objectives to achieve annual goals)

Part B: Strategies and Processes to Implement a COACH-Generated Educational Program
Step 7:   Organizing and Informing the Instructional Planning Team (to ensure the educational plans are carried out)
Step 8:   Scheduling for the Student with Disabilities in the Classroom (to develop a schedule of appropriate activities)
Step 9:   Planning and Adapting Instruction (to ensure that instructional plans are developed and implemented that address student needs and participation in class activities when goals are different from those of classmates)
Step 10:   Evaluating the Impact of Educational Experiences (to ensure the educational plans are evaluated to determine whether they are having a positive impact on the student)

Q3: What are the principles and philosophy on which COACH is based?

A3: A full explanation of the principles and philosophy on which COACH is based can be found in the COACH manual. COACH is based on a set of six guiding principles:

1. **Pursuing valued life outcomes is an important aspect of education.** This means that the ultimate goal of education is to pursue a path leading to an ever-improving life. This will be very individualized because a "good life" means different things to different people.

    We have asked other parents who have children with disabilities what makes a good life for their children. We have broadly categorized their ideas as a set of five valued life outcomes in COACH:

    - Being safe and healthy
    - Having a home in which to live, now and in the future
    - Having meaningful relationships
    - Having choice and control that match one's age and culture
    - Participating in meaningful activities in various places

2. **The family is the cornerstone of educational planning.**
3. **Collaborative teamwork is essential to quality education.**
4. **Coordination among support services providers is essential to appropriate education.**
5. **Using problem-solving methods improves the effectiveness of educational planning.**
6. **Special education is a service, not a place.**

Q4: How does COACH relate to the IEP (individualized education program)?

A4: COACH is used as an IEP planning tool. It is a way to get family input and team involvement in the IEP process. COACH views IEP development as a process rather than an event.

Q5: What is my role, as a parent, in COACH?

A5: First, you will be provided with some information about COACH and asked by school staff if you are interested in participating in a COACH meeting to complete the Family Interview. If you decide to participate, a meeting will be scheduled at a time and place agreed to by you and the school staff.

Q6: If there are two parents, should they both attend the COACH meeting?

A6: We encourage both parents to participate, but COACH can be completed with one parent.

Q7: Should my child be at the COACH meeting?

A7: Students are welcome at COACH meetings but are not required to attend. Whether they attend is an individual decision you make. Participation in COACH typically requires extensive use of language. If accommodations are required to enable your child to participate in the Family Interview (e.g., augmentative communication system, large-print materials), they should be arranged in advance.

Q8: Who else will be at the COACH meeting?

A8: We try to keep COACH meetings small, so not every team member needs to be present. A typical COACH meeting might include the parent(s), special educator, and classroom teacher, but any grouping that makes sense can be used.

Q9: How long will the COACH meeting last?

A9: Typically it takes 1–2 hours to complete COACH Part A (Steps 1, 2, and 3). The time varies based on whether one or two parents are participating and the familiarity and skillfulness of the facilitator in using COACH. The time to complete Part B varies and is spread out over the course of the year rather than being done at a single meeting like Part A.

Q10: What happens at the COACH meeting?

A10: At the COACH meeting you will be asked a series of questions about your child, his or her abilities, and your thoughts about what you think is important for your child to learn this year. This is done on a set of forms used by the person facilitating the COACH meeting. During the Family Interview, the facilitator will direct a series of short questions to you. The professional staff are there to listen to what you have to say and to offer input for your consideration. The questions will call for brief responses. The Family Interview questions move along quickly but should not be rushed. The COACH process is designed to offer you a wide array of possibilities and then help you select which learning outcomes are priorities for your child this year.

Q11: What if I am asked a question I don't know the answer to or don't want to answer?

A11: Most parents find the questions easy to answer and not overly personal. You can choose not to answer certain questions and you need not give any reason. You can simply say, "I don't want to answer that question." A skilled COACH facilitator will not judge your response and will move on to the next question.

Q12: Should I prepare by filling out the forms in advance?

A12: No. Your everyday knowledge of your child is all you will need, so there is no reason to spend time preparing. In fact, filling out forms in advance or coming with a predetermined set of priorities could actually interfere with the COACH process. One of the reasons we think COACH works well is because of the interaction that happens.

Q13:   What happens after we complete the Family Interview?

A13:   After the Family Interview is completed, the facilitator will guide the team through Step 2 (Additional Learning Outcomes) and Step 3 (General Supports). During these two steps, the facilitator will direct questions and get input from all those who are present and strive to reach consensus within the group. By the end of the meeting you will have identified a small set of the learning priorities for your child for this year, a larger set of additional learning outcomes, and a set of general supports. The priorities are used to develop Annual Goals (Step 4). These educational program components then are summarized in a Program-at-a-Glance (Step 5).

Q14:   What happens after the COACH meeting?

A14:   The facilitator will share copies of the Program-at-a-Glance with all the team members, including those who were at the COACH meeting and those who were not. This is done to make sure everyone shares the same understanding about what the educational program is for the student. It is at this point that decisions are made about educational placement and the need for related services. Short-term objectives then are developed by the appropriate group of team members. The team then proceeds to COACH Part B, to make sure that the decisions made at the COACH meeting (Part A) are implemented.

Q15:   Where do specialists (e.g., speech-language pathologists, physical therapists) fit into COACH?

A15:   "Related services" are provided when they are both educationally relevant and necessary in order for the student to access or participate in his or her individualized educational program, or both. Therefore, the need for these specialized supports can only be determined by the team *after* the educational program has been developed, and after an educational placement decision has been made. A companion process to COACH called VISTA *(Vermont Interdependent Services Team Approach)* provides an approach to making team decisions about specialized support services. If you are interested in VISTA, you can find a reference for it in the COACH manual.

Q16:   What if I have other questions that aren't answered here?

A16:   If you have unanswered questions contact the school staff or refer to the COACH manual.

We hope that you find participating in COACH to be helpful and enjoyable, and we wish you good luck!

Michael F. Giangreco, Chigee J. Cloninger, & Virginia Salce Iverson
(co-authors of COACH)

Appendix B

BLANK
COACH FORMS

Student Record

by
Michael F. Giangreco, Ph.D.
Chigee J. Cloninger, Ph.D.
Virginia Salce Iverson, M.Ed.

_____
Student's Name

Planning Is for the _____ School Year

(see COACH manual for complete directions)

Preparation Checklist

The following are important steps to take in preparation for using COACH. In the first column write the initials of the person responsible to ensure completion, and in the second column list the date completed.

	Who?	Date

1. Ensure all team members are sufficiently oriented to the purpose of COACH and directions for using it. (See Appendix A, Questions and Answers for Parents About COACH.)   _____   _____

2. Ensure all team members agree to use COACH to plan the student's educational program.   _____   _____

3. Ensure all team members agree to accept and act upon the educational priorities identified by the family during the Family Interview.   _____   _____

4. Involve the family in determining who will facilitate the Family Interview. List names on the Planning Team Information form.   _____   _____

5. Involve the family in determining when and where the Family Interview will be conducted. List information on the Planning Team Information form.   _____   _____

6. Involve the family in determining who needs to be present at the Family Interview. (Not all team members need to be present. Typically, the Family Interview is a small group of 2–4 people.)   _____   _____

7. Identify by whom, when, and how Steps 2–6 will be facilitated.   _____   _____

8. Ensure all needed forms are ready for use in advance of the Family Interview. List names on the Planning Team Information form.   _____   _____

9. Ensure the person who facilitates the Family Interview is familiar with the directions.   _____   _____

10. Complete the COACH Cover Page, this Checklist, and the Planning Team Information form in advance of the Family Interview.   _____   _____

Planning Team Information

Student's name: _____ Date of birth: _____

Educational placement(s): _____

Family Interview (Step 1)

    Date: _____ Interviewer: _____

    Person(s) being interviewed: _____

Additional Learning Outcomes (Step 2)

    Date: _____ Facilitator: _____

General Supports (Step 3)

    Date: _____ Facilitator: _____

Annual Goals (Step 4)

    Date: _____ Facilitator: _____

Program-at-a-Glance (Step 5)

    Date: _____ Facilitator: _____

Short-Term Objectives (Step 6)

    Date: _____ Facilitator: _____

Team Membership

Name of Team Member	Relationship to Student	Date Steps 1–4 Reviewed
_____	_____	_____
_____	_____	_____
_____	_____	_____
_____	_____	_____
_____	_____	_____
_____	_____	_____
_____	_____	_____
_____	_____	_____
_____	_____	_____
_____	_____	_____

Choosing Outcomes and Accommodations for Children • © 1998 by Michael F. Giangreco •
Baltimore: Paul H. Brookes Publishing Co.

Introducing the Family Interview

Directions: The following headings include sample statements to be shared with participants. *The information must be individualized to match each situation.*

Purpose of the Family Interview

"The purpose of this interview is to identify the top learning priorities for [student's name] that you feel would improve his/her life. The team recognizes the importance of your role in making these decisions."

Content Addressed in the Family Interview

"COACH includes a variety of learning outcomes, many of which typically are not included in the general education curriculum. The learning outcomes in COACH are designed to add to or extend those in the general education curriculum. That is one reason why it is so important to go beyond the priorities you will select today and explore additional learning outcomes from the general education curriculum using Step 2."

Interview Activities and Timelines

"It will take about 1 hour to complete the Family Interview, a bit longer if two or more family members are participating. In the Family Interview you will be asked to consider many possible learning outcomes and to zero in on those you feel are most important to work on **this year**. You will be asked these questions at a steady pace and will be asked to give brief answers. Throughout the interview, please feel free to not answer any questions you don't want to. The overall priority learning outcomes you select will become the focus of ongoing planning by the team."

Outcomes of the Family Interview

"At the end of the Family Interview you will select a small set of the most important learning outcomes for [student's name] to improve his/her life. We will also reach an agreement about which priorities need to be included as IEP goals."

Next Steps

"After the Family Interview is completed, your selections will be shared with the team members who are not here today. The overall priorities you selected to be on the IEP will be restated as annual goals and objectives. Although the Family Interview is an important first step in determining the contents of [student's name] educational program, it will not be complete until a broader set of learning outcomes and general supports has been identified using the rest of COACH."

Choosing Outcomes and Accommodations for Children • © 1998 by Michael F. Giangreco •
Baltimore: Paul H. Brookes Publishing Co.

Part A: Determining a Student's Educational Program

Preparation Checklist

Step 1:   Family Interview

Purpose: to determine family-selected learning priorities for the student through a series of questions asked by an interviewer

Step 2:   Additional Learning Outcomes

Purpose: to determine learning outcomes beyond family priorities

Step 3:   General Supports

Purpose: to determine what supports need to be provided *to or for* the student

Step 4:   Annual Goals

Purpose: to ensure the family's priorities are reflected as IEP goals

Step 5:   Program-at-a-Glance

Purpose: to provide a concise summary of the educational program

****

Determine Least Restrictive Educational Placement and Related Services

****

Step 6:   Short-Term Objectives

Purpose: to develop short-term objectives to achieve annual goals

****

Finalize IEP Document

****

Part B: Strategies and Processes to Implement a COACH-Generated Educational Program

Step 7:   Organizing and Informing the Instructional Planning Team

Purpose: to organize team functioning and ensure IEP implementation

Step 8:   Scheduling for the Student with Disabilities in the Classroom

Purpose: to develop a schedule of activities that meets student needs

Step 9:   Planning and Adapting Instruction

Purpose: to develop and implement instructional plans that address student needs and participation in class activities even when IEP goals differ from those of classmates'

Step 10:   Evaluating the Impact of Educational Experiences

Purpose: to evaluate educational plans to determine their impact on learning outcomes and valued life outcomes

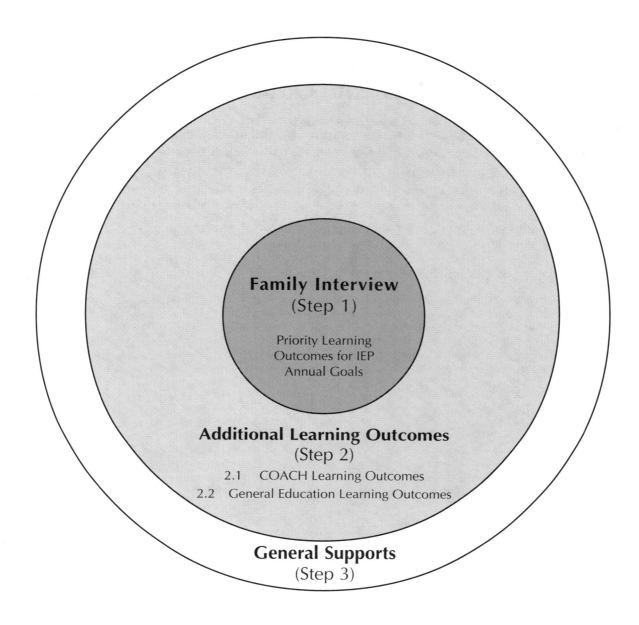

Family Interview
(Step 1)

Priority Learning
Outcomes for IEP
Annual Goals

Additional Learning Outcomes
(Step 2)
2.1   COACH Learning Outcomes
2.2   General Education Learning Outcomes

General Supports
(Step 3)

2.1 COACH Learning Outcomes		**2.2 General Education Learning Outcomes**	
Communication	Home	Reading/Language Arts	Foreign Language
Socialization	School	Math/Science	Community Service
Personal Management	Community	History/Social Studies	Home Economics
Leisure/Recreation	Vocational	Arts/Music	Industrial Arts
Selected Academics	Other	Technology/Computer	Vocational
		Physical/Health Education	Reasoning/Problem Solving

Step 1.1
Valued Life Outcomes

Directions: Review the purpose of this section and the list of Valued Life Outcomes with participants prior to asking questions. All the Valued Life Outcomes are meant to facilitate student independence, interdependence with others, and pursuit of personal growth by expanding access, creating new opportunities, developing individual abilities, and providing ways to contribute to one's community. Terms that are presented in bold are abbreviations for use in Steps 1.5, 10.1, and 10.2.

Being **Safe** and **Healthy**

Having a **Home**, Now and in the Future

Having Meaningful **Relationships**

Having **Choice** and Control that Match One's Age and Culture

Participating in Meaningful **Activities** in Various Places

Choosing Outcomes and Accommodations for Children   •   © 1998 by Michael F. Giangreco   •
Baltimore: Paul H. Brookes Publishing Co.

Being Safe and Healthy

Question: "Are you (family member) interested in
answering questions on this topic?"

Circle   YES   or   NO

1.   What, if anything, would you like to see change in [student's name] current health
     or safety that would help him/her to have a better or more enjoyable life? _____
     _____
     _____
     _____
     _____

Having a Home, Now and in the Future

Question: "Are you (family member) interested in
answering questions on this topic?"

Circle   YES   or   NO

2.   If everything goes as you hope, do you anticipate that [student's name] will continue
     to live where he or she does throughout the school years?

     Circle   YES   or   NO   Where is that? _____

     If NO, where would be a desirable place? _____

3.   Would you like to talk about where a desirable place would be for [student's name]
     to live as an adult? Feel free to answer "No" if you think that decision is too far in
     the future to discuss at this time.

     Circle   YES   or   NO   If YES, where?_____

4.   Is there any place you would not like to have [student's name] live in the future?
     _____
     _____

Having Meaningful Relationships

Question: "Are you (family member) interested in
answering questions on this topic?"

Circle   YES   or   NO

5.   With whom does [student's name] have relationships and friendships? With whom
     does [student's name] like to spend time? _____
     _____
     _____

6.   How, if at all, would you like [student's name] relationships to change or expand in
     the near future? _____
     _____
     _____

Having Choice and Control
that Match One's Age and Culture

Question: "Are you (family member) interested in
answering questions on this topic?"

Circle   YES   or   NO

7.   What kinds of choices and control does [student's name] have now that match his
     or her age and family/community situation? _____
     _____
     _____

8.   How, if at all, would you like to see [student's name] choices and control change or
     expand in the near future? _____
     _____
     _____

Participating in Meaningful Activities in Various Places

Question: "Are you (family member) interested in answering questions on this topic?"

Circle   YES   or   NO

9. What kinds of activities does [student's name] currently do that he or she likes or values? Where does he or she spend time? _____

_____
_____
_____
_____

10. How, if at all, would you like to see these activities and places change or expand in the near future? _____

_____
_____
_____
_____

11. *Usually, you ask this question only if the student is 13 years old or older.* Have you given any thought to what kinds of activities [student's name] might do or places he or she might go as a young adult? For example, in the future how might [student's name] spend his or her time that is now spent in school (e.g., competitive work, supported work, volunteering, continuing education)? _____

_____
_____
_____
_____

Ranking Valued Life Outcomes
to Emphasize this Year

Directions: Ask the person being interviewed, "Please rank the Valued Life Outcomes (where 1 is the most important) to help the team understand which ones you feel are most important for [student's name] this year." Terms that are presented in bold are abbreviations for use in Steps 1.5, 10.1, and 10.2.

Rank

_____   Being **Safe** and **Healthy**

_____   Having a **Home**, Now and in the Future

_____   Having Meaningful **Relationships**

_____   Having **Choice** and Control that Match One's Age and Culture

_____   Participating in Meaningful **Activities** in Various Places

*** Relationship to Next Steps ***

This information about the student's Valued Life Outcomes will set the context for the selection of individualized learning outcomes and general supports.

Notes About Valued Life Outcomes

Communication

Step 1.2

Mark only one box to indicate if the family wants to discuss this set of learning outcomes in:
Step 1 (Family Interview; priority this year?) ☐; Step 2 (Additional Learning Outcomes) ☐; Skip for Now ☐

Currently, in what ways does the student communicate?

Expressively:_____

Receptively: _____

#	Learning Outcomes	Step 1.3 Circle Score	Step 1.3 Needs Work?	Step 1.4 Rank up to 5 Priorities
1	**Expresses Continuation or "More"** (e.g., makes sounds or movement when desired interaction stops to indicate he or she would like eating, playing, etc., to continue)	E P S	N Y	
2	**Makes Choices When Given Options**	E P S	N Y	
3	**Makes Requests** (e.g., for objects, food, interactions, activities, assistance)	E P S	N Y	
4	**Summons Others** (e.g., has a way to call others to him or her)	E P S	N Y	
5	**Expresses Rejection/Refusal** (e.g., indicates when he or she wants something to stop or does not want something to begin)	E P S	N Y	
6	**Expresses Greetings and Farewells**	E P S	N Y	
7	**Follows Instructions** (e.g., one step, multistep)	E P S	N Y	
8	**Sustains Communication with Others** (e.g., takes turns, attends, stays on topic, perseveres)	E P S	N Y	
9	**Initiates Communication with Others**	E P S	N Y	
10	**Responds to Questions** (e.g., if asked a question, he or she attempts to answer)	E P S	N Y	
11	**Comments/Describes** (e.g., expands vocabulary for events, objects, interactions, feelings)	E P S	N Y	
12	**Asks Questions of Others**	E P S	N Y	
		E P S	N Y	

Comments:

Scoring Key (use scores for Step 1.3 alone or in combination):
   E = Early/Emerging Skill (1% – 25%)   **P** = Partial Skill (25% – 80%)   **S** = Skillful (80% – 100%)

Choosing Outcomes and Accommodations for Children • © 1998 by Michael F. Giangreco •
Baltimore: Paul H. Brookes Publishing Co.

Socialization

Step 1.2

Mark only one box to indicate if the family wants to discuss this set of learning outcomes in:
Step 1 (Family Interview; priority this year?) ☐; Step 2 (Additional Learning Outcomes) ☐; Skip for Now ☐

		Step 1.3		Step 1.4
#	Learning Outcomes	Circle Score	Needs Work?	Rank up to 5 Priorities
13	Responds to the Presence and Interactions of Others (e.g., peers, family, adults)	E P S	N Y	
14	Initiates Social Interactions	E P S	N Y	
15	Sustains Social Interactions	E P S	N Y	
16	Terminates Social Interactions	E P S	N Y	
17	Distinguishes and Interacts Differently with Familiar People, Acquaintances, and Strangers	E P S	N Y	
18	Maintains Socially Acceptable Behavior When Alone and with Others	E P S	N Y	
19	Accepts Assistance from Others	E P S	N Y	
20	Offers Assistance to Others	E P S	N Y	
21	Makes Transitions Between Routine Activities	E P S	N Y	
22	Adjusts to Unexpected Changes in Routine	E P S	N Y	
23	Shares with Others	E P S	N Y	
24	Advocates for Self	E P S	N Y	
		E P S	N Y	
		E P S	N Y	
		E P S	N Y	
		E P S	N Y	

Comments:

Scoring Key (use scores for Step 1.3 alone or in combination):
   E = Early/Emerging Skill (1% – 25%)   **P** = Partial Skill (25% – 80%)   **S** = Skillful (80% – 100%)

Choosing Outcomes and Accommodations for Children • © 1998 by Michael F. Giangreco •
Baltimore: Paul H. Brookes Publishing Co.

Personal Management

Step 1.2

Mark only one box to indicate if the family wants to discuss this set of learning outcomes in:
Step 1 (Family Interview; priority this year?) ☐; Step 2 (Additional Learning Outcomes) ☐; Skip for Now ☐

#	Learning Outcomes	Circle Score	Needs Work?	Rank up to 5 Priorities
		Step 1.3		**Step 1.4**
25	Drinks and Eats (e.g., accepts food/drink, chews, swallows)	E P S	N Y	
26	Eats with Hands/Fingers	E P S	N Y	
27	Eats with Utensils (e.g., spoon, fork, knife)	E P S	N Y	
28	Dresses/Undresses	E P S	N Y	
29	Cares for Bowel and Bladder Needs	E P S	N Y	
30	Cares for Hands and Face (e.g., washes, dries, wipes, blows nose, applies lotion, applies lip balm)	E P S	N Y	
31	Combs/Brushes Hair	E P S	N Y	
32	Gives Self-Identification Information (e.g., name, address, phone number)	E P S	N Y	
33	Responds to Emergency Alarm (e.g., leaves building when smoke alarm sounds)	E P S	N Y	
34	Manages Personal Belongings (e.g., toys, clothes, special equipment)	E P S	N Y	
35	Mobile Within and Between Rooms of a Building (e.g., walks, crawls, rolls, moves wheelchair, climbs stairs, uses elevators/escalators, navigates)	E P S	N Y	
36	Recognizes and Avoids Potentially Dangerous Situations	E P S	N Y	
		E P S	N Y	
		E P S	N Y	

Comments:

Scoring Key (use scores for Step 1.3 alone or in combination):
E = Early/Emerging Skill (1% – 25%)   **P** = Partial Skill (25% – 80%)   **S** = Skillful (80% – 100%)

Leisure/Recreation

Step 1.2

Mark only one box to indicate if the family wants to discuss this set of learning outcomes in:
Step 1 (Family Interview; priority this year?) ☐; Step 2 (Additional Learning Outcomes) ☐; Skip for Now ☐

		Step 1.3		Step 1.4
#	Learning Outcomes	Circle Score	Needs Work?	Rank up to 5 Priorities
37	Engages in Individual, Passive Leisure Activities (e.g., listens to music, watches television)	E P S	N Y	
38	Engages in Individual, Active Leisure Activities (e.g., toy play, games, sports, exercise, hobbies)	E P S	N Y	
39	Engages in Passive Leisure Activities with Others (e.g., read to by someone; goes to movies, performances, spectator sports or events with others)	E P S	N Y	
40	Engages in Active Leisure Activities with Others (e.g., group games and activities, sports, exercise, hobbies)	E P S	N Y	
		E P S	N Y	
		E P S	N Y	
		E P S	N Y	
		E P S	N Y	

Comments:

Scoring Key (use scores for Step 1.3 alone or in combination):
  E = Early/Emerging Skill (1% – 25%)   **P** = Partial Skill (25% – 80%)   **S** = Skillful (80% – 100%)

Choosing Outcomes and Accommodations for Children • © 1998 by Michael F. Giangreco •
Baltimore: Paul H. Brookes Publishing Co.

Selected Academics

Step 1.2

Mark only one box to indicate if the family wants to discuss this set of learning outcomes in:
Step 1 (Family Interview; priority this year?) ☐; Step 2 (Additional Learning Outcomes) ☐; Skip for Now ☐

		Step 1.3		Step 1.4
#	Learning Outcomes	Circle Score	Needs Work?	Rank up to 5 Priorities
41	Reacts to Objects, Activities, and/or Interactions by Displaying Some Observable Change in Behavior	E P S	N Y	
42	Directs and Sustains Attention to Activity (e.g., books, toys, class activities)	E P S	N Y	
43	Explores Surroundings (e.g., scans, searches)	E P S	N Y	
44	Differentiates/Discriminates Between Various Things (e.g., objects, activities, symbols, pictures, interactions)	E P S	N Y	
45	Imitates Skills Used in Daily Life	E P S	N Y	
46	Uses Objects for Intended Purposes (e.g., plays with toy, eats with spoon, turns pages of a book, writes/draws with pencil, brushes hair)	E P S	N Y	
47	Identifies Symbols (e.g., letters, words, braille, line drawings, manual signs)	E P S	N Y	
48	Reads to Get Information and/or Follow Instructions	E P S	N Y	
49	Uses Writing Tools to Form Letters and Words (e.g., printing, handwriting, typewriting)	E P S	N Y	
50	Composes Phrases and Sentences	E P S	N Y	
51	Counts with Correspondence	E P S	N Y	
52	Calculates (e.g., adds, subtracts, multiplies, divides)	E P S	N Y	
53	Uses Clock (e.g., face, digital, alarm)	E P S	N Y	
54	Uses Calendar (e.g., days, dates, months, year; notes special events and appointments)	E P S	N Y	
55	Uses Computer	E P S	N Y	
		E P S	N Y	

Scoring Key (use scores for Step 1.3 alone or in combination):
   E = Early/Emerging Skill (1% – 25%)   **P** = Partial Skill (25% – 80%)   **S** = Skillful (80% – 100%)

Choosing Outcomes and Accommodations for Children   •   © 1998 by Michael F. Giangreco   •
Baltimore: Paul H. Brookes Publishing Co.

Step 1.2

Mark only one box to indicate if the family wants to discuss this set of learning outcomes in:
Step 1 (Family Interview; priority this year?) ☐; Step 2 (Additional Learning Outcomes) ☐; Skip for Now ☐

| | | Step 1.3 | | Step 1.4 |
#	Learning Outcomes	Circle Score	Needs Work?	Rank up to 5 Priorities
56	Brushes/Flosses Teeth	E P S	N Y	
57	Selects Appropriate Clothing to Wear (e.g., selects items needed for time of day, weather conditions, style, matching)	E P S	N Y	
58	Cares for Personal Hygiene Needs (e.g., bathes, showers, cares for nails, uses deodorant, shaves)	E P S	N Y	
59	Picks Up After Self	E P S	N Y	
60	Prepares Food (e.g., snacks, cold meals, hot meals)	E P S	N Y	
61	Does Household Chores (e.g., dusts, sweeps, mops, vacuums, washes/dries dishes, takes out garbage, recycles, makes bed, stores groceries, yardwork)	E P S	N Y	
62	Cares for Clothing (e.g., puts laundry in designated place when clean or dirty, washes/dries, folds, irons, mends)	E P S	N Y	
63	Uses Telephone (e.g., answers, calls, uses directory)	E P S	N Y	
		E P S	N Y	
		E P S	N Y	
		E P S	N Y	
		E P S	N Y	

Comments:

Scoring Key (use scores for Step 1.3 alone or in combination):
E = Early/Emerging Skill (1% – 25%)   **P** = Partial Skill (25% – 80%)   **S** = Skillful (80% – 100%)

Choosing Outcomes and Accommodations for Children • © 1998 by Michael F. Giangreco •
Baltimore: Paul H. Brookes Publishing Co.

School

Step 1.2

Mark only one box to indicate if the family wants to discuss this set of learning outcomes in:
Step 1 (Family Interview; priority this year?) ☐ ; Step 2 (Additional Learning Outcomes) ☐ ; Skip for Now ☐

		Step 1.3		Step 1.4
#	Learning Outcomes	Circle Score	Needs Work?	Rank up to 5 Priorities
64	Travels to and from School Safely (e.g., on bus, as a pedestrian)	E P S	N Y	
65	Participates in Small Groups (e.g., tolerates situation, takes turn, is actively involved, responds to instructions)	E P S	N Y	
66	Participates in Large Groups (e.g., tolerates situation, takes turn, is actively involved, responds to instructions)	E P S	N Y	
67	Works at Task Independently (e.g., starts, sustains, completes, at nonfrustrational level)	E P S	N Y	
68	Manages School-Related Belongings (e.g., backpack, materials, books, lockers, gym equipment)	E P S	N Y	
69	Follows School Rules/Routines (e.g., understands and follows class and school rules, changes classes, follows schedule)	E P S	N Y	
70	Uses School Facilities (e.g., playground, cafeteria, library, bookstore)	E P S	N Y	
71	Makes Purchases in School (e.g., cafeteria, bookstore, event tickets)	E P S	N Y	
72	Participates in Extracurricular Activities (e.g., clubs, sports, service organizations, drama, music)	E P S	N Y	
		E P S	N Y	
		E P S	N Y	
		E P S	N Y	

Comments:

Scoring Key (use scores for Step 1.3 alone or in combination):
E = Early/Emerging Skill (1% – 25%)   **P** = Partial Skill (25% – 80%)   **S** = Skillful (80% – 100%)

Choosing Outcomes and Accommodations for Children   •   © 1998 by Michael F. Giangreco   •
Baltimore: Paul H. Brookes Publishing Co.

Community

Step 1.2

Mark only one box to indicate if the family wants to discuss this set of learning outcomes in:
Step 1 (Family Interview; priority this year?) ☐; Step 2 (Additional Learning Outcomes) ☐; Skip for Now ☐

		Step 1.3		Step 1.4
#	Learning Outcomes	Circle Score	Needs Work?	Rank up to 5 Priorities
73	**Travels Safely in the Community** (e.g., crosses intersections, uses crosswalks and sidewalks, acts appropriately with strangers, finds destination)	E P S	N Y	
74	**Uses Restaurants** (e.g., orders food, finds seating, eats meal, pays bill)	E P S	N Y	
75	**Uses Recreational Facilities** (e.g., movies, arcades, parks, recreation centers, fitness clubs)	E P S	N Y	
76	**Makes Purchases of Merchandise or Services** (e.g., food stores, clothing/department stores, specialty stores, post office, hair salon, laundry/cleaner, knows purpose of different kinds of stores, finds merchandise or services desired, pays bill)	E P S	N Y	
77	**Uses Vending Machines** (e.g., drinks, food, stamps, newspaper, public transportation tickets/tokens)	E P S	N Y	
78	**Uses Banking Facilities** (e.g., deposits, withdraws, uses automated teller machines)	E P S	N Y	
79	**Travels by Public Transportation** (e.g., bus, subway, trolley, taxi, ferry)	E P S	N Y	
80	Uses Pay Phone	E P S	N Y	
		E P S	N Y	
		E P S	N Y	
		E P S	N Y	

Comments:

Scoring Key (use scores for Step 1.3 alone or in combination):
  E = Early/Emerging Skill (1% – 25%)   **P** = Partial Skill (25% – 80%)   **S** = Skillful (80% – 100%)

Choosing Outcomes and Accommodations for Children • © 1998 by Michael F. Giangreco •
Baltimore: Paul H. Brookes Publishing Co.

Vocational

Step 1.2

Mark only one box to indicate if the family wants to discuss this set of learning outcomes in:
Step 1 (Family Interview; priority this year?) ☐; Step 2 (Additional Learning Outcomes) ☐; Skip for Now ☐

		Step 1.3		Step 1.4
#	Learning Outcomes	Circle Score	Needs Work?	Rank up to 5 Priorities
81	Does Classroom and/or Home Job(s)	E P S	N Y	
82	Does Job(s) at School, Beyond the Classroom, with Peers without Disabilities (e.g., delivers attendance, messages, lunch money; helps operate bookstore)	E P S	N Y	
For Students at Community Worksites				
83	Travels to and from Worksite	E P S	N Y	
84	Uses Time Clock or Check-In Procedure	E P S	N Y	
85	Interacts Appropriately with Co-workers, Customers, and Supervisors	E P S	N Y	
86	Follows Worksite Rules for Safety, Conduct, and Appearance	E P S	N Y	
87	Works Independently at a Task	E P S	N Y	
88	Works with Others (e.g., cooperates, does enough work, accepts assistance, gives assistance)	E P S	N Y	
89	Follows Schedule of Work Activities	E P S	N Y	
90	Uses Worksite Breaktime Facilities (e.g., engages in appropriate breaktime and lunchtime routines)	E P S	N Y	
91	Applies for Job(s) (e.g., finds potential jobs, contacts employers, fills out forms, participates in job interviews)	E P S	N Y	
		E P S	N Y	

Comments:

Scoring Key (use scores for Step 1.3 alone or in combination):
   E = Early/Emerging Skill (1% – 25%)   **P** = Partial Skill (25% – 80%)   **S** = Skillful (80% – 100%)

Other

Step 1.2

Mark only one box to indicate if the family wants to discuss this set of learning outcomes in:
Step 1 (Family Interview; priority this year?) ☐; Step 2 (Additional Learning Outcomes) ☐; Skip for Now ☐

		Step 1.3		Step 1.4
#	Learning Outcomes	Circle Score	Needs Work?	Rank up to 5 Priorities
		E P S	N Y	
		E P S	N Y	
		E P S	N Y	
		E P S	N Y	
		E P S	N Y	
		E P S	N Y	
		E P S	N Y	
		E P S	N Y	
		E P S	N Y	
		E P S	N Y	
		E P S	N Y	

Comments:

Scoring Key (use scores for Step 1.3 alone or in combination):
   E = Early/Emerging Skill (1% – 25%)   **P** = Partial Skill (25% – 80%)   **S** = Skillful (80% – 100%)

Step 1.5:   Cross-Prioritization

Directions: Transfer priorities, in their ranked order, from each list of learning outcomes (Step 1.4) reviewed with the family.

#	Communication	Socialization	Personal Management	Leisure/ Recreation	Selected Academics
1					
2					
3					
4					
5					

#	Home	School	Community	Vocational	Other
1					
2					
3					
4					
5					

Directions: Referring to the above listings, use the next page (Step 1.5 continued) to have the family member(s) being interviewed:
1. Rank a maximum of the top eight overall priorities, explicitly clarifying the wording to reflect what the student will be expected to learn. Review the overall priority selections to ensure that they accurately reflect student priorities.
2. Verify the reasoning behind the family's selection and record abbreviations corresponding to the valued life outcome(s).
3. Determine the proposed context in which learning of each priority will occur (e.g., classroom, community worksite, cafeteria with peers).
4. Indicate how each priority will be addressed as an IEP annual goal, an additional learning outcome, or primarily as a home responsibility *(check only one of the three boxes for each ranked priority).*

Choosing Outcomes and Accommodations for Children   •   © 1998 by Michael F. Giangreco   •   Baltimore: Paul H. Brookes Publishing Co.

Step 1.5. (*continued*)

Rank	1) Overall Priority Learning Outcomes (word priorities to explicitly clarify what the student will be expected to learn)	2) Write the Abbreviation of Valued Life Outcome(s)	3) List the Context for Learning	4) Check (✔) Only One Box for Each Priority		
				IEP Goal	Additional Learning Outcomes	Home
1						
2						
3						
4						
5						
6						
7						
8						

Directions: The interviewer explains the next steps and the relationship of the Family Interview to the rest of COACH.

Choosing Outcomes and Accommodations for Children • © 1998 by Michael F. Giangreco • Baltimore: Paul H. Brookes Publishing Co.

Step 2.1
Additional Learning Outcomes from COACH

Directions: Consider the learning outcomes on this list and select a subset to be targeted for instruction as Additional Learning Outcomes. These pages may be included as an addendum to the IEP.

Participants: _____

_____

COMMUNICATION

___ 1. Expresses continuation or "more"
___ 2. Makes choices when given options
___ 3. Makes requests
___ 4. Summons others
___ 5. Expresses rejection/refusal
___ 6. Expresses greetings and farewells
___ 7. Follows instructions
___ 8. Sustains communication with others
___ 9. Initiates communication with others
___ 10. Responds to questions
___ 11. Comments/describes
___ 12. Asks questions of others
___ _____
___ _____

SOCIALIZATION

___ 13. Responds to the presence and interactions of others
___ 14. Initiates social interactions
___ 15. Sustains social interactions
___ 16. Terminates social interactions
___ 17. Distinguishes and interacts differently with familiar people, acquaintances, and strangers
___ 18. Maintains socially acceptable behavior when alone and with others
___ 19. Accepts assistance from others
___ 20. Offers assistance to others

___ 21. Makes transitions between routine activities
___ 22. Adjusts to unexpected changes in routine
___ 23. Shares with others
___ 24. Advocates for self
___ _____
___ _____
___ _____

PERSONAL MANAGEMENT

___ 25. Drinks and eats
___ 26. Eats with hands/fingers
___ 27. Eats with utensils
___ 28. Dresses/undresses
___ 29. Cares for bowel and bladder needs
___ 30. Cares for hands and face
___ 31. Combs/brushes hair
___ 32. Gives self-identification information
___ 33. Responds to emergency alarm
___ 34. Manages personal belongings
___ 35. Mobile within and between rooms of a building
___ 36. Recognizes and avoids potentially dangerous situations
___ _____
___ _____
___ _____

LEISURE/RECREATION

___ 37. Engages in individual, passive leisure activities
___ 38. Engages in individual, active leisure activities

___ 39. Engages in passive leisure activities with others
___ 40. Engages in active leisure with others
___ _____
___ _____

SELECTED ACADEMICS

___ 41. Reacts to objects, activities, and/or interactions by displaying some observable change in behavior
___ 42. Directs and sustains attention to activity
___ 43. Explores surroundings
___ 44. Differentiates/discriminates between various things
___ 45. Imitates skills used in daily life
___ 46. Uses objects for intended purposes
___ 47. Identifies symbols
___ 48. Reads to get information and/or follow instructions
___ 49. Uses writing tools to form letters and words
___ 50. Composes phrases and sentences
___ 51. Counts with correspondence
___ 52. Calculates
___ 53. Uses clock
___ 54. Uses calendar
___ 55. Uses computer
___ _____
___ _____
___ _____

(continued)

Choosing Outcomes and Accommodations for Children • © 1998 by Michael F. Giangreco •
Baltimore: Paul H. Brookes Publishing Co.

Step 2.1.   (*continued*)

HOME

___ 56. Brushes/flosses teeth
___ 57. Selects appropriate clothing to wear
___ 58. Cares for personal hygiene needs
___ 59. Picks up after self
___ 60. Prepares food
___ 61. Does household chores
___ 62. Cares for clothing
___ 63. Uses telephone

___ _____
___ _____
___ _____

SCHOOL

___ 64. Travels to and from school safely
___ 65. Participates in small groups
___ 66. Participates in large groups
___ 67. Works at a task independently
___ 68. Manages school-related belongings
___ 69. Follows school rules/ routines
___ 70. Uses school facilities
___ 71. Makes purchases in school
___ 72. Participates in extra-curricular activities

___ _____
___ _____
___ _____
___ _____

COMMUNITY

___ 73. Travels safely in the community
___ 74. Uses restaurants
___ 75. Uses recreational facilities
___ 76. Makes purchases of merchandise or services
___ 77. Uses vending machines
___ 78. Uses banking facilities
___ 79. Travels by public transportation
___ 80. Uses pay phone

___ _____
___ _____
___ _____
___ _____

VOCATIONAL

___ 81. Does classroom and/or home job(s)
___ 82. Does job(s) at school, beyond the classroom, with peers without disabilities

For Students at Community Worksites

___ 83. Travels to and from worksite
___ 84. Uses time clock or check-in procedure
___ 85. Interacts appropriately with co-workers, customers, and supervisors
___ 86. Follows worksite rules for safety, conduct, and appearance
___ 87. Works independently at a task
___ 88. Works with others
___ 89. Follows schedule of work activities
___ 90. Uses worksite breaktime facilities
___ 91. Applies for job(s)

___ _____
___ _____
___ _____

OTHER:

___ _____
___ _____
___ _____
___ _____
___ _____
___ _____
___ _____
___ _____
___ _____
___ _____
___ _____
___ _____
___ _____
___ _____
___ _____
___ _____
___ _____
___ _____
___ _____

OTHER:

___ _____
___ _____
___ _____
___ _____
___ _____
___ _____
___ _____
___ _____
___ _____
___ _____
___ _____
___ _____
___ _____
___ _____
___ _____
___ _____
___ _____
___ _____

OTHER:

___ _____
___ _____
___ _____
___ _____
___ _____
___ _____
___ _____
___ _____
___ _____
___ _____
___ _____
___ _____
___ _____
___ _____
___ _____
___ _____
___ _____
___ _____
___ _____
___ _____
___ _____
___ _____
___ _____

Choosing Outcomes and Accommodations for Children • © 1998 by Michael F. Giangreco •
Baltimore: Paul H. Brookes Publishing Co.

Step 2.2: Additional Learning Outcomes from General Education

Directions: 1) Check all curriculum areas taught in the grade being planned for; 2) beside curriculum areas, clarify subject content; 3) circle the type of participation (same, multilevel, none/curriculum overlapping); 4) if multilevel, indicate if adapted subject content is the same or different by circling your response; and 5) record examples of the student's learning outcomes.

Student Name: **The Grade Placement Being Planned for Is:**   **Date of Meeting:**

Participants:

✓	General Education Curriculum Areas: Class Content	Primary Type?			If Multilevel, Is the Adapted Subject Matter?	
	Reading/Language Arts/Humanities: Individual's Learning Outcomes:	S	ML	N/CO	Same	Different
	Math: Individual's Learning Outcomes:	S	ML	N/CO	Same	Different
	Science: Individual's Learning Outcomes:	S	ML	N/CO	Same	Different
	History/Social Studies: Individual's Learning Outcomes:	S	ML	N/CO	Same	Different
	Arts (Visual/Performing): Individual's Learning Outcomes:	S	ML	N/CO	Same	Different
	Music (Vocal/Instrumental): Individual's Learning Outcomes:	S	ML	N/CO	Same	Different
	Technology/Computer Literacy: Individual's Learning Outcomes:	S	ML	N/CO	Same	Different
	Physical Education: Individual's Learning Outcomes:	S	ML	N/CO	Same	Different

Choosing Outcomes and Accommodations for Children • © 1998 by Michael F. Giangreco • Baltimore: Paul H. Brookes Publishing Co.

Step 2.2. (continued)

✓	General Education Curriculum Areas: Class Content	Primary Type?			If Multilevel, Is the Adapted Subject Matter?	
		S	ML	N/CO	Same	Different
	Health Education: Individual's Learning Outcomes:	S	ML	N/CO	Same	Different
	Foreign Language: Individual's Learning Outcomes:	S	ML	N/CO	Same	Different
	Community Service/Social Responsibility: Individual's Learning Outcomes:	S	ML	N/CO	Same	Different
	Home Economics: Individual's Learning Outcomes:	S	ML	N/CO	Same	Different
	Industrial Arts: Individual's Learning Outcomes:	S	ML	N/CO	Same	Different
	Vocational: Individual's Learning Outcomes:	S	ML	N/CO	Same	Different
	Reasoning and Problem Solving: Individual's Learning Outcomes:	S	ML	N/CO	Same	Different
	Other: Individual's Learning Outcomes:	S	ML	N/CO	Same	Different

Codes: **S** = Same (same learning outcomes as others); **ML** = Multilevel (learning outcomes in the same curriculum area at a different level, such as content, quantity, performance criteria); **N/CO** = None/Curriculum Overlapping (there are no learning outcomes identified for instruction in these curriculum areas, but the student participates in class activities by working on learning outcomes from different curriculum areas).

Choosing Outcomes and Accommodations for Children • © 1998 by Michael F. Giangreco • Baltimore: Paul H. Brookes Publishing Co.

Step 3
General Supports

Directions: Check those items to be included in the student's educational program as "General Supports" (those supports or accommodations provided to or for the student). Space has been provided under each item to allow for clarifying or specifying information individually pertinent to the student. *General Supports are not a comprehensive list of specific instructional supports.* These pages may be included as an addendum to the IEP or the information may be transferred to the IEP in an appropriate section.

Participants: _____

_____

PERSONAL NEEDS

___ 1. Needs to be fed food and drinks

___ 2. Needs to be dressed

___ 3. Needs assistance with bowel and bladder management

___ 4. Needs assistance with personal hygiene

___ 5. Needs to be given medication

___ 6. Needs suctioning and/or postural drainage

Other Personal Needs:

___ _____

___ _____

___ _____

___ _____

___ _____

___ _____

___ _____

PHYSICAL NEEDS

___ 7. Needs to be physically repositioned at regular intervals

___ 8. Needs to have environmental barriers modified to allow access

___ 9. Needs to have physical equipment managed (e.g., wheelchair, braces, orthotics)

___ 10. Needs specialized transportation accommodations

___ 11. Needs to be moved and positioned in specialized ways

___ 12. Needs to be physically moved from place to place

Other Physical Needs:

___ _____

___ _____

___ _____

___ _____

___ _____

TEACHING OTHERS ABOUT THE STUDENT

___ 13. Teach staff and classmates about the student's augmentative communication system and other communicative behaviors

___ 14. Teach staff and students how to communicate with the student

___ 15. Teach staff seizure management procedures

___ 16. Teach staff emergency procedures (e.g., medical, evacuation)

___ 17. Teach staff preventive behavior management procedures

___ 18. Teach staff behavioral crisis intervention procedures

Other Needs Related to Teaching Others About the Student:

___ _____

___ _____

___ _____

___ _____

_____

(continued)

Choosing Outcomes and Accommodations for Children • © 1998 by Michael F. Giangreco • Baltimore: Paul H. Brookes Publishing Co.

Step 3. (*continued*)

SENSORY NEEDS

___ 19. Needs to have hearing aids monitored (e.g., batteries, settings)

___ 20. Needs to have people use FM unit/auditory trainer

___ 21. Needs people to manually communicate (e.g., American Sign Language, common gestures)

___ 22. Needs to have glasses managed (e.g., adjusted, cleaned)

___ 23. Needs tactile materials

___ 24. Needs enlarged materials

___ 25. Needs materials in braille

___ 26. Needs to be positioned to accommodate sensory needs (e.g., specified distance from source)

___ 27. Needs environmental modifications to accommodate for sensory needs (e.g., lighting, location, background, volume, color)

Other Sensory Needs:

___   _____

___   _____

___   _____

___   _____

___   _____

___   _____

___   _____

PROVIDING ACCESS AND OPPORTUNITIES

___ 28. Provide access to general education classes and activities

___ 29. Needs to have instructional accommodations to general education activities and materials prepared in advance to facilitate multilevel instruction and/or curriculum overlapping

___ 30. Provide access to community-based experiences with people without disabilities

___ 31. Provide access to vocational experiences with people without disabilities

___ 32. Provide access to co-curricular activities with people without disabilities

___ 33. Provide access to materials in the student's native language

___ 34. Provide access to materials and activities associated with the student's cultural background as well as other cultures

___ 35. Provide access to nonaversive approaches to dealing with challenging behaviors

Other Needs Related to Providing Access and Opportunities:

___   _____

___   _____

___   _____

OTHER GENERAL SUPPORTS (not listed elsewhere)

___ 36. Needs time limits extended or waived

___ 37. Needs classnotes recorded in any form

___ 38. Needs alternative testing modifications

Other General Supports:

___   _____

___   _____

___   _____

___   _____

___   _____

___   _____

___   _____

___   _____

___   _____

___   _____

___   _____

___   _____

Choosing Outcomes and Accommodations for Children   •   © 1998 by Michael F. Giangreco   •
Baltimore: Paul H. Brookes Publishing Co.

Step 4:   Annual Goals

Priority Learning Outcome (from Step 1.5): _____

Current Level of Functioning Related to the Priority Learning Outcome: _____

_____

_____

Behavior: _____

Context: _____

Team Member Suggestions: _____

Annual Goal: _____

_____

_____

Step 6:   Short-Term Objectives

Clarify the intent/focus of Annual Goal to be reflected in the objectives (check those that apply or determine others):

_____ Decreasing prompts/cues	_____ Increasing response to natural cues
_____ Desensitizing/increasing tolerance	_____ Accepting assistance from others
_____ Acquiring core skills	_____ Initiation of behavior
_____ Preparation for the activity	_____ Quality of performance
_____ Appropriateness of tempo or rate	_____ Extending or reducing duration
_____ Self-monitoring	_____ Problem solving
_____ Termination of the behavior	_____ Assisting others with the behavior
_____ Safety aspects	_____ Expansion of repertoire
_____ Communication aspects	_____ Social behaviors aspects and manners
_____ Indication of choice or preference	_____ Retention over time
_____ Generalization across settings	_____ Generalization across people
_____ Generalization across materials	_____ Generalization across cues

	Conditions	Behavior	Criteria
1			
2			
3			

Choosing Outcomes and Accommodations for Children   •   © 1998 by Michael F. Giangreco   •
Baltimore: Paul H. Brookes Publishing Co.

Step 4:   Annual Goals

Priority Learning Outcome (from Step 1.5): _____

Current Level of Functioning Related to the Priority Learning Outcome: _____

_____

_____

Behavior: _____

Context: _____

Team Member Suggestions: _____

_____

Annual Goal: _____

_____

_____

Step 6:   Short-Term Objectives

Clarify the intent/focus of Annual Goal to be reflected in the objectives (check those that apply or determine others):

_____ Decreasing prompts/cues   _____ Increasing response to natural cues

_____ Desensitizing/increasing tolerance _____ Accepting assistance from others

_____ Acquiring core skills   _____ Initiation of behavior

_____ Preparation for the activity   _____ Quality of performance

_____ Appropriateness of tempo or rate   _____ Extending or reducing duration

_____ Self-monitoring   _____ Problem solving

_____ Termination of the behavior   _____ Assisting others with the behavior

_____ Safety aspects   _____ Expansion of repertoire

_____ Communication aspects   _____ Social behaviors aspects and manners

_____ Indication of choice or preference _____ Retention over time

_____ Generalization across settings   _____ Generalization across people

_____ Generalization across materials   _____ Generalization across cues

	Conditions	Behavior	Criteria
1			
2			
3			

Choosing Outcomes and Accommodations for Children • © 1998 by Michael F. Giangreco •
Baltimore: Paul H. Brookes Publishing Co.

Step 4: Annual Goals

Priority Learning Outcome (from Step 1.5): _____

Current Level of Functioning Related to the Priority Learning Outcome: _____

_____
_____

Behavior: _____

Context: _____

Team Member Suggestions: _____

_____

Annual Goal: _____

_____
_____

Step 6: Short-Term Objectives

Clarify the intent/focus of Annual Goal to be reflected in the objectives (check those that apply or determine others):

_____ Decreasing prompts/cues	_____ Increasing response to natural cues
_____ Desensitizing/increasing tolerance	_____ Accepting assistance from others
_____ Acquiring core skills	_____ Initiation of behavior
_____ Preparation for the activity	_____ Quality of performance
_____ Appropriateness of tempo or rate	_____ Extending or reducing duration
_____ Self-monitoring	_____ Problem solving
_____ Termination of the behavior	_____ Assisting others with the behavior
_____ Safety aspects	_____ Expansion of repertoire
_____ Communication aspects	_____ Social behaviors aspects and manners
_____ Indication of choice or preference	_____ Retention over time
_____ Generalization across settings	_____ Generalization across people
_____ Generalization across materials	_____ Generalization across cues

	Conditions	Behavior	Criteria
1			
2			
3			

Choosing Outcomes and Accommodations for Children • © 1998 by Michael F. Giangreco •
Baltimore: Paul H. Brookes Publishing Co.

Step 4:   Annual Goals

Priority Learning Outcome (from Step 1.5):   _____

Current Level of Functioning Related to the Priority Learning Outcome: _____

_____

_____

Behavior: _____

Context: _____

Team Member Suggestions: _____

_____

Annual Goal: _____

_____

_____

Step 6:   Short-Term Objectives

Clarify the intent/focus of Annual Goal to be reflected in the objectives (check those that apply or determine others):

_____ Decreasing prompts/cues

_____ Desensitizing/increasing tolerance

_____ Acquiring core skills

_____ Preparation for the activity

_____ Appropriateness of tempo or rate

_____ Self-monitoring

_____ Termination of the behavior

_____ Safety aspects

_____ Communication aspects

_____ Indication of choice or preference

_____ Generalization across settings

_____ Generalization across materials

_____ Increasing response to natural cues

_____ Accepting assistance from others

_____ Initiation of behavior

_____ Quality of performance

_____ Extending or reducing duration

_____ Problem solving

_____ Assisting others with the behavior

_____ Expansion of repertoire

_____ Social behaviors aspects and manners

_____ Retention over time

_____ Generalization across people

_____ Generalization across cues

	Conditions	Behavior	Criteria
1			
2			
3			

Choosing Outcomes and Accommodations for Children • © 1998 by Michael F. Giangreco •
Baltimore: Paul H. Brookes Publishing Co.

243

Step 4:   Annual Goals

Priority Learning Outcome (from Step 1.5): _____

Current Level of Functioning Related to the Priority Learning Outcome: _____

_____

_____

Behavior: _____

Context: _____

Team Member Suggestions: _____

_____

Annual Goal: _____

_____

_____

Step 6:   Short-Term Objectives

Clarify the intent/focus of Annual Goal to be reflected in the objectives (check those that apply or determine others):

_____ Decreasing prompts/cues   _____ Increasing response to natural cues
_____ Desensitizing/increasing tolerance   _____ Accepting assistance from others
_____ Acquiring core skills   _____ Initiation of behavior
_____ Preparation for the activity   _____ Quality of performance
_____ Appropriateness of tempo or rate   _____ Extending or reducing duration
_____ Self-monitoring   _____ Problem solving
_____ Termination of the behavior   _____ Assisting others with the behavior
_____ Safety aspects   _____ Expansion of repertoire
_____ Communication aspects   _____ Social behaviors aspects and manners
_____ Indication of choice or preference   _____ Retention over time
_____ Generalization across settings   _____ Generalization across people
_____ Generalization across materials   _____ Generalization across cues

	Conditions	Behavior	Criteria
1			
2			
3			

Choosing Outcomes and Accommodations for Children   •   © 1998 by Michael F. Giangreco   •
Baltimore: Paul H. Brookes Publishing Co.

Step 4:   Annual Goals

Priority Learning Outcome (from Step 1.5): _____

Current Level of Functioning Related to the Priority Learning Outcome: _____

_____

_____

Behavior: _____

Context: _____

Team Member Suggestions: _____

_____

Annual Goal: _____

_____

_____

Step 6:   Short-Term Objectives

Clarify the intent/focus of Annual Goal to be reflected in the objectives (check those that apply or determine others):

_____ Decreasing prompts/cues   _____ Increasing response to natural cues
_____ Desensitizing/increasing tolerance   _____ Accepting assistance from others
_____ Acquiring core skills   _____ Initiation of behavior
_____ Preparation for the activity   _____ Quality of performance
_____ Appropriateness of tempo or rate   _____ Extending or reducing duration
_____ Self-monitoring   _____ Problem solving
_____ Termination of the behavior   _____ Assisting others with the behavior
_____ Safety aspects   _____ Expansion of repertoire
_____ Communication aspects   _____ Social behaviors aspects and manners
_____ Indication of choice or preference   _____ Retention over time
_____ Generalization across settings   _____ Generalization across people
_____ Generalization across materials   _____ Generalization across cues

	Conditions	Behavior	Criteria
1			
2			
3			

Choosing Outcomes and Accommodations for Children   •   © 1998 by Michael F. Giangreco   •
Baltimore: Paul H. Brookes Publishing Co.

245

Step 4:   Annual Goals

Priority Learning Outcome (from Step 1.5): _____
Current Level of Functioning Related to the Priority Learning Outcome: _____
_____
_____

Behavior: _____
Context: _____
Team Member Suggestions: _____
_____

Annual Goal: _____
_____
_____

Step 6:   Short-Term Objectives

Clarify the intent/focus of Annual Goal to be reflected in the objectives (check those that apply or determine others):

_____ Decreasing prompts/cues	_____ Increasing response to natural cues
_____ Desensitizing/increasing tolerance	_____ Accepting assistance from others
_____ Acquiring core skills	_____ Initiation of behavior
_____ Preparation for the activity	_____ Quality of performance
_____ Appropriateness of tempo or rate	_____ Extending or reducing duration
_____ Self-monitoring	_____ Problem solving
_____ Termination of the behavior	_____ Assisting others with the behavior
_____ Safety aspects	_____ Expansion of repertoire
_____ Communication aspects	_____ Social behaviors aspects and manners
_____ Indication of choice or preference	_____ Retention over time
_____ Generalization across settings	_____ Generalization across people
_____ Generalization across materials	_____ Generalization across cues

	Conditions	Behavior	Criteria
1			
2			
3			

Choosing Outcomes and Accommodations for Children   •   © 1998 by Michael F. Giangreco   •
Baltimore: Paul H. Brookes Publishing Co.

Step 4:   Annual Goals

Priority Learning Outcome (from Step 1.5): _____

Current Level of Functioning Related to the Priority Learning Outcome: _____

_____

_____

Behavior: _____

Context: _____

Team Member Suggestions: _____

_____

Annual Goal: _____

_____

_____

Step 6:   Short-Term Objectives

Clarify the intent/focus of Annual Goal to be reflected in the objectives (check those that apply or determine others):

_____ Decreasing prompts/cues	_____ Increasing response to natural cues
_____ Desensitizing/increasing tolerance	_____ Accepting assistance from others
_____ Acquiring core skills	_____ Initiation of behavior
_____ Preparation for the activity	_____ Quality of performance
_____ Appropriateness of tempo or rate	_____ Extending or reducing duration
_____ Self-monitoring	_____ Problem solving
_____ Termination of the behavior	_____ Assisting others with the behavior
_____ Safety aspects	_____ Expansion of repertoire
_____ Communication aspects	_____ Social behaviors aspects and manners
_____ Indication of choice or preference	_____ Retention over time
_____ Generalization across settings	_____ Generalization across people
_____ Generalization across materials	_____ Generalization across cues

	Conditions	Behavior	Criteria
1			
2			
3			

Choosing Outcomes and Accommodations for Children • © 1998 by Michael F. Giangreco •
Baltimore: Paul H. Brookes Publishing Co.

Step 5
Program-at-a-Glance

Student's Name: Date:

List Educational Program Components

Step 5.   (*continued*)

Step 7: Organizing and Informing the Instructional Planning Team

Directions: Write date(s) when each item is completed. Team meeting minutes can be used to document team decisions and actions pertaining to the items.

Date Done

Step 7.1   Reorganize the Team and Clarify Expectations

1. Clarify any changes in team membership and people's relationship to the team (e.g., core, extended, situational resource). _____

2. Establish a team meeting schedule and guidelines (e.g., who needs to attend, dates and time, agenda, rotating roles). _____

3. Develop a way to exchange information and ideas among team members about upcoming classroom instructional activities to facilitate lesson planning, instruction, and evaluation. _____

4. Clarify who will assume service coordination responsibilities (e.g., information sharing among team members, coordinating paperwork requirements, scheduling, contacting parents). _____

5. Clarify who will design and implement the student's instruction. _____

6. Clarify who will train, plan for, and supervise paraprofessionals. _____

7. Clarify who will make and/or adapt instructional materials. _____

8. Clarify who will maintain/care for specialized equipment. _____

Step 7.2   Become Familiar with the Student

9. Ensure that all team members are familiar with the student's Program-at-a-Glance, Annual Goals, and related services. _____

10. Share information among team members about student-specific information (e.g., preferred learning styles, arrangements, motivations, instructional strategies, adaptations). _____

Step 7.3   Become Familiar with the General Education Program

11. Ensure that team members are knowledgeable about the general education program and settings (e.g., schedule, typical routines and activities, physical arrangements, curriculum content, class rules, teacher expectations). _____

12. Ask general class teachers what support they need from various team members, and how they wish to receive support. _____

Choosing Outcomes and Accommodations for Children • © 1998 by Michael F. Giangreco •
Baltimore: Paul H. Brookes Publishing Co.

Step 8.1: Scheduling Matrix

Directions: 1) List the IEP Annual Goals (Step 4), Additional Learning Outcomes categories (Steps 2.1 and 2.2), and class activities in the spaces provided. 2) Use the intersections of the learning outcomes and class activities to note instructional possibilities to assist in scheduling.

Note: General Supports will need to be considered when planning a schedule.

Student name:

Grade:

Class Activities

	IEP Annual Goals

	Additional Learning Outcomes Categories

Step 8.2
Student Schedule

for

_____

(Student Name)

Directions: List classes/activities with corresponding Annual Goals, Additional Learning Outcomes, and General Supports.

Key: **G** = Annual **Goal**   **A** = **Additional** Learning Outcomes   **S** = General **Supports**

_____

(continued)

Key: **G** = Annual **Goal**   **A** = **Additional** Learning Outcomes   **S** = General **Supports**

Step 9
Planning and Adapting Instruction

COACH

Student: _____

Class Activity/Lesson: _____

Short-Term Objective: _____

Materials Needed: _____

Planned by: _____   Implemented by: _____

Describe the sequence of what the instructor will do	Describe what the student will do (in observable terms)	Describe the consequences of correct and incorrect student responses	Describe how student progress will be measured and documented

Choosing Outcomes and Accommodations for Children   •   © 1998 by Michael F. Giangreco   •   Baltimore: Paul H. Brookes Publishing Co.

Step 9
Planning and Adapting Instruction

Student: _____   Planned by: _____   Implemented by: _____

Class Activity/Lesson: _____

Short-Term Objective: _____

Materials Needed: _____

Describe the sequence of what the instructor will do	Describe what the student will do (in observable terms)	Describe the consequences of correct and incorrect student responses	Describe how student progress will be measured and documented

Choosing Outcomes and Accommodations for Children • © 1998 by Michael F. Giangreco • Baltimore: Paul H. Brookes Publishing Co.

Step 9
Planning and Adapting Instruction

Student: _____ Planned by: _____ Implemented by: _____

Class Activity/Lesson: _____

Short-Term Objective: _____

Materials Needed: _____

Describe the sequence of what the instructor will do	Describe what the student will do (in observable terms)	Describe the consequences of correct and incorrect student responses	Describe how student progress will be measured and documented

Choosing Outcomes and Accommodations for Children • © 1998 by Michael F. Giangreco • Baltimore: Paul H. Brookes Publishing Co.

Step 9
Planning and Adapting Instruction

Student: _____   Planned by: _____   Implemented by: _____

Class Activity/Lesson: _____

Short-Term Objective: _____

Materials Needed: _____

Describe the sequence of what the instructor will do	Describe what the student will do (in observable terms)	Describe the consequences of correct and incorrect student responses	Describe how student progress will be measured and documented

Choosing Outcomes and Accommodations for Children • © 1998 by Michael F. Giangreco • Baltimore: Paul H. Brookes Publishing Co.

Step 9
Planning and Adapting Instruction

Planned by: _____   Implemented by: _____

Student: _____

Class Activity/Lesson: _____

Short-Term Objective: _____

Materials Needed: _____

Describe the sequence of what the instructor will do	Describe what the student will do (in observable terms)	Describe the consequences of correct and incorrect student responses	Describe how student progress will be measured and documented

Choosing Outcomes and Accommodations for Children • © 1998 by Michael F. Giangreco • Baltimore: Paul H. Brookes Publishing Co.

Step 9
Planning and Adapting Instruction

COACH

Student: _____   Planned by: _____   Implemented by: _____

Class Activity/Lesson: _____

Short-Term Objective: _____

Materials Needed: _____

Describe the sequence of what the instructor will do	Describe what the student will do (in observable terms)	Describe the consequences of correct and incorrect student responses	Describe how student progress will be measured and documented

Choosing Outcomes and Accommodations for Children • © 1998 by Michael F. Giangreco • Baltimore: Paul H. Brookes Publishing Co.

Step 9
Planning and Adapting Instruction

Student: _____   Planned by: _____   Implemented by: _____

Class Activity/Lesson: _____

Short-Term Objective: _____

Materials Needed: _____

Describe the sequence of what the instructor will do	Describe what the student will do (in observable terms)	Describe the consequences of correct and incorrect student responses	Describe how student progress will be measured and documented

Step 9
Planning and Adapting Instruction

Planned by: _____   Implemented by: _____

Student: _____

Class Activity/Lesson: _____

Short-Term Objective: _____

Materials Needed: _____

Describe the sequence of what the instructor will do	Describe what the student will do (in observable terms)	Describe the consequences of correct and incorrect student responses	Describe how student progress will be measured and documented

Step 10.1
Evaluation of Impact Process
for Learning Outcomes

Directions: Answer the following questions to discuss student progress toward IEP Annual Goals or Additional Learning Outcomes categories.

Student name: _____ Date of team meeting: _____

Team members participating in discussion: _____

_____

1. **Annual Goal** or **Additional Learning Outcome(s)** being discussed: _____
   _____

2. **Valued Life Outcome(s)** being facilitated through the learning outcome(s): _____
   _____
   _____
   _____

3. When was the last time this learning outcome was discussed by the team?
   Date: _____

4. What has been done to teach the student this learning outcome since it was last discussed? _____
   _____
   _____

5. What progress has the student made on the learning outcome?_____
   _____
   _____
   _____
   _____

6. What changes, if any, has the student experienced on the corresponding Valued Life Outcome(s)? _____
   _____
   _____
   _____

7. What changes, if any, need to be made in the educational program to enhance progress or facilitate the corresponding Valued Life Outcome(s)? _____
   _____
   _____
   _____

Choosing Outcomes and Accommodations for Children • © 1998 by Michael F. Giangreco •
Baltimore: Paul H. Brookes Publishing Co.

Step 10.1
Evaluation of Impact Process
for Learning Outcomes

Directions: Answer the following questions to discuss student progress toward IEP Annual Goals or Additional Learning Outcomes categories.

Student name: _____ Date of team meeting: _____

Team members participating in discussion: _____

_____

1. **Annual Goal** or **Additional Learning Outcome(s)** being discussed: _____
   _____

2. **Valued Life Outcome(s)** being facilitated through the learning outcome(s): _____
   _____
   _____
   _____

3. When was the last time this learning outcome was discussed by the team?
   Date: _____

4. What has been done to teach the student this learning outcome since it was last discussed? _____
   _____
   _____

5. What progress has the student made on the learning outcome? _____
   _____
   _____
   _____
   _____

6. What changes, if any, has the student experienced on the corresponding Valued Life Outcome(s)? _____
   _____
   _____
   _____

7. What changes, if any, need to be made in the educational program to enhance progress or facilitate the corresponding Valued Life Outcome(s)? _____
   _____
   _____
   _____

Choosing Outcomes and Accommodations for Children • © 1998 by Michael F. Giangreco •
Baltimore: Paul H. Brookes Publishing Co.

Step 10.1
Evaluation of Impact Process
for Learning Outcomes

Directions: Answer the following questions to discuss student progress toward IEP Annual Goals or Additional Learning Outcomes categories.

Student name: _____ Date of team meeting: _____

Team members participating in discussion: _____

_____

1. **Annual Goal** or **Additional Learning Outcome(s)** being discussed: _____
   _____

2. **Valued Life Outcome(s)** being facilitated through the learning outcome(s):_____
   _____
   _____
   _____

3. When was the last time this learning outcome was discussed by the team?
   Date: _____

4. What has been done to teach the student this learning outcome since it was last
   discussed? _____
   _____
   _____

5. What progress has the student made on the learning outcome?_____
   _____
   _____
   _____
   _____

6. What changes, if any, has the student experienced on the corresponding Valued Life
   Outcome(s)? _____
   _____
   _____
   _____

7. What changes, if any, need to be made in the educational program to enhance
   progress or facilitate the corresponding Valued Life Outcome(s)? _____
   _____
   _____
   _____

Choosing Outcomes and Accommodations for Children • © 1998 by Michael F. Giangreco •
Baltimore: Paul H. Brookes Publishing Co.

Step 10.1
Evaluation of Impact Process
for Learning Outcomes

Directions: Answer the following questions to discuss student progress toward IEP Annual Goals or Additional Learning Outcomes categories.

Student name: _____ Date of team meeting: _____

Team members participating in discussion: _____

_____

---

1. **Annual Goal** or **Additional Learning Outcome(s)** being discussed: _____
_____

2. **Valued Life Outcome(s)** being facilitated through the learning outcome(s): _____
_____
_____
_____

---

3. When was the last time this learning outcome was discussed by the team?
Date: _____

4. What has been done to teach the student this learning outcome since it was last discussed? _____
_____
_____

5. What progress has the student made on the learning outcome? _____
_____
_____
_____
_____

6. What changes, if any, has the student experienced on the corresponding Valued Life Outcome(s)? _____
_____
_____
_____

7. What changes, if any, need to be made in the educational program to enhance progress or facilitate the corresponding Valued Life Outcome(s)? _____
_____
_____
_____

Choosing Outcomes and Accommodations for Children • © 1998 by Michael F. Giangreco •
Baltimore: Paul H. Brookes Publishing Co.

Step 10.1
Evaluation of Impact Process
for Learning Outcomes

Directions: Answer the following questions to discuss student progress toward IEP Annual Goals or Additional Learning Outcomes categories.

Student name: _____   Date of team meeting: _____

Team members participating in discussion: _____

_____

1. **Annual Goal** or **Additional Learning Outcome(s)** being discussed: _____
    _____

2. **Valued Life Outcome(s)** being facilitated through the learning outcome(s): _____
    _____
    _____
    _____

3. When was the last time this learning outcome was discussed by the team?
    Date: _____

4. What has been done to teach the student this learning outcome since it was last
    discussed? _____
    _____
    _____

5. What progress has the student made on the learning outcome?_____
    _____
    _____
    _____
    _____

6. What changes, if any, has the student experienced on the corresponding Valued Life
    Outcome(s)? _____
    _____
    _____
    _____

7. What changes, if any, need to be made in the educational program to enhance
    progress or facilitate the corresponding Valued Life Outcome(s)? _____
    _____
    _____
    _____

Choosing Outcomes and Accommodations for Children   •   © 1998 by Michael F. Giangreco   •
Baltimore: Paul H. Brookes Publishing Co.

Step 10.1
Evaluation of Impact Process
for Learning Outcomes

Directions: Answer the following questions to discuss student progress toward IEP Annual Goals or Additional Learning Outcomes categories.

Student name: _____ Date of team meeting: _____

Team members participating in discussion: _____

_____

1. **Annual Goal** or **Additional Learning Outcome(s)** being discussed: _____
   _____

2. **Valued Life Outcome(s)** being facilitated through the learning outcome(s): _____
   _____
   _____
   _____

3. When was the last time this learning outcome was discussed by the team?
   Date: _____

4. What has been done to teach the student this learning outcome since it was last
   discussed? _____
   _____
   _____

5. What progress has the student made on the learning outcome?_____
   _____
   _____
   _____
   _____

6. What changes, if any, has the student experienced on the corresponding Valued Life
   Outcome(s)? _____
   _____
   _____
   _____

7. What changes, if any, need to be made in the educational program to enhance
   progress or facilitate the corresponding Valued Life Outcome(s)? _____
   _____
   _____
   _____

Choosing Outcomes and Accommodations for Children • © 1998 by Michael F. Giangreco •
Baltimore: Paul H. Brookes Publishing Co.

Step 10.1
Evaluation of Impact Process
for Learning Outcomes

Directions: Answer the following questions to discuss student progress toward IEP Annual Goals or Additional Learning Outcomes categories.

Student name: _____ Date of team meeting: _____

Team members participating in discussion: _____

_____

1. **Annual Goal** or **Additional Learning Outcome(s)** being discussed: _____
   _____

2. **Valued Life Outcome(s)** being facilitated through the learning outcome(s): _____
   _____
   _____
   _____

3. When was the last time this learning outcome was discussed by the team?
   Date: _____

4. What has been done to teach the student this learning outcome since it was last
   discussed? _____
   _____
   _____

5. What progress has the student made on the learning outcome? _____
   _____
   _____
   _____
   _____

6. What changes, if any, has the student experienced on the corresponding Valued Life
   Outcome(s)? _____
   _____
   _____
   _____

7. What changes, if any, need to be made in the educational program to enhance
   progress or facilitate the corresponding Valued Life Outcome(s)? _____
   _____
   _____
   _____

Choosing Outcomes and Accommodations for Children • © 1998 by Michael F. Giangreco •
Baltimore: Paul H. Brookes Publishing Co.

Step 10.1
Evaluation of Impact Process
for Learning Outcomes

Directions: Answer the following questions to discuss student progress toward IEP Annual Goals or Additional Learning Outcomes categories.

Student name: _____ Date of team meeting: _____

Team members participating in discussion: _____

_____

1. **Annual Goal** or **Additional Learning Outcome(s)** being discussed: _____
   _____

2. **Valued Life Outcome(s)** being facilitated through the learning outcome(s): _____
   _____
   _____
   _____

3. When was the last time this learning outcome was discussed by the team?
   Date: _____

4. What has been done to teach the student this learning outcome since it was last
   discussed? _____
   _____
   _____

5. What progress has the student made on the learning outcome? _____
   _____
   _____
   _____
   _____

6. What changes, if any, has the student experienced on the corresponding Valued Life
   Outcome(s)? _____
   _____
   _____
   _____

7. What changes, if any, need to be made in the educational program to enhance
   progress or facilitate the corresponding Valued Life Outcome(s)? _____
   _____
   _____
   _____

Choosing Outcomes and Accommodations for Children • © 1998 by Michael F. Giangreco •
Baltimore: Paul H. Brookes Publishing Co.

Step 10.2
Evaluation of Impact Process
for General Supports

Directions: Answer the following questions to discuss the student's status regarding the identified General Supports category; use one page for each area.

Student name: _____ Date of team meeting: _____

Team members participating in discussion: _____

_____

1. **General Supports** category being discussed: _____
   Items: _____
   _____
   _____

2. **Valued Life Outcome(s)** being facilitated through these general supports: _____
   _____
   _____
   _____

3. When was the last time these general supports were discussed by the team?
   Date: _____

4. What has been done since then related to these general supports? _____
   _____
   _____
   _____

5. What is the current status of these general supports? _____
   _____
   _____

6. What changes, if any, has the student experienced on the corresponding Valued Life Outcome(s) as a result of having these general supports provided? _____
   _____
   _____
   _____

7. What changes, if any, need to be made in the educational program regarding these general supports to facilitate the corresponding Valued Life Outcome(s)? _____
   _____
   _____
   _____

Step 10.2
Evaluation of Impact Process
for General Supports

Directions: Answer the following questions to discuss the student's status regarding the identified General Supports category; use one page for each area.

Student name: _____ Date of team meeting: _____

Team members participating in discussion: _____

_____

1. **General Supports** category being discussed: _____
   Items: _____
   _____
   _____

2. **Valued Life Outcome(s)** being facilitated through these general supports: _____
   _____
   _____
   _____

3. When was the last time these general supports were discussed by the team?
   Date: _____

4. What has been done since then related to these general supports? _____
   _____
   _____
   _____

5. What is the current status of these general supports? _____
   _____
   _____

6. What changes, if any, has the student experienced on the corresponding Valued Life Outcome(s) as a result of having these general supports provided? _____
   _____
   _____
   _____

7. What changes, if any, need to be made in the educational program regarding these general supports to facilitate the corresponding Valued Life Outcome(s)? _____
   _____
   _____
   _____

Choosing Outcomes and Accommodations for Children • © 1998 by Michael F. Giangreco •
Baltimore: Paul H. Brookes Publishing Co.

Step 10.2
Evaluation of Impact Process
for General Supports

Directions: Answer the following questions to discuss the student's status regarding the identified General Supports category; use one page for each area.

Student name: _____ Date of team meeting: _____

Team members participating in discussion: _____

---

1. **General Supports** category being discussed: _____
   Items: _____
   _____
   _____

2. **Valued Life Outcome(s)** being facilitated through these general supports: _____
   _____
   _____
   _____

---

3. When was the last time these general supports were discussed by the team?
   Date: _____

4. What has been done since then related to these general supports? _____
   _____
   _____
   _____

5. What is the current status of these general supports? _____
   _____
   _____

6. What changes, if any, has the student experienced on the corresponding Valued Life Outcome(s) as a result of having these general supports provided? _____
   _____
   _____
   _____

7. What changes, if any, need to be made in the educational program regarding these general supports to facilitate the corresponding Valued Life Outcome(s)? _____
   _____
   _____
   _____

Step 10.2
Evaluation of Impact Process
for General Supports

Directions: Answer the following questions to discuss the student's status regarding the identified General Supports category; use one page for each area.

Student name: _____ Date of team meeting: _____

Team members participating in discussion: _____

_____

1. **General Supports** category being discussed: _____
   Items: _____
   _____
   _____

2. **Valued Life Outcome(s)** being facilitated through these general supports: _____
   _____
   _____
   _____

3. When was the last time these general supports were discussed by the team?
   Date: _____

4. What has been done since then related to these general supports? _____
   _____
   _____
   _____

5. What is the current status of these general supports? _____
   _____
   _____

6. What changes, if any, has the student experienced on the corresponding Valued Life Outcome(s) as a result of having these general supports provided? _____
   _____
   _____
   _____

7. What changes, if any, need to be made in the educational program regarding these general supports to facilitate the corresponding Valued Life Outcome(s)? _____
   _____
   _____
   _____

Choosing Outcomes and Accommodations for Children   •   © 1998 by Michael F. Giangreco   •
Baltimore: Paul H. Brookes Publishing Co.

Step 10.2
Evaluation of Impact Process
for General Supports

Directions: Answer the following questions to discuss the student's status regarding the identified General Supports category; use one page for each area.

Student name: _____ Date of team meeting: _____

Team members participating in discussion: _____

_____

---

1. **General Supports** category being discussed: _____
   Items: _____
   _____
   _____

2. **Valued Life Outcome(s)** being facilitated through these general supports: _____
   _____
   _____
   _____

---

3. When was the last time these general supports were discussed by the team?
   Date: _____

4. What has been done since then related to these general supports? _____
   _____
   _____
   _____

5. What is the current status of these general supports? _____
   _____
   _____

6. What changes, if any, has the student experienced on the corresponding Valued Life Outcome(s) as a result of having these general supports provided? _____
   _____
   _____
   _____

7. What changes, if any, need to be made in the educational program regarding these general supports to facilitate the corresponding Valued Life Outcome(s)? _____
   _____
   _____
   _____

Step 10.2
Evaluation of Impact Process
for General Supports

Directions: Answer the following questions to discuss the student's status regarding the identified General Supports category; use one page for each area.

Student name: _____ Date of team meeting: _____

Team members participating in discussion: _____

_____

1. **General Supports** category being discussed: _____
   Items: _____
   _____
   _____

2. **Valued Life Outcome(s)** being facilitated through these general supports: _____
   _____
   _____
   _____

3. When was the last time these general supports were discussed by the team?
   Date: _____

4. What has been done since then related to these general supports? _____
   _____
   _____
   _____

5. What is the current status of these general supports? _____
   _____
   _____

6. What changes, if any, has the student experienced on the corresponding Valued Life Outcome(s) as a result of having these general supports provided? _____
   _____
   _____
   _____

7. What changes, if any, need to be made in the educational program regarding these general supports to facilitate the corresponding Valued Life Outcome(s)? _____
   _____
   _____
   _____

Step 10.2
Evaluation of Impact Process
for General Supports

Directions: Answer the following questions to discuss the student's status regarding the identified General Supports category; use one page for each area.

Student name: _____ Date of team meeting: _____

Team members participating in discussion: _____

_____

---

1. **General Supports** category being discussed: _____
   Items: _____
   _____
   _____

2. **Valued Life Outcome(s)** being facilitated through these general supports: _____
   _____
   _____
   _____

---

3. When was the last time these general supports were discussed by the team?
   Date: _____

4. What has been done since then related to these general supports? _____
   _____
   _____
   _____

5. What is the current status of these general supports? _____
   _____
   _____

6. What changes, if any, has the student experienced on the corresponding Valued Life Outcome(s) as a result of having these general supports provided? _____
   _____
   _____
   _____

7. What changes, if any, need to be made in the educational program regarding these general supports to facilitate the corresponding Valued Life Outcome(s)? _____
   _____
   _____
   _____

Step 10.2
Evaluation of Impact Process
for General Supports

Directions: Answer the following questions to discuss the student's status regarding the identified General Supports category; use one page for each area.

Student name: _____ Date of team meeting: _____

Team members participating in discussion: _____

_____

1. **General Supports** category being discussed: _____
   Items: _____
   _____
   _____

2. **Valued Life Outcome(s)** being facilitated through these general supports: _____
   _____
   _____
   _____

3. When was the last time these general supports were discussed by the team?
   Date: _____

4. What has been done since then related to these general supports? _____
   _____
   _____
   _____

5. What is the current status of these general supports? _____
   _____
   _____

6. What changes, if any, has the student experienced on the corresponding Valued Life Outcome(s) as a result of having these general supports provided? _____
   _____
   _____
   _____

7. What changes, if any, need to be made in the educational program regarding these general supports to facilitate the corresponding Valued Life Outcome(s)? _____
   _____
   _____
   _____

Appendix C

COACH EXAMPLE
FOR A
KINDERGARTEN STUDENT
WITH
MULTIPLE DISABILITIES

STUDENT DESCRIPTION

Keisha Springer is a 5-year-old girl who lives at home with her father, mother, 10-year-old sister, and 8-year-old brother in an urban neighborhood. Her house is two blocks from the school and about a mile from the nearest city park. Keisha has dual sensory impairments. She is legally blind, with vision acuity of 20/400; she also has a moderate to severe hearing loss. She wears corrective lenses and bilateral hearing aids. Keisha communicates using gesture, signs, fingerspelling, and vocalizations. She understands a little spoken language. Gestures, fingerspelling, and signs must be done within 12 inches of her face or into her hand. Keisha is able to get around most places once familiar with them. She really likes playing active games; she especially enjoys swimming and using playground equipment, such as swings. She functions in the moderate range of cognitive impairment. Keisha is fond of listening to stories and has recently begun showing an interest in learning letters in large print.

At the beginning of the school year, Keisha made the transition from an early childhood special education program to the kindergarten in her neighborhood. She walks to school with her sister and brother, who attend the same school, and some neighborhood friends. Keisha's kindergarten teacher receives support from a special educator who serves as an inclusion facilitator, an itinerant teacher with expertise in deaf-blindness, an orientation and mobility specialist, and a speech pathologist with a background in hearing impairments. A teacher assistant is assigned to the classroom full time to support the range of students. The kindergarten teacher, the classroom assistant, and the deaf-blindness specialist know and use sign language; others on the team are learning it.

Keisha's COACH for the current school year appears on the following pages. Only completed forms are shown. Assistive information and diagrams, such as "Introducing the Family Interview" and "Parts of COACH," are not shown even though they are included in Appendix B. For some steps in Part B, examples, rather than all completed forms, are presented.

Student Record

by
Michael F. Giangreco, Ph.D.
Chigee J. Cloninger, Ph.D.
Virginia Salce Iverson, M.Ed.

Keisha Springer
Student's Name

Planning Is for the *1997-98* **School Year**

(see COACH manual for complete directions)

Choosing Outcomes and Accommodations for Children • © 1998 by Michael F. Giangreco •
Baltimore: Paul H. Brookes Publishing Co.

Preparation Checklist

The following are important steps to take in preparation for using COACH. In the first column write the initials of the person responsible to ensure completion, and in the second column list the date completed.

	Who?	Date
1. Ensure all team members are sufficiently oriented to the purpose of COACH and directions for using it. (See Appendix A, Questions and Answers for Parents About COACH.)	J.M.	5-1-97
2. Ensure all team members agree to use COACH to plan the student's educational program.	D.L.	5-1-97
3. Ensure all team members agree to accept and act upon the educational priorities identified by the family during the Family Interview.	D.L.	5-10-97
4. Involve the family in determining who will facilitate the Family Interview. List names on the Planning Team Information form.	D.L.	5-25-97
5. Involve the family in determining when and where the Family Interview will be conducted. List information on the Planning Team Information form.	D.L.	5-25-97
6. Involve the family in determining who needs to be present at the Family Interview. (Not all team members need to be present. Typically, the Family Interview is a small group of 2–4 people.)	D.L.	5-25-97
7. Identify by whom, when, and how Steps 2–6 will be facilitated.	D.L.	5-10-97
8. Ensure all needed forms are ready for use in advance of the Family Interview. List names on the Planning Team Information form.	D.L./J.M.	6-10-97
9. Ensure the person who facilitates the Family Interview is familiar with the directions.	D.L./J.M.	5-10-97
10. Complete the COACH Cover Page, this Checklist, and the Planning Team Information form in advance of the Family Interview.	D.L.	5-10-97

Planning Team Information

Student's name: _Keisha Springer_ Date of birth: _1-13-92_

Educational placement(s): _Kindergarten, Magnolia St. School_

Family Interview (Step 1)

    Date: _6-6-97_ Interviewer: _Debbie Lamkin_

    Person(s) being interviewed: _Jane & Henry Springer_

Additional Learning Outcomes (Step 2)

    Date: _6-10-97_ Facilitator: _D.L._

General Supports (Step 3)

    Date: _6-10-97_ Facilitator: _D.L._

Annual Goals (Step 4)

    Date: _6-10-97_ Facilitator: _D.L._

Program-at-a-Glance (Step 5)

    Date: _6-10-97_ Facilitator: _D.L._

Short-Term Objectives (Step 6)

    Date: _6-10-97_ Facilitator: _D.L._

Team Membership

Name of Team Member	Relationship to Student	Date Steps 1–4 Reviewed
Jane Springer	Mother	6-10-97
Henry Springer	Father	6-10-97
Debbie Lamkin	Special Educator/Inclusion Facilitator	6-10-97
Val Rigling	Kindergarten Teacher	6-10-97
Robert Arrington	Speech-Language Pathologist	6-12-97
Jan Murphy	Special Educator/Deaf-Blind Specialist	6-10-97
Kay Cotrane	Orientation & Mobility Specialist	6-16-97
Willa Blake	Instructional Assistant	6-10-97
Marjorie Beasley	Principal	6-15-97

Choosing Outcomes and Accommodations for Children • © 1998 by Michael F. Giangreco •
Baltimore: Paul H. Brookes Publishing Co.

Step 1.1
Valued Life Outcomes

Directions: Review the purpose of this section and the list of Valued Life Outcomes with participants prior to asking questions. All the Valued Life Outcomes are meant to facilitate student independence, interdependence with others, and pursuit of personal growth by expanding access, creating new opportunities, developing individual abilities, and providing ways to contribute to one's community. Terms that are presented in bold are abbreviations for use in Steps 1.5, 10.1, and 10.2.

Being **Safe** and **Healthy**

Having a **Home**, Now and in the Future

Having Meaningful **Relationships**

Having **Choice** and Control that Match One's Age and Culture

Participating in Meaningful **Activities** in Various Places

Being Safe and Healthy

Question: "Are you (family member) interested in answering questions on this topic?"

Circle (YES) or NO

1. What, if anything, would you like to see change in [student's name] current health or safety that would help him/her to have a better or more enjoyable life? *She's pretty healthy; needs more exercise, activity, and mobility. She's cautious, seems fearful of new places. Needs to know more about streets.*

Having a Home, Now and in the Future

Question: "Are you (family member) interested in answering questions on this topic?"

Circle (YES) or NO

2. If everything goes as you hope, do you anticipate that [student's name] will continue to live where he or she does throughout the school years?

   Circle (YES) or NO   Where is that? *At home with parents, brother, sister*
   If NO, where would be a desirable place? _____

3. Would you like to talk about where a desirable place would be for [student's name] to live as an adult? Feel free to answer "No" if you think that decision is too far in the future to discuss at this time.

   Circle YES or (NO)   If YES, where? _____

4. Is there any place you would not like to have [student's name] live in the future?
   Not in big institution-type place. Not with brother or sister unless it's OK with them.

Choosing Outcomes and Accommodations for Children • © 1998 by Michael F. Giangreco •
Baltimore: Paul H. Brookes Publishing Co.

Having Meaningful Relationships

Question: "Are you (family member) interested in answering questions on this topic?"

Circle (YES) or NO

5. With whom does [student's name] have relationships and friendships? With whom does [student's name] like to spend time? *Gets along with most kids. Boy next door, cousins (older). Has a "Big Sister," visits deaf couple and family some.*

6. How, if at all, would you like [student's name] relationships to change or expand in the near future? *A few more friends outside of school, although she's pretty busy now.*

Having Choice and Control that Match One's Age and Culture

Question: "Are you (family member) interested in answering questions on this topic?"

Circle (YES) or NO

7. What kinds of choices and control does [student's name] have now that match his or her age and family/community situation? *Lots! Food, clothes she wears, things to do/play with. Try to give her same choices and decisions as brother and sister.*

8. How, if at all, would you like to see [student's name] choices and control change or expand in the near future? *Able to get around school, playground better. Maybe think about a guide dog some day. "Talk" to more people - more people understand and talk to her.*

Choosing Outcomes and Accommodations for Children • © 1998 by Michael F. Giangreco • Baltimore: Paul H. Brookes Publishing Co.

Participating in Meaningful Activities in Various Places

Question: "Are you (family member) interested in answering questions on this topic?"

Circle (YES) or NO

9. What kinds of activities does [student's name] currently do that he or she likes or values? Where does he or she spend time? _Goes most places the family does, except if it's a place she can't move around or make some noise. Likes to swim, go to the park, go to grocery store, go for ice cream._

10. How, if at all, would you like to see these activities and places change or expand in the near future? _Go to more recreation places, play more games with others._

11. _Usually, you ask this question only if the student is 13 years old or older._ Have you given any thought to what kinds of activities [student's name] might do or places he or she might go as a young adult? For example, in the future how might [student's name] spend his or her time that is now spent in school (e.g., competitive work, supported work, volunteering, continuing education)? _N/A_

Choosing Outcomes and Accommodations for Children • © 1998 by Michael F. Giangreco • Baltimore: Paul H. Brookes Publishing Co.

Ranking Valued Life Outcomes to Emphasize this Year

Directions: Ask the person being interviewed, "Please rank the Valued Life Outcomes (where 1 is the most important) to help the team understand which ones you feel are most important for [student's name] this year." Terms that are presented in bold are abbreviations for use in Steps 1.5, 10.1, and 10.2.

Rank

_5_   Being **Safe** and **Healthy**

_4_   Having a **Home**, Now and in the Future

_3_   Having Meaningful **Relationships**

_2_   Having **Choice** and Control that Match One's Age and Culture

_1_   Participating in Meaningful **Activities** in Various Places

*** Relationship to Next Steps ***

This information about the student's Valued Life Outcomes will set the context for the selection of individualized learning outcomes and general supports.

Choosing Outcomes and Accommodations for Children • © 1998 by Michael F. Giangreco •
Baltimore: Paul H. Brookes Publishing Co.

Notes About Valued Life Outcomes

1st, 2nd, & 3rd choices seen as very interrelated. Difficult to rank. If she goes to more places and does more things, then she will meet people who will communicate with her and be friends.

Communication

Mark only one box to indicate if the family wants to discuss this set of learning outcomes in:
Step 1 (Family Interview; priority this year?) ☒; Step 2 (Additional Learning Outcomes) ☐; Skip for Now ☐

Currently, in what ways does the student communicate?

Expressively: *Gestures, vocalizations, signing*

Receptively: *Gestures, signing (near face and/or in hand), a little speech*

#	Learning Outcomes	Step 1.3 Circle Score	Needs Work?	Step 1.4 Rank up to 5 Priorities
1	Expresses Continuation or "More" (e.g., makes sounds or movement when desired interaction stops to indicate he or she would like eating, playing, etc., to continue)	E P (S)	(N) Y	
2	Makes Choices When Given Options	E P (S)	(N) Y	
3	Makes Requests (e.g., for objects, food, interactions, activities, assistance)	E P (S)	N (Y)	
4	Summons Others (e.g., has a way to call others to him or her)	E P (S)	(N) Y	
5	Expresses Rejection/Refusal (e.g., indicates when he or she wants something to stop or does not want something to begin)	E P (S)	(N) Y	
6	Expresses Greetings and Farewells	E (P) S	N (Y)	5
7	Follows Instructions (e.g., one step, multistep)	E (P) S	N (Y)	
8	Sustains Communication with Others (e.g., takes turns, attends, stays on topic, perseveres)	E (P) S	N (Y)	4
9	Initiates Communication with Others	E (P) S	N (Y)	3
10	Responds to Questions (e.g., if asked a question, he or she attempts to answer)	E (P) S	N (Y)	
11	Comments/Describes (e.g., expands vocabulary for events, objects, interactions, feelings)	(E) P S	N (Y)	1
12	Asks Questions of Others	(E) P S	N (Y)	2
		E P S	N Y	

Comments: *Others need to know her signs to understand her. Also uses some unique gestures, vocalizations/speech.*

Scoring Key (use scores for Step 1.3 alone or in combination):
E = Early/Emerging Skill (1% – 25%)   **P** = Partial Skill (25% – 80%)   **S** = Skillful (80% – 100%)

Choosing Outcomes and Accommodations for Children • © 1998 by Michael F. Giangreco • Baltimore: Paul H. Brookes Publishing Co.

Socialization

Step 1.2

Mark only one box to indicate if the family wants to discuss this set of learning outcomes in:
Step 1 (Family Interview; priority this year?) ☒; Step 2 (Additional Learning Outcomes) ☐; Skip for Now ☐

		Step 1.3		Step 1.4
#	Learning Outcomes	Circle Score	Needs Work?	Rank up to 5 Priorities
13	Responds to the Presence and Interactions of Others (e.g., peers, family, adults)	E P (S)	(N) Y	
14	Initiates Social Interactions	E (P) S	N (Y)	5
15	Sustains Social Interactions	E (P) S	N (Y)	2
16	Terminates Social Interactions	E (P) S	N (Y)	
17	Distinguishes and Interacts Differently with Familiar People, Acquaintances, and Strangers	(E) P S	(N) Y	
18	Maintains Socially Acceptable Behavior When Alone and with Others	E P (S)	N (Y)	3
19	Accepts Assistance from Others	E P (S)	(N) Y	
20	Offers Assistance to Others	E (P) S	N (Y)	4
21	Makes Transitions Between Routine Activities	E P (S)	(N) Y	
22	Adjusts to Unexpected Changes in Routine	E (P) S	N (Y)	
23	Shares with Others	E (P) S	N (Y)	1
24	Advocates for Self	(E) P S	(N) Y	
		E P S	N Y	
		E P S	N Y	
		E P S	N Y	
		E P S	N Y	

Comments: Understands concept of sharing but sometimes gets into disagreements with others. Happens when child approaches and asks to share but Keisha does not get the message. When child stops asking & tries to take toy, K's response may be aggressive. Kids need to know how to be sure she gets the message.
K needs to use signs to get others to interact, not just use gestures or objects.

Scoring Key (use scores for Step 1.3 alone or in combination):
E = Early/Emerging Skill (1% – 25%)   **P** = Partial Skill (25% – 80%)   **S** = Skillful (80% – 100%)

Personal Management

Step 1.2

Mark only one box to indicate if the family wants to discuss this set of learning outcomes in:
Step 1 (Family Interview; priority this year?) ☒; Step 2 (Additional Learning Outcomes) ☐; Skip for Now ☐

		Step 1.3		Step 1.4
#	**Learning Outcomes**	Circle Score	Needs Work?	Rank up to 5 Priorities
25	Drinks and Eats (e.g., accepts food/drink, chews, swallows)	E P (S)	(N) Y	
26	Eats with Hands/Fingers	E P (S)	(N) Y	
27	Eats with Utensils (e.g., spoon, fork, knife)	E P (S)	N (Y)	3
28	Dresses/Undresses	E (P) S	N (Y)	
29	Cares for Bowel and Bladder Needs	E P (S)	(N) Y	
30	Cares for Hands and Face (e.g., washes, dries, wipes, blows nose, applies lotion, applies lip balm)	E P (S)	(N) Y	
31	Combs/Brushes Hair	E (P) S	(N) Y	
32	Gives Self-Identification Information (e.g., name, address, phone number)	E (P) S	N (Y)	4
33	Responds to Emergency Alarm (e.g., leaves building when smoke alarm sounds)	E (P) S	N (Y)	
34	Manages Personal Belongings (e.g., toys, clothes, special equipment)	E (P) S	N (Y)	2
35	Mobile Within and Between Rooms of a Building (e.g., walks, crawls, rolls, moves wheel-chair, climbs stairs, uses elevators/escalators, navigates)	E (P) S	N (Y)	1
36	Recognizes and Avoids Potentially Dangerous Situations	(E) P S	N (Y)	5
		E P S	N Y	
		E P S	N Y	

Comments:
27 – uses utensils, but is a bit messy
28 – puts some clothes on inside out, has favorites she wants to wear all the time
34 – needs to learn to care for hearing aids & glasses
35, 36 – O & M needs to continue

Scoring Key (use scores for Step 1.3 alone or in combination):
E = Early/Emerging Skill (1% – 25%)   **P** = Partial Skill (25% – 80%)   **S** = Skillful (80% – 100%)

Leisure/Recreation

Step 1.2

Mark only one box to indicate if the family wants to discuss this set of learning outcomes in:
Step 1 (Family Interview; priority this year?) ☐; Step 2 (Additional Learning Outcomes) ☐; Skip for Now ☒

		Step 1.3		Step 1.4
#	Learning Outcomes	Circle Score	Needs Work?	Rank up to 5 Priorities
37	Engages in Individual, Passive Leisure Activities (e.g., listens to music, watches television)	E P S	N Y	
38	Engages in Individual, Active Leisure Activities (e.g., toy play, games, sports, exercise, hobbies)	E P S	N Y	
39	Engages in Passive Leisure Activities with Others (e.g., read to by someone; goes to movies, performances, spectator sports or events with others)	E P S	N Y	
40	Engages in Active Leisure Activities with Others (e.g., group games and activities, sports, exercise, hobbies)	E P S	N Y	
		E P S	N Y	
		E P S	N Y	
		E P S	N Y	
		E P S	N Y	

Comments:

Scoring Key (use scores for Step 1.3 alone or in combination):
  E = Early/Emerging Skill (1% – 25%) **P** = Partial Skill (25% – 80%) **S** = Skillful (80% – 100%)

Selected Academics

Step 1.2

Mark only one box to indicate if the family wants to discuss this set of learning outcomes in:
Step 1 (Family Interview; priority this year?) ☒; Step 2 (Additional Learning Outcomes) ☐; Skip for Now ☐

#	Learning Outcomes	Step 1.3 Circle Score	Step 1.3 Needs Work?	Step 1.4 Rank up to 5 Priorities
41	Reacts to Objects, Activities, and/or Interactions by Displaying Some Observable Change in Behavior	E P Ⓢ	Ⓝ Y	
42	Directs and Sustains Attention to Activity (e.g., books, toys, class activities)	E P Ⓢ	N Ⓨ	
43	Explores Surroundings (e.g., scans, searches)	E Ⓟ S	Ⓝ Y	
44	Differentiates/Discriminates Between Various Things (e.g., objects, activities, symbols, pictures, interactions)	E P Ⓢ	N Ⓨ	
45	Imitates Skills Used in Daily Life	E Ⓟ S	N Ⓨ	
46	Uses Objects for Intended Purposes (e.g., plays with toy, eats with spoon, turns pages of a book, writes/draws with pencil, brushes hair)	E Ⓟ S	Ⓝ Y	
47	Identifies Symbols (e.g., letters, words, braille, line drawings, manual signs)	Ⓔ P S	N Ⓨ	1
48	Reads to Get Information and/or Follow Instructions	Ⓔ P S	N Ⓨ	
49	Uses Writing Tools to Form Letters and Words (e.g., printing, handwriting, typewriting)	Ⓔ P S	N Ⓨ	2
50	Composes Phrases and Sentences	Ⓔ P S	Ⓝ Y	
51	Counts with Correspondence	Ⓔ P S	N Ⓨ	3
52	Calculates (e.g., adds, subtracts, multiplies, divides)	Ⓔ P S	Ⓝ Y	
53	Uses Clock (e.g., face, digital, alarm)	Ⓔ P S	N Ⓨ	
54	Uses Calendar (e.g., days, dates, months, year; notes special events and appointments)	Ⓔ P S	N Ⓨ	
55	Uses Computer	Ⓔ P S	N Ⓨ	4
	Uses some large print with good contrast Needs to learn to use TDD			

Scoring Key (use scores for Step 1.3 alone or in combination):
   E = Early/Emerging Skill (1% – 25%)   **P** = Partial Skill (25% – 80%)   **S** = Skillful (80% – 100%)

Home

Step 1.2

Mark only one box to indicate if the family wants to discuss this set of learning outcomes in:
Step 1 (Family Interview; priority this year?) ☐; Step 2 (Additional Learning Outcomes) ☐; Skip for Now ☒

#	Learning Outcomes	Step 1.3 Circle Score	Needs Work?	Step 1.4 Rank up to 5 Priorities
56	Brushes/Flosses Teeth	E P S	N Y	
57	Selects Appropriate Clothing to Wear (e.g., selects items needed for time of day, weather conditions, style, matching)	E P S	N Y	
58	Cares for Personal Hygiene Needs (e.g., bathes, showers, cares for nails, uses deodorant, shaves)	E P S	N Y	
59	Picks Up After Self	E P S	N Y	
60	Prepares Food (e.g., snacks, cold meals, hot meals)	E P S	N Y	
61	Does Household Chores (e.g., dusts, sweeps, mops, vacuums, washes/dries dishes, takes out garbage, recycles, makes bed, stores groceries, yardwork)	E P S	N Y	
62	Cares for Clothing (e.g., puts laundry in designated place when clean or dirty, washes/dries, folds, irons, mends)	E P S	N Y	
63	Uses Telephone (e.g., answers, calls, uses directory)	E P S	N Y	
		E P S	N Y	
		E P S	N Y	
		E P S	N Y	
		E P S	N Y	

Comments:

Scoring Key (use scores for Step 1.3 alone or in combination):
E = Early/Emerging Skill (1% – 25%)   **P** = Partial Skill (25% – 80%)   **S** = Skillful (80% – 100%)

Choosing Outcomes and Accommodations for Children   •   © 1998 by Michael F. Giangreco   •
Baltimore: Paul H. Brookes Publishing Co.

School

Step 1.2

Mark only one box to indicate if the family wants to discuss this set of learning outcomes in:
Step 1 (Family Interview; priority this year?) ☐; Step 2 (Additional Learning Outcomes) ☒; Skip for Now ☐

		Step 1.3		Step 1.4
#	Learning Outcomes	Circle Score	Needs Work?	Rank up to 5 Priorities
64	Travels to and from School Safely (e.g., on bus, as a pedestrian)	E P S	N Y	
65	Participates in Small Groups (e.g., tolerates situation, takes turn, is actively involved, responds to instructions)	E P S	N Y	
66	Participates in Large Groups (e.g., tolerates situation, takes turn, is actively involved, responds to instructions)	E P S	N Y	
67	Works at Task Independently (e.g., starts, sustains, completes, at nonfrustrational level)	E P S	N Y	
68	Manages School-Related Belongings (e.g., backpack, materials, books, lockers, gym equipment)	E P S	N Y	
69	Follows School Rules/Routines (e.g., understands and follows class and school rules, changes classes, follows schedule)	E P S	N Y	
70	Uses School Facilities (e.g., playground, cafeteria, library, bookstore)	E P S	N Y	
71	Makes Purchases in School (e.g., cafeteria, bookstore, event tickets)	E P S	N Y	
72	Participates in Extracurricular Activities (e.g., clubs, sports, service organizations, drama, music)	E P S	N Y	
		E P S	N Y	
		E P S	N Y	
		E P S	N Y	

Comments:

Scoring Key (use scores for Step 1.3 alone or in combination):
E = Early/Emerging Skill (1% – 25%)   **P** = Partial Skill (25% – 80%)   **S** = Skillful (80% – 100%)

Community

Step 1.2

Mark only one box to indicate if the family wants to discuss this set of learning outcomes in:
Step 1 (Family Interview; priority this year?) ☐; Step 2 (Additional Learning Outcomes) ☐; Skip for Now ☒

		Step 1.3		Step 1.4
#	Learning Outcomes	Circle Score	Needs Work?	Rank up to 5 Priorities
73	Travels Safely in the Community (e.g., crosses intersections, uses crosswalks and sidewalks, acts appropriately with strangers, finds destination)	E P S	N Y	
74	Uses Restaurants (e.g., orders food, finds seating, eats meal, pays bill)	E P S	N Y	
75	Uses Recreational Facilities (e.g., movies, arcades, parks, recreation centers, fitness clubs)	E P S	N Y	
76	Makes Purchases of Merchandise or Services (e.g., food stores, clothing/department stores, specialty stores, post office, hair salon, laundry/cleaner, knows purpose of different kinds of stores, finds merchandise or services desired, pays bill)	E P S	N Y	
77	Uses Vending Machines (e.g., drinks, food, stamps, newspaper, public transportation tickets/tokens)	E P S	N Y	
78	Uses Banking Facilities (e.g., deposits, withdraws, uses automated teller machines)	E P S	N Y	
79	Travels by Public Transportation (e.g., bus, subway, trolley, taxi, ferry)	E P S	N Y	
80	Uses Pay Phone	E P S	N Y	
		E P S	N Y	
		E P S	N Y	
		E P S	N Y	

Comments:

Scoring Key (use scores for Step 1.3 alone or in combination):
  E = Early/Emerging Skill (1% – 25%)   **P** = Partial Skill (25% – 80%)   **S** = Skillful (80% – 100%)

Choosing Outcomes and Accommodations for Children • © 1998 by Michael F. Giangreco •
Baltimore: Paul H. Brookes Publishing Co.

Vocational

Step 1.2

Mark only one box to indicate if the family wants to discuss this set of learning outcomes in:
Step 1 (Family Interview; priority this year?) ☐; Step 2 (Additional Learning Outcomes) ☒; Skip for Now ☐

#	Learning Outcomes	Step 1.3 Circle Score	Needs Work?	Step 1.4 Rank up to 5 Priorities
81	Does Classroom and/or Home Job(s)	E P S	N Y	
82	Does Job(s) at School, Beyond the Classroom, with Peers without Disabilities (e.g., delivers attendance, messages, lunch money; helps operate bookstore)	E P S	N Y	
For Students at Community Worksites				
83	Travels to and from Worksite	E P S	N Y	
84	Uses Time Clock or Check-In Procedure	E P S	N Y	
85	Interacts Appropriately with Co-workers, Customers, and Supervisors	E P S	N Y	
86	Follows Worksite Rules for Safety, Conduct, and Appearance	E P S	N Y	
87	Works Independently at a Task	E P S	N Y	
88	Works with Others (e.g., cooperates, does enough work, accepts assistance, gives assistance)	E P S	N Y	
89	Follows Schedule of Work Activities	E P S	N Y	
90	Uses Worksite Breaktime Facilities (e.g., engages in appropriate breaktime and lunchtime routines)	E P S	N Y	
91	Applies for Job(s) (e.g., finds potential jobs, contacts employers, fills out forms, participates in job interviews)	E P S	N Y	
		E P S	N Y	

Comments:

Scoring Key (use scores for Step 1.3 alone or in combination):
    E = Early/Emerging Skill (1% – 25%)   **P** = Partial Skill (25% – 80%)   **S** = Skillful (80% – 100%)

Choosing Outcomes and Accommodations for Children • © 1998 by Michael F. Giangreco •
Baltimore: Paul H. Brookes Publishing Co.

Other

Step 1.2

Mark only one box to indicate if the family wants to discuss this set of learning outcomes in:
Step 1 (Family Interview; priority this year?) ☐; Step 2 (Additional Learning Outcomes) ☐; Skip for Now ☒

#	Learning Outcomes	Step 1.3 Circle Score	Needs Work?	Step 1.4 Rank up to 5 Priorities
		E P S	N Y	
		E P S	N Y	
		E P S	N Y	
		E P S	N Y	
		E P S	N Y	
		E P S	N Y	
		E P S	N Y	
		E P S	N Y	
		E P S	N Y	
		E P S	N Y	
		E P S	N Y	

Comments:

Scoring Key (use scores for Step 1.3 alone or in combination):
E = Early/Emerging Skill (1% – 25%)   **P** = Partial Skill (25% – 80%)   **S** = Skillful (80% – 100%)

Choosing Outcomes and Accommodations for Children • © 1998 by Michael F. Giangreco •
Baltimore: Paul H. Brookes Publishing Co.

Step 1.5:   Cross-Prioritization

Directions: Transfer priorities, in their ranked order, from each list of learning outcomes (Step 1.4) reviewed with the family.

#	Communication	Socialization	Personal Management	Leisure/Recreation	Selected Academics
1	Comments/describes	Shares with others	Mobile around school		Identifies symbols
2	Asks questions	Sustains social interactions	Manages personal belongings	Skip for Now	Uses writing tools
3	Initiates communication	Acceptable behavior with others	Eats with utensils		Counts with correspondence
4	Sustains communication	Assistance to others	Gives self-identification		Uses computer
5	Greetings & farewells	Initiates social interactions	Recognizes/avoids dangerous situations		

#	School	Community	Vocational	Home	Other
1					
2	Assess as Additional Learning Outcomes	Skip for Now	Assess as Additional Learning Outcomes	Skip for Now	Not Assessed
3					
4					
5					

Directions: Referring to the above listings, use the next page (Step 1.5 continued) to have the family member(s) being interviewed:
1. Rank a maximum of the top eight overall priorities, explicitly clarifying the wording to reflect what the student will be expected to learn. Review the overall priority selections to ensure that they accurately reflect student priorities.
2. Verify the reasoning behind the family's selection and record abbreviations corresponding to the valued life outcome(s).
3. Determine the proposed context in which learning of each priority will occur (e.g., classroom, community worksite, cafeteria with peers).
4. Indicate how each priority will be addressed as an IEP annual goal, an additional learning outcome, or primarily as a home responsibility (check only one of the three boxes for each ranked priority).

Choosing Outcomes and Accommodations for Children   •   © 1998 by Michael F. Giangreco   •   Baltimore: Paul H. Brookes Publishing Co.

Step 1.5. (continued)

Rank	1) Overall Priority Learning Outcomes (word priorities to explicitly clarify what the student will be expected to learn)	2) Write the Abbreviation of Valued Life Outcome(s)	3) List the Context for Learning	4) Check (✔) Only One Box for Each Priority		
				IEP Goal	Additional Learning Outcomes	Home
1	Shares with others (responds to and uses signs/gestures)	Relationships, Activities	Kindergarten activities & lessons	✔		
2	Comments on and describes events, objects, feelings (expand vocabulary)	Choice	"	✔		
3	Mobile around school, uses O & M strategies and equipment (e.g. modified cane)	Choice, Activities	"	✔		
4	Manages personal belongings – cleans, checks batteries, etc. for aids, glasses	Choice	Home & school			✔
5	Ask questions of others	Relationships, Choice, Activities	Kindergarten activities & lessons	✔		
6	Reads symbols (large print, beginning braille, fingerspelling, signs)	Choice, Activities	"		✔	
7	Expresses greetings & farewells	Relationships	"		✔	
8	Eats with utensils – uses to eat neatly, uses napkin	Choice	Home & school			

Choosing Outcomes and Accommodations for Children • © 1998 by Michael F. Giangreco • Baltimore: Paul H. Brookes Publishing Co.

Directions: The interviewer explains the next steps and the relationship of the Family Interview to the rest of COACH.

Step 2.1
Additional Learning Outcomes from COACH

Directions: Consider the learning outcomes on this list and select a subset to be targeted for instruction as Additional Learning Outcomes. These pages may be included as an addendum to the IEP.

Participants: *Debbie Lamkin, Jane & Henry Springer, Val Rigling, Jan Murphy, Willa Blake*

COMMUNICATION

____ 1. Expresses continuation or "more"
____ 2. Makes choices when given options
____ 3. Makes requests
____ 4. Summons others
____ 5. Expresses rejection/refusal
✓ 6. Expresses greetings and farewells
____ 7. Follows instructions
✓ 8. Sustains communication with others
✓ 9. Initiates communication with others
____ 10. Responds to questions
____ 11. Comments/describes
____ 12. Asks questions of others
____ _____
____ _____

SOCIALIZATION

____ 13. Responds to the presence and interactions of others
✓ 14. Initiates social interactions
✓ 15. Sustains social interactions
____ 16. Terminates social interactions
____ 17. Distinguishes and interacts differently with familiar people, acquaintances, and strangers
✓ 18. Maintains socially acceptable behavior when alone and with others
____ 19. Accepts assistance from others
____ 20. Offers assistance to others

____ 21. Makes transitions between routine activities
____ 22. Adjusts to unexpected changes in routine
____ 23. Shares with others
✓ 24. Advocates for self
____ _____
____ _____
____ _____

PERSONAL MANAGEMENT

____ 25. Drinks and eats
____ 26. Eats with hands/fingers
✓ 27. Eats with utensils
____ 28. Dresses/undresses
____ 29. Cares for bowel and bladder needs
____ 30. Cares for hands and face
____ 31. Combs/brushes hair
✓ 32. Gives self-identification information
✓ 33. Responds to emergency alarm
✓ 34. Manages personal belongings
____ 35. Mobile within and between rooms of a building
✓ 36. Recognizes and avoids potentially dangerous situations
____ _____
____ _____
____ _____

LEISURE/RECREATION

____ 37. Engages in individual, passive leisure activities
____ 38. Engages in individual, active leisure activities

____ 39. Engages in passive leisure activities with others
____ 40. Engages in active leisure with others
____ _____
____ _____

SELECTED ACADEMICS
(see Kindergarten curriculum)

____ 41. Reacts to objects, activities, and/or interactions by displaying some observable change in behavior
____ 42. Directs and sustains attention to activity
____ 43. Explores surroundings
____ 44. Differentiates/discriminates between various things
____ 45. Imitates skills used in daily life
____ 46. Uses objects for intended purposes
____ 47. Identifies symbols
____ 48. Reads to get information and/or follow instructions
____ 49. Uses writing tools to form letters and words
____ 50. Composes phrases and sentences
____ 51. Counts with correspondence
____ 52. Calculates
____ 53. Uses clock
____ 54. Uses calendar
____ 55. Uses computer
____ _____
____ _____
____ _____

(continued)

Choosing Outcomes and Accommodations for Children • © 1998 by Michael F. Giangreco •
Baltimore: Paul H. Brookes Publishing Co.

Step 2.1. (continued)

HOME

___ 56. Brushes/flosses teeth
___ 57. Selects appropriate
      clothing to wear
___ 58. Cares for personal
      hygiene needs
___ 59. Picks up after self
___ 60. Prepares food
___ 61. Does household chores
___ 62. Cares for clothing
___ 63. Uses telephone

___ _____
___ _____
___ _____

SCHOOL

___ 64. Travels to and from
      school safely
___ 65. Participates in small
      groups
___ 66. Participates in large
      groups
___ 67. Works at a task
      independently
___ 68. Manages school-related
      belongings
___ 69. Follows school rules/
      routines
___ 70. Uses school facilities
___ 71. Makes purchases in
      school
___ 72. Participates in extra-
      curricular activities

___ _____
___ _____
___ _____

COMMUNITY

___ 73. Travels safely in the
      community
___ 74. Uses restaurants
___ 75. Uses recreational
      facilities
___ 76. Makes purchases of
      merchandise or services
___ 77. Uses vending machines
___ 78. Uses banking facilities
___ 79. Travels by public
      transportation
___ 80. Uses pay phone

___ _____
___ _____
___ _____
___ _____

VOCATIONAL

___ 81. Does classroom and/or
      home job(s)
___ 82. Does job(s) at school,
      beyond the classroom,
      with peers without
      disabilities

*For Students at Community
Worksites*

___ 83. Travels to and from
      worksite
___ 84. Uses time clock or
      check-in procedure
___ 85. Interacts appropriately
      with co-workers,
      customers, and
      supervisors
___ 86. Follows worksite rules
      for safety, conduct, and
      appearance
___ 87. Works independently at
      a task
___ 88. Works with others
___ 89. Follows schedule of
      work activities
___ 90. Uses worksite breaktime
      facilities
___ 91. Applies for job(s)

___ _____
___ _____

OTHER:

___ _____
___ _____
___ _____
___ _____
___ _____
___ _____
___ _____
___ _____
___ _____
___ _____
___ _____
___ _____
___ _____
___ _____
___ _____
___ _____
___ _____
___ _____

OTHER:

___ _____
___ _____
___ _____
___ _____
___ _____
___ _____
___ _____
___ _____
___ _____
___ _____
___ _____
___ _____
___ _____
___ _____
___ _____
___ _____
___ _____
___ _____

OTHER:

___ _____
___ _____
___ _____
___ _____
___ _____
___ _____
___ _____
___ _____
___ _____
___ _____
___ _____
___ _____
___ _____
___ _____
___ _____
___ _____
___ _____
___ _____
___ _____
___ _____

Step 2.2: Additional Learning Outcomes from General Education

Directions: 1) Check all curriculum areas taught in the grade being planned for; 2) beside curriculum areas, clarify subject content; 3) circle the type of participation (**same, multilevel, none/curriculum overlapping**); 4) if multilevel, indicate if adapted subject content is the same or different by circling your response; and 5) record examples of the student's learning outcomes.

Student Name: Keisha Springer   **The Grade Placement Being Planned for Is:** K   **Date of Meeting:** June 10, 1997

Participants: DL, J & HS, VR, JM, WB

✓	General Education Curriculum Areas: Class Content	Primary Type?			If Multilevel, Is the Adapted Subject Matter?	
		S	ML	N/CO	Same	Different
✓	(Reading) Language Arts: *Name, sequencing, directions, story telling*	(S)	ML	N/CO	Same	Different
	Individual's Learning Outcomes: *Recognizes name, tells story*					
✓	Math: *Counting, matching numerals, shapes, positions, patterns*	(S)	ML	N/CO	Same	Different
	Individual's Learning Outcomes: *counts from 1-10; names shapes*					
✓	Science: *Plants & animal differences; simple machines; solar system*	S	ML	(N/CO)	Same	Different
	Individual's Learning Outcomes:					
	History/Social Studies:	S	ML	N/CO	Same	Different
	Individual's Learning Outcomes:					
✓	Arts (Visual) Performing: *Colors, composition, space, texture, vocabulary*	S	ML	(N/CO)	Same	Different
	Individual's Learning Outcomes:					
✓	Music (Vocal/Instrumental): *Rhythms, listening skills, signing, instruments*	S	ML	(N/CO)	Same	Different
	Individual's Learning Outcomes:					
✓	Technology (Computer Literacy): *Computer parts, terms, functions*	(S)	ML	N/CO	Same	Different
	Individual's Learning Outcomes: *As above*					
✓	Physical Education: *Movements, balance, uses equipment, games*	(S)	ML	N/CO	Same	Different
	Individual's Learning Outcomes: *plays active games*					

Choosing Outcomes and Accommodations for Children • © 1998 by Michael F. Giangreco • Baltimore: Paul H. Brookes Publishing Co.

Step 2.2. (continued)

✓	General Education Curriculum Areas: Class Content	Primary Type?			If Multilevel, Is the Adapted Subject Matter?	
		S	ML	N/CO	Same	Different
✓	**Health Education:** *Poisons, Drugs, Meaning of health, safe routes/touch, safe choices, feelings, senses* Individual's Learning Outcomes: *As above*	(S)	ML	N/CO	Same	Different
	Foreign Language: Individual's Learning Outcomes:	S	ML	N/CO	Same	Different
	Community Service/Social Responsibility: Individual's Learning Outcomes:	S	ML	N/CO	Same	Different
	Home Economics: Individual's Learning Outcomes:	S	ML	N/CO	Same	Different
	Industrial Arts: Individual's Learning Outcomes:	S	ML	N/CO	Same	Different
	Vocational: Individual's Learning Outcomes:	S	ML	N/CO	Same	Different
	Reasoning and Problem Solving: Individual's Learning Outcomes:	S	ML	N/CO	Same	Different
	Other: Individual's Learning Outcomes:	S	ML	N/CO	Same	Different

Codes: **S** = Same (same learning outcomes as others); **ML** = Multilevel (learning outcomes in the same curriculum area at a different level, such as content, quantity, performance criteria); **N/CO** = None/Curriculum Overlapping (there are no learning outcomes identified for instruction in these curriculum areas, but the student participates in class activities by working on learning outcomes from different curriculum areas).

Choosing Outcomes and Accommodations for Children • © 1998 by Michael F. Giangreco • Baltimore: Paul H. Brookes Publishing Co.

Step 3
General Supports

Directions: Check those items to be included in the student's educational program as "General Supports" (those supports or accommodations provided to or for the student). Space has been provided under each item to allow for clarifying or specifying information individually pertinent to the student. *General Supports are not a comprehensive list of specific instructional supports.* These pages may be included as an addendum to the IEP or the information may be transferred to the IEP in an appropriate section.

Participants: *DL, J & HS, VR, JM, WB*

PERSONAL NEEDS

___ 1. Needs to be fed food and drinks

___ 2. Needs to be dressed

___ 3. Needs assistance with bowel and bladder management

___ 4. Needs assistance with personal hygiene

___ 5. Needs to be given medication

___ 6. Needs suctioning and/or postural drainage

Other Personal Needs:

___ _____

___ _____

___ _____

___ _____

___ _____

___ _____

___ _____

PHYSICAL NEEDS

___ 7. Needs to be physically repositioned at regular intervals

___ 8. Needs to have environmental barriers modified to allow access

___ 9. Needs to have physical equipment managed (e.g., wheelchair, braces, orthotics)

___ 10. Needs specialized transportation accommodations

___ 11. Needs to be moved and positioned in specialized ways

___ 12. Needs to be physically moved from place to place

Other Physical Needs:

___ _____

___ _____

___ _____

___ _____

___ _____

TEACHING OTHERS ABOUT THE STUDENT

✓ 13. Teach staff and class-mates about the student's augmentative communi-cation system and other communicative behaviors

✓ 14. Teach staff and students how to communicate with the student

___ 15. Teach staff seizure management procedures

✓ 16. Teach staff emergency procedures (e.g., medical, evacuation)

___ 17. Teach staff preventive behavior management procedures

___ 18. Teach staff behavioral crisis intervention procedures

Other Needs Related to Teaching Others About the Student:

___ _____

___ _____

___ _____

_____

(continued)

Step 3. (*continued*)

SENSORY NEEDS

✓ 19. Needs to have hearing aids monitored (e.g., batteries, settings)

✓ 20. Needs to have people use FM unit/auditory trainer

✓ 21. Needs people to manually communicate (e.g., American Sign Language, common gestures)

✓ 22. Needs to have glasses managed (e.g., adjusted, cleaned)

✓ 23. Needs tactile materials

✓ 24. Needs enlarged materials

___ 25. Needs materials in braille

✓ 26. Needs to be positioned to accommodate sensory needs (e.g., specified distance from source)

✓ 27. Needs environmental modifications to accommodate for sensory needs (e.g., lighting, location, background, volume, color)

Other Sensory Needs:

___ _____

___ _____

___ _____

___ _____

___ _____

___ _____

___ _____

___ _____

PROVIDING ACCESS AND OPPORTUNITIES

✓ 28. Provide access to general education classes and activities

✓ 29. Needs to have instructional accommodations to general education activities and materials prepared in advance to facilitate multilevel instruction and/or curriculum overlapping

___ 30. Provide access to community-based experiences with people without disabilities

___ 31. Provide access to vocational experiences with people without disabilities

___ 32. Provide access to co-curricular activities with people without disabilities

___ 33. Provide access to materials in the student's native language

___ 34. Provide access to materials and activities associated with the student's cultural background as well as other cultures

___ 35. Provide access to nonaversive approaches to dealing with challenging behaviors

Other Needs Related to Providing Access and Opportunities:

___ _____

___ _____

___ _____

OTHER GENERAL SUPPORTS
(not listed elsewhere)

___ 36. Needs time limits extended or waived

___ 37. Needs classnotes recorded in any form

___ 38. Needs alternative testing modifications

Other General Supports:

___ _____

___ _____

___ _____

___ _____

___ _____

___ _____

___ _____

___ _____

___ _____

___ _____

___ _____

___ _____

___ _____

___ _____

Choosing Outcomes and Accommodations for Children • © 1998 by Michael F. Giangreco •
Baltimore: Paul H. Brookes Publishing Co.

Step 4: Annual Goals

Priority Learning Outcome (from Step 1.5): _Shares with others_

Current Level of Functioning Related to the Priority Learning Outcome: _Shares at times – more with adults, older children. May grab. Child not skillful in saying "No, not now" (shakes head & pulls object away). Vocalizes displeasure_

Behavior: _giving objects, include others in activities_

Context: _Class activities and lessons, in classroom & playground_

Team Member Suggestions: _specify events, objects, "given approached appropriately"_

Annual Goal: _Keisha will share with others or communicate a "No" response._

Step 6: Short-Term Objectives

Clarify the intent/focus of Annual Goal to be reflected in the objectives (check those that apply or determine others):

_____ Decreasing prompts/cues	_____ Increasing response to natural cues
_____ Desensitizing/increasing tolerance	_____ Accepting assistance from others
_____ Acquiring core skills	_____ Initiation of behavior
_____ Preparation for the activity	_____ Quality of performance
_____ Appropriateness of tempo or rate	_____ Extending or reducing duration
_____ Self-monitoring	_____ Problem solving
_____ Termination of the behavior	_____ Assisting others with the behavior
_____ Safety aspects	_____ Expansion of repertoire
✓ Communication aspects	✓ Social behaviors aspects and manners
_____ Indication of choice or preference	_____ Retention over time
✓ Generalization across settings	✓ Generalization across people
✓ Generalization across materials	_____ Generalization across cues

	Conditions	Behavior	Criteria
1	Approached with signed appropriate communication (e.g., "May I use . . . ?") at appropriate distance (6–12 inches) & low-preference object/activity by adult	Keisha hands object to another or moves to include other in activity <u>or</u> signs "No"	90% of the time over 6 weeks
2	Approached with signed appropriate communication and higher-preference object/activity by adult or peer	"	"
3	Approached with signed appropriate communication and high-preference object/activity by adult or peer	"	"

Choosing Outcomes and Accommodations for Children • © 1998 by Michael F. Giangreco •
Baltimore: Paul H. Brookes Publishing Co.

Step 4:   Annual Goals

Priority Learning Outcome (from Step 1.5): _Comments, describes_

Current Level of Functioning Related to the Priority Learning Outcome: _Uses many one-word signs for objects and events, very few for feelings. Uses vocalizations for feelings (happy, pain, frustration). Very few two-sign phrases/sentences._

Behavior: _Comments, describes using signs_

Context: _in class activities_

Team Member Suggestions: _add various modes of communication_

Annual Goal: _Keisha will increase her vocabulary to comment and describe events, objects, and feelings._

Step 6:   Short-Term Objectives

Clarify the intent/focus of Annual Goal to be reflected in the objectives (check those that apply or determine others):

_____ Decreasing prompts/cues	_____ Increasing response to natural cues
_____ Desensitizing/increasing tolerance	_____ Accepting assistance from others
✓ Acquiring core skills	_____ Initiation of behavior
_____ Preparation for the activity	_____ Quality of performance
_____ Appropriateness of tempo or rate	_____ Extending or reducing duration
_____ Self-monitoring	_____ Problem solving
_____ Termination of the behavior	_____ Assisting others with the behavior
_____ Safety aspects	✓ Expansion of repertoire
✓ Communication aspects	_____ Social behaviors aspects and manners
_____ Indication of choice or preference	_____ Retention over time
✓ Generalization across settings	✓ Generalization across people
✓ Generalization across materials	_____ Generalization across cues

	Conditions	Behavior	Criteria
1	With communication partners (peers & adults), Keisha will use	sign or touch symbol to describe/comment on events, objects, feelings presently occurring, using	20 signs/symbols per day over 6 weeks with at least 3 "feelings" words
2	"	" that will occur or has occurred, using	"
3	"	2 or more signs/symbols (2+ word phrases/sentences)	10 combinations per day over 6 weeks

Choosing Outcomes and Accommodations for Children • © 1998 by Michael F. Giangreco •
Baltimore: Paul H. Brookes Publishing Co.

Step 4: Annual Goals

Priority Learning Outcome (from Step 1.5): _Mobile around school_

Current Level of Functioning Related to the Priority Learning Outcome: _Independently walks around when comfortable with environment. Uses sighted guide technique & trailing. Often does not stop at curbs._

Behavior: _mobile around school_

Context: _school building and playground_

Team Member Suggestions: _using various ways to orient and travel_

Annual Goal: _Walking/running, Keisha will use various ways to safely get around school building and playground, to/from bus._

Step 6: Short-Term Objectives

Clarify the intent/focus of Annual Goal to be reflected in the objectives (check those that apply or determine others):

_____ Decreasing prompts/cues		_____ Increasing response to natural cues	
_____ Desensitizing/increasing tolerance		_____ Accepting assistance from others	
✓ Acquiring core skills		_____ Initiation of behavior	
_____ Preparation for the activity		_____ Quality of performance	
_____ Appropriateness of tempo or rate		_____ Extending or reducing duration	
_____ Self-monitoring		✓ Problem solving	
_____ Termination of the behavior		_____ Assisting others with the behavior	
✓ Safety aspects		✓ Expansion of repertoire	
✓ Communication aspects		_____ Social behaviors aspects and manners	
_____ Indication of choice or preference		_____ Retention over time	
✓ Generalization across settings		_____ Generalization across people	
_____ Generalization across materials		_____ Generalization across cues	

	Conditions	Behavior	Criteria
1	With class arrangement (tables, centers) and hallways, remaining stable, Keisha	walks around classroom, to/from bathroom, gym, library, music, bus, playground	using trailing, sighted guide with less than 25% cues over 6 weeks
2	With some variation (e.g., obstacles), Keisha	" and runs in gym	"
3	"	" & runs on playground	using adapted cane

Choosing Outcomes and Accommodations for Children • © 1998 by Michael F. Giangreco •
Baltimore: Paul H. Brookes Publishing Co.

312

Step 4: Annual Goals

Priority Learning Outcome (from Step 1.5): _Asks questions_

Current Level of Functioning Related to the Priority Learning Outcome: _Does make requests for items/activities using one sign or symbol. Will ask "who" of new people she meets_

Behavior: _signs or uses symbols to ask questions_

Context: _lessons, activities_

Team Member Suggestions: _emphasize signing, with peers and adults_

Annual Goal: _Keisha will ask questions related to class activities and events of peers and adults using signs and symbols._

Step 6: Short-Term Objectives

Clarify the intent/focus of Annual Goal to be reflected in the objectives (check those that apply or determine others):

_____ Decreasing prompts/cues	_____ Increasing response to natural cues
_____ Desensitizing/increasing tolerance	_____ Accepting assistance from others
✓ Acquiring core skills	✓ Initiation of behavior
_____ Preparation for the activity	_____ Quality of performance
_____ Appropriateness of tempo or rate	_____ Extending or reducing duration
_____ Self-monitoring	_____ Problem solving
_____ Termination of the behavior	_____ Assisting others with the behavior
_____ Safety aspects	✓ Expansion of repertoire
✓ Communication aspects	_____ Social behaviors aspects and manners
_____ Indication of choice or preference	_____ Retention over time
✓ Generalization across settings	✓ Generalization across people
✓ Generalization across materials	_____ Generalization across cues

	Conditions	Behavior	Criteria
1	With communication partner (peer & adult), Keisha	signs or touches symbol to ask about immediate events, objects	uses 15 who, what, how signs/symbols per day over 6 weeks (each at least 2 times)
2	"	" . . . and upcoming events	" . . . and when, where
3	"	. . . and past events	"

Choosing Outcomes and Accommodations for Children • © 1998 by Michael F. Giangreco •
Baltimore: Paul H. Brookes Publishing Co.

Step 5
Program-at-a-Glance

Student's Name: *Keisha Springer*   Date: *6-10-97*

List Educational Program Components

Annual Goals
(from Family-Selected Priority Learning Outcomes)

1. *Shares objects, activities when asked; uses "No"*
2. *Increase vocabulary to comment, describe events, objects, feelings*
3. *Walks, runs around school, playground, to/from bus*
4. *Asks questions related to class activities and events*

General Supports
(list by area, e.g., Personal, Physical, Sensory)

Teaching Others About Student:

5. *Teach others communication system*
6. *Teach others how to communicate (signs, symbols)*
7. *Teach evacuation procedures to others*

Sensory Needs:

8. *Check hearing aids and glasses daily*
9. *Use FM unit*
10. *Use manual communication*
11. *Use tactile materials, enlarged materials/print, contrasted materials*
12. *Position in front row for groups*
13. *Face Keisha when speaking, signing*
14. *Provide good lighting, no glare or reflection*

Providing Access & Opportunities:

15. *Access to general education and activities*
16. *Prepare materials in advance*

Additional Learning Outcomes

17. Expresses greetings, farewells
18. Initiates and sustains communication
19. Initiates and sustains social interactions
20. Maintains socially acceptable behavior with others
21. Advocates for self
22. Eats with utensils
23. Responds to emergency alarm
24. Gives self-identification information
25. Manages personal belongings
26. Recognizes & avoids potentially dangerous situations
27. Recognizes name
28. Tells story
29. Counts, names shapes, colors
30. Uses computer keyboard, prepared for programs
31. Engages in active/leisure games with others

Choosing Outcomes and Accommodations for Children • © 1998 by Michael F. Giangreco •
Baltimore: Paul H. Brookes Publishing Co.

Step 7: Organizing and Informing the Instructional Planning Team

Directions: Write date(s) when each item is completed. Team meeting minutes can be used to document team decisions and actions pertaining to the items.

Step 7.1   Reorganize the Team and Clarify Expectations

	Date Done
1. Clarify any changes in team membership and people's relationship to the team (e.g., core, extended, situational resource).	*8/25*
2. Establish a team meeting schedule and guidelines (e.g., who needs to attend, dates and time, agenda, rotating roles).	*8/30*
3. Develop a way to exchange information and ideas among team members about upcoming classroom instructional activities to facilitate lesson planning, instruction, and evaluation.	*8/30*
4. Clarify who will assume service coordination responsibilities (e.g., information sharing among team members, coordinating paperwork requirements, scheduling, contacting parents).	*8/30*
5. Clarify who will design and implement the student's instruction.	*8/30*
6. Clarify who will train, plan for, and supervise paraprofessionals.	*8/30*
7. Clarify who will make and/or adapt instructional materials.	*8/30*
8. Clarify who will maintain/care for specialized equipment.	*8/30*

Step 7.2   Become Familiar with the Student

9. Ensure that all team members are familiar with the student's Program-at-a-Glance, Annual Goals, and related services.	*8/30*
10. Share information among team members about student-specific information (e.g., preferred learning styles, arrangements, motivations, instructional strategies, adaptations).	*9/15*

Step 7.3   Become Familiar with the General Education Program

11. Ensure that team members are knowledgeable about the general education program and settings (e.g., schedule, typical routines and activities, physical arrangements, curriculum content, class rules, teacher expectations).	*9/15*
12. Ask general class teachers what support they need from various team members, and how they wish to receive support.	*9/15*

Choosing Outcomes and Accommodations for Children   •   © 1998 by Michael F. Giangreco   •
Baltimore: Paul H. Brookes Publishing Co.

Step 8.1: Scheduling Matrix

Directions: 1) List the IEP Annual Goals (Step 4), Additional Learning Outcomes categories (Steps 2.1 and 2.2), and class activities in the spaces provided. 2) Use the intersections of the learning outcomes and class activities to note instructional possibilities to assist in scheduling.

Note: General Supports will need to be considered when planning a schedule.

Student name: *Keisha Springer*

Grade: *K (morning)*

Class Activities

	Arrival	Opening Circle	Learning Ctrs	Journals	PE/library	Snack	Recess	Art/Music	Group Project	Departure		
	15	15	30	15	20	15	20	20	20	10		
IEP Annual Goals												
Shares/uses "No"	✓	✓	✓	✓	✓	✓	✓	✓				
Comments, describes (vocabulary)	✓	✓	✓	✓	✓	✓	✓	✓				
Mobile around school	✓	✓		✓	✓	✓	✓		✓			
Asks questions	✓	✓		✓		✓	✓	✓	✓			
Additional Learning Outcomes Categories												
Greetings, farewells	✓		✓		✓	✓				✓		
Initiates & sustains communication	✓	✓	✓		✓			✓				
Initiates & sustains social interactions	✓	✓	✓	✓	✓	✓		✓				
Socially acceptable behavior with others	✓	✓		✓	✓	✓	✓	✓	✓			
Advocates for self	✓	✓		✓	✓	✓		✓	✓			
Eats with utensils					✓	✓						
Responds to emergency alarm/dangers	✓	✓		✓	✓	✓			✓	*(and as occurs)*		
Gives self-ID info/recognizes name	✓	✓	✓	✓	✓		✓	✓	✓			
Manages personal belongings	✓			✓	✓	✓			✓			
Tells story		✓	✓	✓				✓				
Counts, names shapes, colors		✓	✓	✓	✓	✓	✓	✓				
Uses computer		✓	✓				✓	✓				
Active leisure with others	✓			✓		✓	✓					

Step 8.2
Student Schedule

for

Keisha Springer

(Student Name)

Directions: List classes/activities with corresponding Annual Goals, Additional Learning Outcomes, and General Supports.

To Be Addressed in All Activities
    Use signs, symbols (S)
    Use FM unit (S)
    Use tactile/enlarged materials, contrast (S)
    Position near teacher, action (S)
    Provide good lighting (no glare, reflection) (S)
    Prepare materials in advance (S)
    Face Keisha when speaking/signing (S)
    Walks around school, playground, etc. (G)
    Responds to emergency alarm/safety procedures (A)
    Participates in kindergarten curriculum (A)

Arrival
    Manages belongings (A)   Initiates & sustains social
    Advocates for self (A)   interactions (A)
    Checks hearing aid, glasses, FM units (S)

Opening Circle
    Shares (G)   Initiates & sustains communication (A)
    Comments, describes (G)   Tells story (A)
    Asks questions (G)   Counts, names colors, shapes (A)
    Manages belongings (A)

Learning Centers
    Comments, describes (G)   Counts, names shapes, colors (A)
    Shares (G)
    Recognizes name in symbol (A)
    Advocates for self (A)
    Uses computer (A)

Key: **G** = Annual **Goal** **A** = **Additional** Learning Outcomes **S** = General **Supports**

(continued)

Choosing Outcomes and Accommodations for Children • © 1998 by Michael F. Giangreco •
Baltimore: Paul H. Brookes Publishing Co.

Step 8.2. (continued)

COACH 2

Journals
- Comments/describes (G)
- Recognizes name (A)
- Manages belongings (A)
- Tells story (A)
- Uses computer (A)

PE
- Shares (G)
- Plays active games with peers (A)
- Manages belongings (A)
- Initiates & sustains social interactions (S)

Library
- Asks questions (G)
- Tells story (S)

Snack
- Shares, uses "No" (G)
- Asks questions (G)
- Advocates for self (A)
- Uses utensil (S)
- Initiates & sustains communication (S)

Recess
- Shares, uses "No" (G)
- Advocates for self (A)
- Plays active games with others (A)
- Initiates & sustains social interactions (S)

Art/Music
- Shares (G)
- Asks questions (G)
- Names shapes, colors (A)
- Recognizes names (A)
- Uses computer (A)

Group Project
- Shares (G)
- Comments, describes (G)
- Asks questions (G)
- Initiates & sustains communication (S)
- Recognizes names (A)
- Uses computer (A)

Departure
- Manages belongings (A)

Key: **G** = Annual **Goal**   **A** = **Additional** Learning Outcomes   **S** = General **Supports**

Choosing Outcomes and Accommodations for Children • © 1998 by Michael F. Giangreco •
Baltimore: Paul H. Brookes Publishing Co.

Step 9
Planning and Adapting Instruction

Student: _Keisha Springer_   Planned by: _D.L., V.R., W.B._   Implemented by: _V.R. & W.B._

Class Activity/Lesson: _Group project – Learning About Your School_

Short-Term Objective: _Sign to describe, comment on event & feelings, ask questions_

Materials Needed: _Map with raised lines, bright markers, sticky dots_

Describe the sequence of what the instructor will do	Describe what the student will do (in observable terms)	Describe the consequences of correct and incorrect student responses	Describe how student progress will be measured and documented
1. Using large map, with locations marked in various colors, students will color a small map to match. 2. Tour school and mark places visited while hearing about that place (e.g. art, Principal's office). 3. In classroom students will answer questions and demonstrate routes about school, using their maps.	1. Color raised-lines map, using signs (e.g. colors, places) to comment and ask questions. 2. Put sticky dots on places visited 3. Respond to questions and participate in role-play situations.	Use questions and word prompts if Keisha does not spontaneously use. Prompt peer conversation. Give feedback "Yes." "No." Correct answer, model sign.	Uses 3 different signs to ask questions. Uses 5 different signs to respond to questions. Record words used and frequency of each.

Choosing Outcomes and Accommodations for Children • © 1998 by Michael F. Giangreco • Baltimore: Paul H. Brookes Publishing Co.

Step 9
Planning and Adapting Instruction

Student: _Keisha Springer_   Planned by: _D.L., V.R., W.B._   Implemented by: _V.R., W.B._

Class Activity/Lesson: _Color wheel – Mixing and naming primary and secondary colors_

Short-Term Objective: _Shares objects, asks questions, describes_

Materials Needed: _Large print & darkened worksheet, larger pieces of clay_

Describe the sequence of what the instructor will do	Describe what the student will do (in observable terms)	Describe the consequences of correct and incorrect student responses	Describe how student progress will be measured and documented
1) Three children per group. Each child receives a piece of either blue, yellow, or red clay.	1) When asked for piece of clay, hands it to peer.	Same as others, give feedback on correct signs, descriptions. Use "conversation" to discuss activity.	Uses: 6 color words, "mix," "color," "give," "please." Gives clay when asked.
2) Each child breaks her/his piece into 3 and shares with others in group, asking for appropriate color.	2) Asks peer for the colored clay, signing the color and "please."		Record words and frequency of use.
3) On basic color wheel sheet, each presses 1 small piece of red clay above the word "red." Same for blue, yellow.	3) Names colors and describes how mixed colors together	If does not "share" after being asked twice, first remind that she'll get pieces when she gives. If needed, remove materials from in front of her, and/or physically prompt to hand out the pieces.	Record number of times "shared" and latency of action.
4) Mix small pieces of yellow & blue until green; press on above word "green." Do for blue & red = purple, red & yellow = orange.			
5) Review names and mixtures			

Choosing Outcomes and Accommodations for Children • © 1998 by Michael F. Giangreco • Baltimore: Paul H. Brookes Publishing Co.

Step 10.1
Evaluation of Impact Process
for Learning Outcomes

Directions: Answer the following questions to discuss student progress toward IEP Annual Goals or Additional Learning Outcomes categories.

Student name: _Keisha_ Date of team meeting: _11-8-97_

Team members participating in discussion: _D.L., V.R., W.B., J.S., R.A._

_____

1. **Annual Goal** or **Additional Learning Outcome(s)** being discussed: _____
   Comment, describe events, objects, feelings with signs, symbols, speech

2. **Valued Life Outcome(s)** being facilitated through the learning outcome(s):_____
   Choice & Control
   _____
   _____

3. When was the last time this learning outcome was discussed by the team?
   Date: _10-8-97_

4. What has been done to teach the student this learning outcome since it was last discussed? _Lots of conversation with adults, peers. Uses computer_
   programs.

5. What progress has the student made on the learning outcome? _Little speech;_
   uses 40 signs; 1, 2 & 3 signs together. Understands at least 60
   signs. Uses 20 symbols spontaneously. Understands at least 30
   symbols.

6. What changes, if any, has the student experienced on the corresponding Valued Life Outcome(s)? _Chooses computer programs, free time activities; asks to go_
   places, uses items.
   _____
   _____

7. What changes, if any, need to be made in the educational program to enhance progress or facilitate the corresponding Valued Life Outcome(s)? _Move_
   instructional assistant out of peer interactions; teach more students
   and adults more signs
   _____

Choosing Outcomes and Accommodations for Children • © 1998 by Michael F. Giangreco •
Baltimore: Paul H. Brookes Publishing Co.

Step 10.1
Evaluation of Impact Process
for Learning Outcomes

Directions: Answer the following questions to discuss student progress toward IEP Annual Goals or Additional Learning Outcomes categories.

Student name: ___*Keisha*___ Date of team meeting: ___*11-8-97*___

Team members participating in discussion: ___*D.L., V.R, W.B., J.S., R.A.*___

---

1. **Annual Goal** or **Additional Learning Outcome(s)** being discussed: _____
   Shares with others

2. **Valued Life Outcome(s)** being facilitated through the learning outcome(s): _____
   Meaningful relationships
   Meaningful activities in various places

---

3. When was the last time this learning outcome was discussed by the team?
   Date: ___*10-8-97*___

4. What has been done to teach the student this learning outcome since it was last discussed? *modeling by adults and peers, using "give and get"*

5. What progress has the student made on the learning outcome? *About 90% for any items with adults; 90% for low preference with peers; 50% for high preference. Says "No." Only 1 time grabbed child.*

6. What changes, if any, has the student experienced on the corresponding Valued Life Outcome(s)? *Children ask her to play more. She is welcome in groups more. Can go to office & cafeteria to deliver items.*

7. What changes, if any, need to be made in the educational program to enhance progress or facilitate the corresponding Valued Life Outcome(s)? *More on giving and responding with signs for high-preference items ("No," "Not now," "5 minutes, etc.").*

Choosing Outcomes and Accommodations for Children • © 1998 by Michael F. Giangreco •
Baltimore: Paul H. Brookes Publishing Co.

Step 10.2
Evaluation of Impact Process
for General Supports

Directions: Answer the following questions to discuss the student's status regarding the identified General Supports category; use one page for each area.

Student name: _Keisha_   Date of team meeting: _11-8-97_

Team members participating in discussion: _DL, VR, WB, JS, RA_

---

1. **General Supports** category being discussed: _Teaching others_
   Items: _Others learning signs_

2. **Valued Life Outcome(s)** being facilitated through these general supports: _____
   Meaningful relationships, meaningful activities/places

---

3. When was the last time these general supports were discussed by the team?
   Date: _10-8-97_

4. What has been done since then related to these general supports? _Val and Willa sign for all class activities. Two "formal" sign classes for children every day (5 minutes)._

5. What is the current status of these general supports? _Ongoing implementation_

6. What changes, if any, has the student experienced on the corresponding Valued Life Outcome(s) as a result of having these general supports provided? _Signs more with peers and Val both receptively and expressively._

7. What changes, if any, need to be made in the educational program regarding these general supports to facilitate the corresponding Valued Life Outcome(s)? _Others in school need more instruction. Short lessons "on-the-fly" and at faculty meetings. Teach in other classes, especially of same grade._

Choosing Outcomes and Accommodations for Children   •   © 1998 by Michael F. Giangreco   •
Baltimore: Paul H. Brookes Publishing Co.

Step 10.2
Evaluation of Impact Process
for General Supports

Directions: Answer the following questions to discuss the student's status regarding the identified General Supports category; use one page for each area.

Student name: _Keisha_ Date of team meeting: _11-8-97_

Team members participating in discussion: _Debbie, Val, Jane, Willa, Robert_

---

1. **General Supports** category being discussed: _Materials preparation_
   Items: _advance preparation_

2. **Valued Life Outcome(s)** being facilitated through these general supports: _____
   Choice & Control, Meaningful activities

---

3. When was the last time these general supports were discussed by the team?
   Date: _10-8-97_

4. What has been done since then related to these general supports? _Regularly used_
   materials have been duplicated, some laminated.

5. What is the current status of these general supports? _ongoing_

6. What changes, if any, has the student experienced on the corresponding Valued Life Outcome(s) as a result of having these general supports provided? _Meaningful_
   participation occurs in most lessons, activities. She has more choices of
   materials to use during center time.

7. What changes, if any, need to be made in the educational program regarding these general supports to facilitate the corresponding Valued Life Outcome(s)? _When need_
   adjustments on unplanned activities, need access to materials. Keep box
   of "stuff" handy. Research software for upcoming units.

Choosing Outcomes and Accommodations for Children • © 1998 by Michael F. Giangreco •
Baltimore: Paul H. Brookes Publishing Co.

Appendix D

COACH EXAMPLE
FOR A
HIGH SCHOOL STUDENT
WITH
MODERATE DISABILITIES

STUDENT DESCRIPTION

Chelsea Ross is 17 years old and a junior at Columbus High School. She lives at home with her mother Margaret, and her 14-year-old brother, Mark. Chelsea enjoys school and is a hard worker. She is very sociable and has several friends with whom she spends time. Chelsea enjoys a busy lifestyle. Upon graduation, she plans to get a job and hopes to live in an apartment with a friend. Her current educational program includes job training experiences designed to give her opportunities to explore various employment options. She presently works 3 half-days a week at the Little Tikes Preschool assisting the teachers with a group of 3- and 4-year-old children.

Chelsea reads at approximately a third-grade level. She is capable of participating in all activities of daily living but has physical delays in fine and gross motor skills that affect the quality of her participation. Heart problems related to Down syndrome require Chelsea to take short rests during more strenuous activities such as brisk walks and some household chores. Her physician has recommended that she begin a health and fitness program, under supervision, designed to build her strength and stamina.

Chelsea's COACH for the current school year appears on the following pages. Only completed forms are shown. Assistive information and diagrams, such as "Introducing the Family Interview" and "Parts of COACH," are not shown even though they are included in Appendix B. For some steps in Part B, examples, rather than all completed forms, are presented.

Student Record

by
Michael F. Giangreco, Ph.D.
Chigee J. Cloninger, Ph.D.
Virginia Salce Iverson, M.Ed.

Chelsea Ross

Student's Name

Planning Is for the *1997-98* **School Year**

(see COACH manual for complete directions)

Choosing Outcomes and Accommodations for Children • © 1998 by Michael F. Giangreco •
Baltimore: Paul H. Brookes Publishing Co.

Preparation Checklist

The following are important steps to take in preparation for using COACH. In the first column write the initials of the person responsible to ensure completion, and in the second column list the date completed.

	Who?	Date
1. Ensure all team members are sufficiently oriented to the purpose of COACH and directions for using it. (See Appendix A, Questions and Answers for Parents About COACH.)	*JS*	*5/97*
2. Ensure all team members agree to use COACH to plan the student's educational program.	*JS*	*5/97*
3. Ensure all team members agree to accept and act upon the educational priorities identified by the family during the Family Interview.	*JS*	*5/97*
4. Involve the family in determining who will facilitate the Family Interview. List names on the Planning Team Information form.	*JS*	*5/97*
5. Involve the family in determining when and where the Family Interview will be conducted. List information on the Planning Team Information form.	*JS*	*5/97*
6. Involve the family in determining who needs to be present at the Family Interview. (Not all team members need to be present. Typically, the Family Interview is a small group of 2–4 people.)	*JS*	*5/97*
7. Identify by whom, when, and how Steps 2–6 will be facilitated.	*JS*	*6/97*
8. Ensure all needed forms are ready for use in advance of the Family Interview. List names on the Planning Team Information form.	*JS*	*6/97*
9. Ensure the person who facilitates the Family Interview is familiar with the directions.	*JS*	*6/97*
10. Complete the COACH Cover Page, this Checklist, and the Planning Team Information form in advance of the Family Interview.	*JS*	*6/97*

Planning Team Information

Student's name: _Chelsea Ross_   Date of birth: _1-18-80_

Educational placement(s): _11th grade Columbus High_

Family Interview (Step 1)

     Date: _6/2/97_   Interviewer: _Johanna Stiles_

     Person(s) being interviewed: _Chelsea & Margaret Ross_

Additional Learning Outcomes (Step 2)

     Date: _8/25/97_   Facilitator: _Johanna Stiles_

General Supports (Step 3)

     Date: _8/25/97_   Facilitator: _Johanna Stiles_

Annual Goals (Step 4)

     Date: _8/25/97_   Facilitator: _Johanna Stiles_

Program-at-a-Glance (Step 5)

     Date: _9/9/97_   Facilitator: _Johanna Stiles_

Short-Term Objectives (Step 6)

     Date: _9/9/97_   Facilitator: _Johanna Stiles_

Team Membership

Name of Team Member	Relationship to Student	Date Steps 1–4 Reviewed
Chelsea Ross	Student	8-25-97
Margaret Ross	Mother	8-25-97
Johanna Stiles	Special Educator	8-25-97
Dave Pratt	Employment Specialist	9-9-97
Ben Ackert	Physical Education	9-9-97
Mary Jo Jensen	Health Education	9-9-97
Samantha Meade	English	9-9-97
Karen Green	Music Education	9-9-97
Donna Huber	Home Economics	9-9-97

Choosing Outcomes and Accommodations for Children • © 1998 by Michael F. Giangreco •
Baltimore: Paul H. Brookes Publishing Co.

Step 1.1
Valued Life Outcomes

Directions: Review the purpose of this section and the list of Valued Life Outcomes with participants prior to asking questions. All the Valued Life Outcomes are meant to facilitate student independence, interdependence with others, and pursuit of personal growth by expanding access, creating new opportunities, developing individual abilities, and providing ways to contribute to one's community. Terms that are presented in bold are abbreviations for use in Steps 1.5, 10.1, and 10.2.

Being **Safe** and **Healthy**

Having a **Home**, Now and in the Future

Having Meaningful **Relationships**

Having **Choice** and Control that Match One's Age and Culture

Participating in Meaningful **Activities** in Various Places

Choosing Outcomes and Accommodations for Children • © 1998 by Michael F. Giangreco •
Baltimore: Paul H. Brookes Publishing Co.

Being Safe and Healthy

Question: "Are you (family member) interested in answering questions on this topic?"

Circle (YES) or   NO

1. What, if anything, would you like to see change in [student's name] current health or safety that would help him/her to have a better or more enjoyable life? _Better endurance and strength so Chelsea can safely participate in more active recreational, work, and community activities. Close monitoring of heart condition._

Having a Home, Now and in the Future

Question: "Are you (family member) interested in answering questions on this topic?"

Circle (YES) or   NO

2. If everything goes as you hope, do you anticipate that [student's name] will continue to live where he or she does throughout the school years?

Circle (YES) or   NO   Where is that? _home_

If NO, where would be a desirable place? _____

3. Would you like to talk about where a desirable place would be for [student's name] to live as an adult? Feel free to answer "No" if you think that decision is too far in the future to discuss at this time.

Circle (YES) or   NO   If YES, where? _Apartment with friend_

4. Is there any place you would not like to have [student's name] live in the future? _Not in a group home or nursing home_

Choosing Outcomes and Accommodations for Children • © 1998 by Michael F. Giangreco •
Baltimore: Paul H. Brookes Publishing Co.

Having Meaningful Relationships

Question: "Are you (family member) interested in answering questions on this topic?"

Circle (YES) or   NO

5.   With whom does [student's name] have relationships and friendships? With whom does [student's name] like to spend time? _family, relatives; has 3 close girlfriends at school; has many school acquaintances._

6.   How, if at all, would you like [student's name] relationships to change or expand in the near future? _Some of her friends may move away after high school so she needs to develop a wider local network of relationships. Chelsea says she wants a "boyfriend."_

Having Choice and Control
that Match One's Age and Culture

Question: "Are you (family member) interested in answering questions on this topic?"

Circle (YES) or   NO

7.   What kinds of choices and control does [student's name] have now that match his or her age and family/community situation? _Chelsea has the opportunity to make many of her own choices, but she tends to be passive and waits for others to make decisions for her._

8.   How, if at all, would you like to see [student's name] choices and control change or expand in the near future? _More confidence and assertiveness to make her own choices and advocate for herself._

Choosing Outcomes and Accommodations for Children   •   © 1998 by Michael F. Giangreco   •
Baltimore: Paul H. Brookes Publishing Co.

Participating in Meaningful Activities in Various Places

Question: "Are you (family member) interested in answering questions on this topic?"

Circle (YES) or NO

9. What kinds of activities does [student's name] currently do that he or she likes or values? Where does he or she spend time? _Being outside, gardening, swimming, walks, shopping, hanging out with friends, family gatherings, movies, reading magazines, school events (e.g., dances, plays, sports events)_

10. How, if at all, would you like to see these activities and places change or expand in the near future? _Continue with her full schedule having her make more of the choices herself. More active things for her to do._

11. *Usually, you ask this question only if the student is 13 years old or older.* Have you given any thought to what kinds of activities [student's name] might do or places he or she might go as a young adult? For example, in the future how might [student's name] spend his or her time that is now spent in school (e.g., competitive work, supported work, volunteering, continuing education)? _Plans to get a job. Would like to work in a restaurant or store. Also would like a job working with young children, like in a preschool._

Choosing Outcomes and Accommodations for Children • © 1998 by Michael F. Giangreco • Baltimore: Paul H. Brookes Publishing Co.

Ranking Valued Life Outcomes to Emphasize this Year

Directions: Ask the person being interviewed, "Please rank the Valued Life Outcomes (where 1 is the most important) to help the team understand which ones you feel are most important for [student's name] this year." Terms that are presented in bold are abbreviations for use in Steps 1.5, 10.1, and 10.2.

Rank

_3_   Being **Safe** and **Healthy**

_5_   Having a **Home**, Now and in the Future

_4_   Having Meaningful **Relationships**

_2_   Having **Choice** and Control that Match One's Age and Culture

_1_   Participating in Meaningful **Activities** in Various Places

*** Relationship to Next Steps ***

This information about the student's Valued Life Outcomes will set the context for the selection of individualized learning outcomes and general supports.

Choosing Outcomes and Accommodations for Children • © 1998 by Michael F. Giangreco •
Baltimore: Paul H. Brookes Publishing Co.

Notes About Valued Life Outcomes

Overall, Chelsea has a full and busy life. Her valued life outcomes may change significantly as she and her friends approach high school graduation. It is possible that many of her relationships and activities will change over the next 2 or 3 years.

Communication

Step 1.2

Mark only one box to indicate if the family wants to discuss this set of learning outcomes in:
Step 1 (Family Interview; priority this year?) ☐; Step 2 (Additional Learning Outcomes) ☒; Skip for Now ☐

Currently, in what ways does the student communicate?

Expressively: _____

Receptively: _____

#	Learning Outcomes	Step 1.3 Circle Score	Needs Work?	Step 1.4 Rank up to 5 Priorities
1	Expresses Continuation or "More" (e.g., makes sounds or movement when desired interaction stops to indicate he or she would like eating, playing, etc., to continue)	E P S	N Y	
2	Makes Choices When Given Options	E P S	N Y	
3	Makes Requests (e.g., for objects, food, interactions, activities, assistance)	E P S	N Y	
4	Summons Others (e.g., has a way to call others to him or her)	E P S	N Y	
5	Expresses Rejection/Refusal (e.g., indicates when he or she wants something to stop or does not want something to begin)	E P S	N Y	
6	Expresses Greetings and Farewells	E P S	N Y	
7	Follows Instructions (e.g., one step, multistep)	E P S	N Y	
8	Sustains Communication with Others (e.g., takes turns, attends, stays on topic, perseveres)	E P S	N Y	
9	Initiates Communication with Others	E P S	N Y	
10	Responds to Questions (e.g., if asked a question, he or she attempts to answer)	E P S	N Y	
11	Comments/Describes (e.g., expands vocabulary for events, objects, interactions, feelings)	E P S	N Y	
12	Asks Questions of Others	E P S	N Y	
		E P S	N Y	

Comments:

Scoring Key (use scores for Step 1.3 alone or in combination):
   E = Early/Emerging Skill (1% – 25%)   **P** = Partial Skill (25% – 80%)   **S** = Skillful (80% – 100%)

Choosing Outcomes and Accommodations for Children • © 1998 by Michael F. Giangreco •
Baltimore: Paul H. Brookes Publishing Co.

Socialization

Step 1.2

Mark only one box to indicate if the family wants to discuss this set of learning outcomes in:
Step 1 (Family Interview; priority this year?) ☒; Step 2 (Additional Learning Outcomes) ☐; Skip for Now ☐

		Step 1.3		Step 1.4
#	Learning Outcomes	Circle Score	Needs Work?	Rank up to 5 Priorities
13	Responds to the Presence and Interactions of Others (e.g., peers, family, adults)	E P (S)	(N) Y	
14	Initiates Social Interactions	E (P) S	N (Y)	3
15	Sustains Social Interactions	E P (S)	(N) Y	
16	Terminates Social Interactions	E (P) S	N (Y)	4
17	Distinguishes and Interacts Differently with Familiar People, Acquaintances, and Strangers	E (P) S	N (Y)	2
18	Maintains Socially Acceptable Behavior When Alone and with Others	E P (S)	(N) Y	
19	Accepts Assistance from Others	E P (S)	(N) Y	
20	Offers Assistance to Others	E P (S)	(N) Y	
21	Makes Transitions Between Routine Activities	E P (S)	(N) Y	
22	Adjusts to Unexpected Changes in Routine	E P (S)	(N) Y	
23	Shares with Others	E P (S)	(N) Y	
24	Advocates for Self	E (P) S	N (Y)	1
		E P S	N Y	
		E P S	N Y	
		E P S	N Y	
		E P S	N Y	

Comments: (17) Margaret is concerned that Chelsea's friendly, trusting manner may put her at risk in new situations unless she learns to interact differently with new acquaintances.
(24) Needs to advocate for self, develop more confidence to initiate rather than being passive.

Scoring Key (use scores for Step 1.3 alone or in combination):
E = Early/Emerging Skill (1% – 25%) **P** = Partial Skill (25% – 80%) **S** = Skillful (80% – 100%)

Choosing Outcomes and Accommodations for Children • © 1998 by Michael F. Giangreco •
Baltimore: Paul H. Brookes Publishing Co.

Personal Management

Mark only one box to indicate if the family wants to discuss this set of learning outcomes in:
Step 1 (Family Interview; priority this year?) ☐; Step 2 (Additional Learning Outcomes) ☐; Skip for Now ☒

		Step 1.3		Step 1.4
#	Learning Outcomes	Circle Score	Needs Work?	Rank up to 5 Priorities
25	Drinks and Eats (e.g., accepts food/drink, chews, swallows)	E P S	N Y	
26	Eats with Hands/Fingers	E P S	N Y	
27	Eats with Utensils (e.g., spoon, fork, knife)	E P S	N Y	
28	Dresses/Undresses	E P S	N Y	
29	Cares for Bowel and Bladder Needs	E P S	N Y	
30	Cares for Hands and Face (e.g., washes, dries, wipes, blows nose, applies lotion, applies lip balm)	E P S	N Y	
31	Combs/Brushes Hair	E P S	N Y	
32	Gives Self-Identification Information (e.g., name, address, phone number)	E P S	N Y	
33	Responds to Emergency Alarm (e.g., leaves building when smoke alarm sounds)	E P S	N Y	
34	Manages Personal Belongings (e.g., toys, clothes, special equipment)	E P S	N Y	
35	Mobile Within and Between Rooms of a Building (e.g., walks, crawls, rolls, moves wheelchair, climbs stairs, uses elevators/escalators, navigates)	E P S	N Y	
36	Recognizes and Avoids Potentially Dangerous Situations	E P S	N Y	
		E P S	N Y	
		E P S	N Y	

Comments:

Scoring Key (use scores for Step 1.3 alone or in combination):
   E = Early/Emerging Skill (1% – 25%)   **P** = Partial Skill (25% – 80%)   **S** = Skillful (80% – 100%)

Choosing Outcomes and Accommodations for Children • © 1998 by Michael F. Giangreco •
Baltimore: Paul H. Brookes Publishing Co.

Leisure/Recreation

Step 1.2

Mark only one box to indicate if the family wants to discuss this set of learning outcomes in:
Step 1 (Family Interview; priority this year?) ☒; Step 2 (Additional Learning Outcomes) ☐; Skip for Now ☐

		Step 1.3		Step 1.4
#	Learning Outcomes	Circle Score	Needs Work?	Rank up to 5 Priorities
37	Engages in Individual, Passive Leisure Activities (e.g., listens to music, watches television)	E P (S)	(N) Y	
38	Engages in Individual, Active Leisure Activities (e.g., toy play, games, sports, exercise, hobbies)	E (P) S	N (Y)	1
39	Engages in Passive Leisure Activities with Others (e.g., read to by someone; goes to movies, performances, spectator sports or events with others)	E P (S)	(N) Y	
40	Engages in Active Leisure Activities with Others (e.g., group games and activities, sports, exercise, hobbies)	E (P) S	N (Y)	2
		E P S	N Y	
		E P S	N Y	
		E P S	N Y	
		E P S	N Y	

Comments: (38) *Needs to engage in a personal fitness program that can be done partially on her own and may be done partially with others.*
It was suggested that Chelsea might join a fitness center to both get fit and meet new friends.

Scoring Key (use scores for Step 1.3 alone or in combination):
E = Early/Emerging Skill (1% – 25%)   **P** = Partial Skill (25% – 80%)   **S** = Skillful (80% – 100%)

Choosing Outcomes and Accommodations for Children • © 1998 by Michael F. Giangreco •
Baltimore: Paul H. Brookes Publishing Co.

Selected Academics

Step 1.2

Mark only one box to indicate if the family wants to discuss this set of learning outcomes in:
Step 1 (Family Interview; priority this year?) ☒ ; Step 2 (Additional Learning Outcomes) ☐ ; Skip for Now ☐

		Step 1.3		Step 1.4
#	Learning Outcomes	Circle Score	Needs Work?	Rank up to 5 Priorities
41	Reacts to Objects, Activities, and/or Interactions by Displaying Some Observable Change in Behavior	E P (S)	(N) Y	
42	Directs and Sustains Attention to Activity (e.g., books, toys, class activities)	E P (S)	(N) Y	
43	Explores Surroundings (e.g., scans, searches)	E P (S)	(N) Y	
44	Differentiates/Discriminates Between Various Things (e.g., objects, activities, symbols, pictures, interactions)	E P (S)	(N) Y	
45	Imitates Skills Used in Daily Life	E P (S)	(N) Y	
46	Uses Objects for Intended Purposes (e.g., plays with toy, eats with spoon, turns pages of a book, writes/draws with pencil, brushes hair)	E P (S)	(N) Y	
47	Identifies Symbols (e.g., letters, words, braille, line drawings, manual signs)	E P (S)	(N) Y	
48	Reads to Get Information and/or Follow Instructions	E (P) S	N (Y)	2
49	Uses Writing Tools to Form Letters and Words (e.g., printing, handwriting, typewriting)	E P (S)	N (Y)	
50	Composes Phrases and Sentences	E (P) S	N (Y)	3
51	Counts with Correspondence	E P (S)	(N) Y	
52	Calculates (e.g., adds, subtracts, multiplies, divides)	E (P) S	N (Y)	4
53	Uses Clock (e.g., face, digital, alarm)	E P (S)	(N) Y	
54	Uses Calendar (e.g., days, dates, months, year; notes special events and appointments)	E (P) S	N (Y)	1
55	Uses Computer	E (P) S	N (Y)	5

Scoring Key (use scores for Step 1.3 alone or in combination):
E = Early/Emerging Skill (1% – 25%)   **P** = Partial Skill (25% – 80%)   **S** = Skillful (80% – 100%)

Choosing Outcomes and Accommodations for Children • © 1998 by Michael F. Giangreco •
Baltimore: Paul H. Brookes Publishing Co.

Home

Step 1.2

Mark only one box to indicate if the family wants to discuss this set of learning outcomes in:
Step 1 (Family Interview; priority this year?) ☒ ; Step 2 (Additional Learning Outcomes) ☐ ; Skip for Now ☐

		Step 1.3		Step 1.4
#	Learning Outcomes	Circle Score	Needs Work?	Rank up to 5 Priorities
56	Brushes/Flosses Teeth	E P Ⓢ	Ⓝ Y	
57	Selects Appropriate Clothing to Wear (e.g., selects items needed for time of day, weather conditions, style, matching)	E P Ⓢ	Ⓝ Y	
58	Cares for Personal Hygiene Needs (e.g., bathes, showers, cares for nails, uses deodorant, shaves)	E P Ⓢ	Ⓝ Y	
59	Picks Up After Self	E P Ⓢ	Ⓝ Y	
60	Prepares Food (e.g., snacks, cold meals, hot meals)	E Ⓟ S	N Ⓨ	1
61	Does Household Chores (e.g., dusts, sweeps, mops, vacuums, washes/dries dishes, takes out garbage, recycles, makes bed, stores groceries, yardwork)	E Ⓟ S	N Ⓨ	2
62	Cares for Clothing (e.g., puts laundry in designated place when clean or dirty, washes/dries, folds, irons, mends)	E Ⓟ S	N Ⓨ	3
63	Uses Telephone (e.g., answers, calls, uses directory)	E P Ⓢ	Ⓝ Y	
		E P S	N Y	
		E P S	N Y	
		E P S	N Y	
		E P S	N Y	

Comments: *Chelsea needs to learn more of the household skills that will allow her to contribute to living in an apartment with a friend.*

Scoring Key (use scores for Step 1.3 alone or in combination):
E = Early/Emerging Skill (1% – 25%)   **P** = Partial Skill (25% – 80%)   **S** = Skillful (80% – 100%)

Choosing Outcomes and Accommodations for Children • © 1998 by Michael F. Giangreco •
Baltimore: Paul H. Brookes Publishing Co.

School

Step 1.2

Mark only one box to indicate if the family wants to discuss this set of learning outcomes in:
Step 1 (Family Interview; priority this year?) ☐; Step 2 (Additional Learning Outcomes) ☒; Skip for Now ☐

#	Learning Outcomes	Step 1.3 Circle Score	Needs Work?	Step 1.4 Rank up to 5 Priorities
64	Travels to and from School Safely (e.g., on bus, as a pedestrian)	E P S	N Y	
65	Participates in Small Groups (e.g., tolerates situation, takes turn, is actively involved, responds to instructions)	E P S	N Y	
66	Participates in Large Groups (e.g., tolerates situation, takes turn, is actively involved, responds to instructions)	E P S	N Y	
67	Works at Task Independently (e.g., starts, sustains, completes, at nonfrustrational level)	E P S	N Y	
68	Manages School-Related Belongings (e.g., backpack, materials, books, lockers, gym equipment)	E P S	N Y	
69	Follows School Rules/Routines (e.g., understands and follows class and school rules, changes classes, follows schedule)	E P S	N Y	
70	Uses School Facilities (e.g., playground, cafeteria, library, bookstore)	E P S	N Y	
71	Makes Purchases in School (e.g., cafeteria, bookstore, event tickets)	E P S	N Y	
72	Participates in Extracurricular Activities (e.g., clubs, sports, service organizations, drama, music)	E P S	N Y	
		E P S	N Y	
		E P S	N Y	
		E P S	N Y	

Comments:

Scoring Key (use scores for Step 1.3 alone or in combination):
E = Early/Emerging Skill (1% – 25%)   **P** = Partial Skill (25% – 80%)   **S** = Skillful (80% – 100%)

Choosing Outcomes and Accommodations for Children • © 1998 by Michael F. Giangreco •
Baltimore: Paul H. Brookes Publishing Co.

Community

Step 1.2

Mark only one box to indicate if the family wants to discuss this set of learning outcomes in:
Step 1 (Family Interview; priority this year?) ☒ ; Step 2 (Additional Learning Outcomes) ☐ ; Skip for Now ☐

#	Learning Outcomes	Step 1.3 Circle Score	Needs Work?	Step 1.4 Rank up to 5 Priorities
73	Travels Safely in the Community (e.g., crosses intersections, uses crosswalks and sidewalks, acts appropriately with strangers, finds destination)	E (P) S	N (Y)	2
74	Uses Restaurants (e.g., orders food, finds seating, eats meal, pays bill)	E P (S)	(N) Y	
75	Uses Recreational Facilities (e.g., movies, arcades, parks, recreation centers, fitness clubs)	E (P) S	N (Y)	3
76	Makes Purchases of Merchandise or Services (e.g., food stores, clothing/department stores, specialty stores, post office, hair salon, laundry/cleaner, knows purpose of different kinds of stores, finds merchandise or services desired, pays bill)	E (P) S	N (Y)	4
77	Uses Vending Machines (e.g., drinks, food, stamps, newspaper, public transportation tickets/tokens)	E P (S)	(N) Y	
78	Uses Banking Facilities (e.g., deposits, withdraws, uses automated teller machines)	E (P) S	N (Y)	5
79	Travels by Public Transportation (e.g., bus, subway, trolley, taxi, ferry)	(E) P S	N (Y)	1
80	Uses Pay Phone	E P (S)	(N) Y	
		E P S	N Y	
		E P S	N Y	
		E P S	N Y	

Comments:

Scoring Key (use scores for Step 1.3 alone or in combination):
E = Early/Emerging Skill (1% – 25%)   **P** = Partial Skill (25% – 80%)   **S** = Skillful (80% – 100%)

Choosing Outcomes and Accommodations for Children • © 1998 by Michael F. Giangreco •
Baltimore: Paul H. Brookes Publishing Co.

Vocational

Mark only one box to indicate if the family wants to discuss this set of learning outcomes in:
Step 1 (Family Interview; priority this year?) ☒; Step 2 (Additional Learning Outcomes) ☐; Skip for Now ☐

		Step 1.3		Step 1.4
#	Learning Outcomes	Circle Score	Needs Work?	Rank up to 5 Priorities
81	Does Classroom and/or Home Job(s)	E P Ⓢ	Ⓝ Y	
82	Does Job(s) at School, Beyond the Classroom, with Peers without Disabilities (e.g., delivers attendance, messages, lunch money; helps operate bookstore)	E P Ⓢ	Ⓝ Y	
For Students at Community Worksites				
83	Travels to and from Worksite	E Ⓟ S	N Ⓨ	3
84	Uses Time Clock or Check-In Procedure	E P Ⓢ	Ⓝ Y	
85	Interacts Appropriately with Co-workers, Customers, and Supervisors	E P Ⓢ	Ⓝ Y	
86	Follows Worksite Rules for Safety, Conduct, and Appearance	E P Ⓢ	Ⓝ Y	
87	Works Independently at a Task	E Ⓟ S	N Ⓨ	2
88	Works with Others (e.g., cooperates, does enough work, accepts assistance, gives assistance)	E P Ⓢ	Ⓝ Y	
89	Follows Schedule of Work Activities	E Ⓟ S	N Ⓨ	1
90	Uses Worksite Breaktime Facilities (e.g., engages in appropriate breaktime and lunchtime routines)	E Ⓟ S	N Ⓨ	4
91	Applies for Job(s) (e.g., finds potential jobs, contacts employers, fills out forms, participates in job interviews)	E Ⓟ S	N Ⓨ	5
		E P S	N Y	

Comments: ⑧③ Needs to travel by bus and walking to get to jobsites.
⑧⑦ Can work at some tasks independently, but needs to increase number and complexity.
⑨⓪ Socializes well at break if others initiate – needs to initiate her own choices (e.g., read magazine, take walk, visit with friends).

Scoring Key (use scores for Step 1.3 alone or in combination):
  E = Early/Emerging Skill (1% – 25%)   **P** = Partial Skill (25% – 80%)   **S** = Skillful (80% – 100%)

Choosing Outcomes and Accommodations for Children • © 1998 by Michael F. Giangreco •
Baltimore: Paul H. Brookes Publishing Co.

Other

Mark only one box to indicate if the family wants to discuss this set of learning outcomes in:
Step 1 (Family Interview; priority this year?) ☐; Step 2 (Additional Learning Outcomes) ☐; Skip for Now ☒

#	Learning Outcomes	Step 1.3 Circle Score	Needs Work?	Step 1.4 Rank up to 5 Priorities
		E P S	N Y	
		E P S	N Y	
		E P S	N Y	
		E P S	N Y	
		E P S	N Y	
		E P S	N Y	
		E P S	N Y	
		E P S	N Y	
		E P S	N Y	
		E P S	N Y	
		E P S	N Y	

Comments:

Scoring Key (use scores for Step 1.3 alone or in combination):
E = Early/Emerging Skill (1% – 25%)   **P** = Partial Skill (25% – 80%)   **S** = Skillful (80% – 100%)

Step 1.5: Cross-Prioritization

Directions: Transfer priorities, in their ranked order, from each list of learning outcomes (Step 1.4) reviewed with the family.

#	Communication	Socialization	Personal Management	Leisure/ Recreation	Selected Academics
1	*Assessed as Additional Learning Outcomes*	Advocates for self	*Skip for Now*	Engages in Individual Active Leisure	Uses Calendar
2		Interacts Differently w/ Strangers/Acquaintances		Engages in Active Leisure with Others	Reads to Get Info
3		Initiates Social Interactions			Composes Phrases . . .
4		Terminates Social Interactions			Calculates
5					Uses Computer

#	Home	School	Community	Vocational	Other
1	Prepares Food	*Assessed as Additional Learning Outcomes*	Travels by Public Bus	Follows Schedule of Work Activities	*Skip for Now*
2	Household Chores		Finds Destination	Works Independently at a Task	
3	Cares for Clothing		Uses Recreational Facilities	Travels to and from Worksite	
4			Makes Purchases	Uses Worksite Breaktime Facilities	
5			Uses Banking Facilities	Applies for Jobs	

Directions: Referring to the above listings, use the next page (Step 1.5 continued) to have the family member(s) being interviewed:
1. Rank a maximum of the top eight overall priorities, explicitly clarifying the wording to reflect what the student will be expected to learn. Review the overall priority selections to ensure that they accurately reflect student priorities.
2. Verify the reasoning behind the family's selection and record abbreviations corresponding to the valued life outcome(s).
3. Determine the proposed context in which learning of each priority will occur (e.g., classroom, community worksite, cafeteria with peers).
4. Indicate how each priority will be addressed as an IEP annual goal, an additional learning outcome, or primarily as a home responsibility (check only one of the three boxes for each ranked priority).

Choosing Outcomes and Accommodations for Children • © 1998 by Michael F. Giangreco • Baltimore: Paul H. Brookes Publishing Co.

350

Step 1.5. (continued)

Rank	1) Overall Priority Learning Outcomes (word priorities to explicitly clarify what the student will be expected to learn)	2) Write the Abbreviation of Valued Life Outcome(s)	3) List the Context for Learning	4) Check (✔) Only One Box for Each Priority		
				IEP Goal	Additional Learning Outcomes	Home
1	Engages in personal fitness plan when alone and with others	Health, Activities, Relationships	Gym, Home, Fitness Center	✔		
2	Advocates for self	Choice	School, Home, Work, Community		✔	
3	Prepares meals that are "heart healthy"	Health	Home, School	✔		
4	Uses calendar to schedule work activities with friends, & fitness	Activities, Choice, Relationships	Home, School, Community	✔		
5	Travels safely in the community by public bus & walking	Activities, Safety, Choice	Community	✔		
6	Reads to get information	Activities, Choice	School, Community, Work		✔	
7	Follows schedule of work activities	Activities, Choice	Work		✔	
8	Makes purchases	Activities, Choice, Home	Community	✔		

Directions: The interviewer explains the next steps and the relationship of the Family Interview to the rest of COACH.

Choosing Outcomes and Accommodations for Children • © 1998 by Michael F. Giangreco • Baltimore: Paul H. Brookes Publishing Co.

Step 2.1
Additional Learning
Outcomes from COACH

Directions: Consider the learning outcomes on this list and select a subset to be targeted for instruction as Additional Learning Outcomes. These pages may be included as an addendum to the IEP.

Participants: _Chelsea R., Margaret R., Johanna S., Dave P._

COMMUNICATION

___ 1. Expresses continuation or "more"
___ 2. Makes choices when given options
___ 3. Makes requests
___ 4. Summons others
___ 5. Expresses rejection/refusal
___ 6. Expresses greetings and farewells
✓ 7. Follows instructions
___ 8. Sustains communication with others
___ 9. Initiates communication with others
___ 10. Responds to questions
___ 11. Comments/describes
✓ 12. Asks questions of others
___ _____
___ _____

SOCIALIZATION

___ 13. Responds to the presence and interactions of others
✓ 14. Initiates social interactions
___ 15. Sustains social interactions
✓ 16. Terminates social interactions
✓ 17. Distinguishes and interacts differently with familiar people, acquaintances, and strangers
___ 18. Maintains socially acceptable behavior when alone and with others
___ 19. Accepts assistance from others
___ 20. Offers assistance to others

___ 21. Makes transitions between routine activities
___ 22. Adjusts to unexpected changes in routine
___ 23. Shares with others
✓ 24. Advocates for self
___ _____
___ _____
___ _____

PERSONAL MANAGEMENT

___ 25. Drinks and eats
___ 26. Eats with hands/fingers
___ 27. Eats with utensils
___ 28. Dresses/undresses
___ 29. Cares for bowel and bladder needs
___ 30. Cares for hands and face
___ 31. Combs/brushes hair
___ 32. Gives self-identification information
___ 33. Responds to emergency alarm
___ 34. Manages personal belongings
___ 35. Mobile within and between rooms of a building
___ 36. Recognizes and avoids potentially dangerous situations
___ _____
___ _____
___ _____

LEISURE/RECREATION

___ 37. Engages in individual, passive leisure activities
___ 38. Engages in individual, active leisure activities

___ 39. Engages in passive leisure activities with others
___ 40. Engages in active leisure with others
___ _____
___ _____

SELECTED ACADEMICS

___ 41. Reacts to objects, activities, and/or interactions by displaying some observable change in behavior
___ 42. Directs and sustains attention to activity
___ 43. Explores surroundings
___ 44. Differentiates/discriminates between various things
___ 45. Imitates skills used in daily life
___ 46. Uses objects for intended purposes
___ 47. Identifies symbols
✓ 48. Reads to get information and/or follow instructions
___ 49. Uses writing tools to form letters and words
✓ 50. Composes phrases and sentences
___ 51. Counts with correspondence
✓ 52. Calculates
___ 53. Uses clock
___ 54. Uses calendar
✓ 55. Uses computer
___ _____
___ _____

(continued)

Step 2.1. (continued)

HOME

___ 56. Brushes/flosses teeth
___ 57. Selects appropriate clothing to wear
___ 58. Cares for personal hygiene needs
___ 59. Picks up after self
___ 60. Prepares food
✓ 61. Does household chores
✓ 62. Cares for clothing
___ 63. Uses telephone

___ _____
___ _____
___ _____
___ _____

SCHOOL

___ 64. Travels to and from school safely
___ 65. Participates in small groups
___ 66. Participates in large groups
___ 67. Works at a task independently
___ 68. Manages school-related belongings
___ 69. Follows school rules/ routines
___ 70. Uses school facilities
✓ 71. Makes purchases in school
✓ 72. Participates in extra-curricular activities

___ _____
___ _____
___ _____
___ _____

COMMUNITY

___ 73. Travels safely in the community
___ 74. Uses restaurants
___ 75. Uses recreational facilities
___ 76. Makes purchases of merchandise or services
___ 77. Uses vending machines
___ 78. Uses banking facilities
___ 79. Travels by public transportation
___ 80. Uses pay phone

___ _____
___ _____
___ _____
___ _____

VOCATIONAL

___ 81. Does classroom and/or home job(s)
___ 82. Does job(s) at school, beyond the classroom, with peers without disabilities

For Students at Community Worksites

___ 83. Travels to and from worksite
___ 84. Uses time clock or check-in procedure
___ 85. Interacts appropriately with co-workers, customers, and supervisors
___ 86. Follows worksite rules for safety, conduct, and appearance
✓ 87. Works independently at a task
___ 88. Works with others
___ 89. Follows schedule of work activities
✓ 90. Uses worksite breaktime facilities
✓ 91. Applies for job(s)

___ _____
___ _____
___ _____

OTHER:

___ _____
___ _____
___ _____
___ _____
___ _____
___ _____
___ _____
___ _____
___ _____
___ _____
___ _____
___ _____
___ _____
___ _____
___ _____
___ _____
___ _____
___ _____
___ _____
___ _____
___ _____
___ _____

OTHER:

___ _____
___ _____
___ _____
___ _____
___ _____
___ _____
___ _____
___ _____
___ _____
___ _____
___ _____
___ _____
___ _____
___ _____
___ _____
___ _____
___ _____
___ _____
___ _____
___ _____
___ _____

OTHER:

___ _____
___ _____
___ _____
___ _____
___ _____
___ _____
___ _____
___ _____
___ _____
___ _____
___ _____
___ _____
___ _____
___ _____
___ _____
___ _____
___ _____
___ _____
___ _____
___ _____
___ _____
___ _____
___ _____

Choosing Outcomes and Accommodations for Children   •   © 1998 by Michael F. Giangreco   •
Baltimore: Paul H. Brookes Publishing Co.

Step 2.2: Additional Learning Outcomes from General Education

Directions: 1) Check all curriculum areas taught in the grade being planned for; 2) beside curriculum areas, clarify subject content; 3) circle the type of participation (**same, multilevel, none/curriculum overlapping**); 4) if multilevel, indicate if adapted subject content is the same or different by circling your response; and 5) record examples of the student's learning outcomes.

Student Name: _Chelsea Ross_   **The Grade Placement Being Planned for Is:** _11th_   **Date of Meeting:** _August 25, 1997_

Participants: _Chelsea, Johanna, Samantha, Dave, Ben_

✓	General Education Curriculum Areas: Class Content	Primary Type?			If Multilevel, Is the Adapted Subject Matter?	
✓	Reading/Language Arts/Humanities: _English Literature_ Individual's Learning Outcomes: _Reads to get info; reads for leisure, composes sentences and phrases_	S	(ML)	N/CO	(Same)	Different
✓	Math: _Algebra_ Individual's Learning Outcomes: _calculates, estimates amounts_	S	(ML)	N/CO	Same	(Different)
✓	Science: _Chemistry_ Individual's Learning Outcomes:	S	ML	(N/CO)	Same	Different
✓	History/Social Studies: _Asian Studies_ Individual's Learning Outcomes:	S	ML	(N/CO)	Same	Different
	Arts (Visual/Performing): Individual's Learning Outcomes:	S	ML	N/CO	Same	Different
✓	Music (Vocal/Instrumental): _11th & 12th grade Chorus_ Individual's Learning Outcomes: _group singing_	(S)	ML	N/CO	Same	Different
	Technology/Computer Literacy: Individual's Learning Outcomes:	S	ML	N/CO	Same	Different
✓	Physical Education: _Sports, Fitness, Dance, Swimming_ Individual's Learning Outcomes: _hiking, weights, swimming, aerobics_	S	(ML)	N/CO	(Same)	Different

Choosing Outcomes and Accommodations for Children • © 1998 by Michael F. Giangreco • Baltimore: Paul H. Brookes Publishing Co.

Step 2.2. (continued)

✓	General Education Curriculum Areas: Class Content	Primary Type?			If Multilevel, Is the Adapted Subject Matter?	
✓	**Health Education:** *Human Body, Relationships, Wellness* Individual's Learning Outcomes: *human relationships, personal health and wellness; health effects of smoking, alcohol, drugs*	S	(ML)	N/CO	(Same)	Different
	Foreign Language: Individual's Learning Outcomes:	S	ML	N/CO	Same	Different
	Community Service/Social Responsibility: Individual's Learning Outcomes:	S	ML	N/CO	Same	Different
✓	**Home Economics:** *Cooking, Household Planning, Nutrition* Individual's Learning Outcomes: *Meal planning, budgeting for household expenses*	S	(ML)	N/CO	(Same)	Different
	Industrial Arts: Individual's Learning Outcomes:	S	ML	N/CO	Same	Different
	Vocational: Individual's Learning Outcomes:	S	ML	N/CO	Same	Different
	Reasoning and Problem Solving: Individual's Learning Outcomes:	S	ML	N/CO	Same	Different
	Other: Individual's Learning Outcomes:	S	ML	N/CO	Same	Different

Codes: **S** = Same (same learning outcomes as others); **ML** = Multilevel (learning outcomes in the same curriculum area at a different level, such as content, quantity, performance criteria); **N/CO** = None/Curriculum Overlapping (there are no learning outcomes identified for instruction in these curriculum areas, but the student participates in class activities by working on learning outcomes from different curriculum areas).

Choosing Outcomes and Accommodations for Children • © 1998 by Michael F. Giangreco • Baltimore: Paul H. Brookes Publishing Co.

Step 3
General Supports

Directions: Check those items to be included in the student's educational program as "General Supports" (those supports or accommodations provided to or for the student). Space has been provided under each item to allow for clarifying or specifying information individually pertinent to the student. *General Supports are not a comprehensive list of specific instructional supports.* These pages may be included as an addendum to the IEP or the information may be transferred to the IEP in an appropriate section.

Participants: *Chelsea, Margaret, Johanna*

PERSONAL NEEDS

___ 1. Needs to be fed food and drinks

___ 2. Needs to be dressed

___ 3. Needs assistance with bowel and bladder management

___ 4. Needs assistance with personal hygiene

___ 5. Needs to be given medication

___ 6. Needs suctioning and/or postural drainage

Other Personal Needs:

___ _____

___ _____

___ _____

___ _____

___ _____

___ _____

PHYSICAL NEEDS

___ 7. Needs to be physically repositioned at regular intervals

___ 8. Needs to have environmental barriers modified to allow access

___ 9. Needs to have physical equipment managed (e.g., wheelchair, braces, orthotics)

___ 10. Needs specialized transportation accommodations

___ 11. Needs to be moved and positioned in specialized ways

___ 12. Needs to be physically moved from place to place

Other Physical Needs:

___ _____

___ _____

___ _____

___ _____

TEACHING OTHERS ABOUT THE STUDENT

___ 13. Teach staff and classmates about the student's augmentative communication system and other communicative behaviors

___ 14. Teach staff and students how to communicate with the student

___ 15. Teach staff seizure management procedures

✓ 16. Teach staff emergency procedures (e.g., medical, evacuation) *(heart problem symptoms)*

___ 17. Teach staff preventive behavior management procedures

___ 18. Teach staff behavioral crisis intervention procedures

Other Needs Related to Teaching Others About the Student:

___ _____

___ _____

___ _____

___ _____

(continued)

Step 3.   (*continued*)

SENSORY NEEDS

___ 19. Needs to have hearing aids monitored (e.g., batteries, settings)

___ 20. Needs to have people use FM unit/auditory trainer

___ 21. Needs people to manually communicate (e.g., American Sign Language, common gestures)

___ 22. Needs to have glasses managed (e.g., adjusted, cleaned)

___ 23. Needs tactile materials

___ 24. Needs enlarged materials

___ 25. Needs materials in braille

___ 26. Needs to be positioned to accommodate sensory needs (e.g., specified distance from source)

___ 27. Needs environmental modifications to accommodate for sensory needs (e.g., lighting, location, background, volume, color)

Other Sensory Needs:

___ _____

___ _____

___ _____

___ _____

___ _____

___ _____

___ _____

PROVIDING ACCESS AND OPPORTUNITIES

✓ 28. Provide access to general education classes and activities

✓ 29. Needs to have instructional accommodations to general education activities and materials prepared in advance to facilitate multilevel instruction and/or curriculum overlapping

✓ 30. Provide access to community-based experiences with people without disabilities

✓ 31. Provide access to vocational experiences with people without disabilities

✓ 32. Provide access to co-curricular activities with people without disabilities

___ 33. Provide access to materials in the student's native language

___ 34. Provide access to materials and activities associated with the student's cultural background as well as other cultures

___ 35. Provide access to nonaversive approaches to dealing with challenging behaviors

Other Needs Related to Providing Access and Opportunities:

___ _____

___ _____

___ _____

___ _____

OTHER GENERAL SUPPORTS
(not listed elsewhere)

✓ 36. Needs time limits extended or waived

___ 37. Needs classnotes recorded in any form

✓ 38. Needs alternative testing modifications

Other General Supports:

___ _____

___ _____

___ _____

___ _____

___ _____

___ _____

___ _____

___ _____

___ _____

___ _____

___ _____

___ _____

___ _____

Choosing Outcomes and Accommodations for Children   •   © 1998 by Michael F. Giangreco   •
Baltimore: Paul H. Brookes Publishing Co.

357

Step 4:   Annual Goals

COACH 2

Priority Learning Outcome (from Step 1.5): _Engages in Personal Fitness Plan when alone and with others_

Current Level of Functioning Related to the Priority Learning Outcome: _Currently engages in mostly passive activities and a few activities that require some walking. Limited cardiovascular endurance._

Behavior: _engage in personal fitness activities_

Context: _In school and community gym_

Team Member Suggestions: _identify peer with similar interests; review activities with physician for appropriateness in advance_

Annual Goal: _In school and community gymnasiums, Chelsea will engage in a personal fitness routine._

Step 6:   Short-Term Objectives

Clarify the intent/focus of Annual Goal to be reflected in the objectives (check those that apply or determine others):

_____ Decreasing prompts/cues	_____ Increasing response to natural cues
_____ Desensitizing/increasing tolerance	_____ Accepting assistance from others
✓ Acquiring core skills	_____ Initiation of behavior
_____ Preparation for the activity	_____ Quality of performance
_____ Appropriateness of tempo or rate	✓ Extending or reducing duration
✓ Self-monitoring	_____ Problem solving
_____ Termination of the behavior	_____ Assisting others with the behavior
_____ Safety aspects	✓ Expansion of repertoire
_____ Communication aspects	_____ Social behaviors aspects and manners
_____ Indication of choice or preference	_____ Retention over time
_____ Generalization across settings	_____ Generalization across people
_____ Generalization across materials	_____ Generalization across cues

	Conditions	Behavior	Criteria
1	Following "warm-ups" and monitoring heart rate (at rest)	Chelsea will use a sequence card to engage in her individualized fitness routine	for 10 consecutive mins. followed by heart monitoring and a 5-min rest before repeating once; 3 days/wk for 3 weeks
2	"	"	As above for 15 min.
3	"	Chelsea will engage in her individualized fitness routine (without sequence card)	As above for 20 min.

Choosing Outcomes and Accommodations for Children   •   © 1998 by Michael F. Giangreco   •
Baltimore: Paul H. Brookes Publishing Co.

359

Step 4: Annual Goals

Priority Learning Outcome (from Step 1.5): _Prepares meals that are "heart healthy"_

Current Level of Functioning Related to the Priority Learning Outcome: _Chelsea currently can prepare simple, cold foods (e.g., cereal & milk, peanut butter sandwich). Without monitoring she will select heart-unhealthy foods._

Behavior: _Prepares hot and cold heart-healthy meals for one or two_

Context: _In a kitchen, prior to mealtime_

Team Member Suggestions: _Give homework to prepare part of dinner; schedule Home Ec prior to lunch; eat with a friend for lunch_

Annual Goal: _In a kitchen prior to mealtime, Chelsea will prepare simple hot and cold heart-healthy meals for one or two._

Step 6: Short-Term Objectives

Clarify the intent/focus of Annual Goal to be reflected in the objectives (check those that apply or determine others):

_____ Decreasing prompts/cues		_____	Increasing response to natural cues
_____ Desensitizing/increasing tolerance		_____	Accepting assistance from others
✓ Acquiring core skills		_____	Initiation of behavior
✓ Preparation for the activity		_____	Quality of performance
_____ Appropriateness of tempo or rate		_____	Extending or reducing duration
_____ Self-monitoring		_____	Problem solving
_____ Termination of the behavior		_____	Assisting others with the behavior
✓ Safety aspects		✓	Expansion of repertoire
_____ Communication aspects		_____	Social behaviors aspects and manners
✓ Indication of choice or preference		_____	Retention over time
_____ Generalization across settings		_____	Generalization across people
_____ Generalization across materials		_____	Generalization across cues

	Conditions	Behavior	Criteria
1	Given a choice of fruits & vegetables	Chelsea will prepare a heart-healthy salad for one or two people	of sufficient quality that a classmate would rate it desirable to eat and eat it, 3 consecutive meals
2	Given a choice of canned soups and sandwich fixings	Chelsea will prepare a heart-healthy soup-and-sandwich combination for two	"
3	For homework, given access to ingredients and materials before school	Chelsea will prepare a hot cereal (e.g., oatmeal) and select other items (e.g., fruit) to make breakfast	so that the quantities and ingredients (documented in writing) meet heart-healthy standards, 5 consecutive meals

Choosing Outcomes and Accommodations for Children • © 1998 by Michael F. Giangreco •
Baltimore: Paul H. Brookes Publishing Co.

Step 4: Annual Goals

COACH 2

Priority Learning Outcome (from Step 1.5): _Uses calendar to schedule work, activities, with friends, fitness_

Current Level of Functioning Related to the Priority Learning Outcome: _Knows time, days of the week, months, time of day, but does not currently use calendar as a reminder of activities – forgets supplies or dates._

Behavior: _Uses calendar to prepare items (e.g., money) and show ups as scheduled_

Context: _Across school, work, and personal engagements_

Team Member Suggestions: _keeps "day planner"_

Annual Goal: _Using a personal calendar book, Chelsea will be prepared for and show up for scheduled school, work, and personal engagements._

Step 6: Short-Term Objectives

Clarify the intent/focus of Annual Goal to be reflected in the objectives (check those that apply or determine others):

✓ Decreasing prompts/cues	____ Increasing response to natural cues
____ Desensitizing/increasing tolerance	____ Accepting assistance from others
✓ Acquiring core skills	____ Initiation of behavior
✓ Preparation for the activity	____ Quality of performance
____ Appropriateness of tempo or rate	____ Extending or reducing duration
✓ Self-monitoring	____ Problem solving
____ Termination of the behavior	____ Assisting others with the behavior
____ Safety aspects	____ Expansion of repertoire
____ Communication aspects	____ Social behaviors aspects and manners
____ Indication of choice or preference	____ Retention over time
____ Generalization across settings	____ Generalization across people
____ Generalization across materials	____ Generalization across cues

	Conditions	Behavior	Criteria
1	Using a calendar book	Chelsea will write standard engagements (e.g., work M, W, F 12–3³⁰) in her calendar book	at least 1 week in advance without prompting and will show up as scheduled 2 consecutive weeks
2	Using a calendar book	Chelsea will write all non-standard engagements (e.g., dates with friends, Dr. appointment) in her calendar book	within 10 minutes of making the arrangements without prompting and will show up as scheduled, 2 consecutive weeks
3	Using a calendar book	Chelsea will write any changes in standard or nonstandard engagements in her calendar book	within 10 minutes of knowing about the change and will show up at the rescheduled time, 2 consecutive weeks

Choosing Outcomes and Accommodations for Children • © 1998 by Michael F. Giangreco •
Baltimore: Paul H. Brookes Publishing Co.

Step 4: Annual Goals

COACH 2

Priority Learning Outcome (from Step 1.5): _Travels safely in the community by public bus and walking_

Current Level of Functioning Related to the Priority Learning Outcome: _Can safely cross streets at stop signs and traffic lights but gets lost going more than a couple blocks from home; has no experience with public bus._

Behavior: _Rides bus and walks to worksite_

Context: _In local community_

Team Member Suggestions: _from home rather than school_

Annual Goal: _In the local community, Chelsea will walk and ride the bus from her home to worksite and back home._

Step 6: Short-Term Objectives

Clarify the intent/focus of Annual Goal to be reflected in the objectives (check those that apply or determine others):

_____ Decreasing prompts/cues	_____ Increasing response to natural cues
_____ Desensitizing/increasing tolerance	_____ Accepting assistance from others
✓ Acquiring core skills	_____ Initiation of behavior
_____ Preparation for the activity	_____ Quality of performance
_____ Appropriateness of tempo or rate	_____ Extending or reducing duration
_____ Self-monitoring	_____ Problem solving
_____ Termination of the behavior	_____ Assisting others with the behavior
✓ Safety aspects	_____ Expansion of repertoire
_____ Communication aspects	_____ Social behaviors aspects and manners
_____ Indication of choice or preference	_____ Retention over time
_____ Generalization across settings	_____ Generalization across people
_____ Generalization across materials	_____ Generalization across cues

	Conditions	Behavior	Criteria
1	Given a simple map and written directions	Chelsea will walk from her house to the bus stop	Safely, and in time to catch the appropriate bus to get to work on time, 5 consecutive days
2	Given a simple map and written directions	Chelsea will walk from her house to the bus stop, board the correct bus, and exit near work	Safely, and in time to arrive at work on time, 5 consecutive days
3	Given a simple map and written directions	Chelsea will walk from her house to the bus stop, ride the bus to the stop near work, and walk to work	Safely, and in time to arrive at work on time, 5 consecutive days

Choosing Outcomes and Accommodations for Children • © 1998 by Michael F. Giangreco •
Baltimore: Paul H. Brookes Publishing Co.

Step 4: Annual Goals

Priority Learning Outcome (from Step 1.5): ___*Makes purchases*___

Current Level of Functioning Related to the Priority Learning Outcome: ___*Knows how to exchange money for goods, but only for amounts less than $5; often leaves cashier before getting change.*___

Behavior: ___*Makes purchases of goods and/or services*___

Context: ___*In community settings (e.g., stores, hair salon)*___

Team Member Suggestions: ___*Work with family to identify purchases that would be made anyway (food, hair cut, clothes)*___

Annual Goal: ___*In community setting (e.g., stores, hair salon, restaurants) Chelsea will make purchases of goods and/or services.*___

Step 6: Short-Term Objectives

Clarify the intent/focus of Annual Goal to be reflected in the objectives (check those that apply or determine others):

_____ Decreasing prompts/cues	_____ Increasing response to natural cues
_____ Desensitizing/increasing tolerance	_____ Accepting assistance from others
✓ Acquiring core skills	_____ Initiation of behavior
_____ Preparation for the activity	_____ Quality of performance
_____ Appropriateness of tempo or rate	_____ Extending or reducing duration
_____ Self-monitoring	_____ Problem solving
_____ Termination of the behavior	_____ Assisting others with the behavior
_____ Safety aspects	_____ Expansion of repertoire
_____ Communication aspects	_____ Social behaviors aspects and manners
_____ Indication of choice or preference	_____ Retention over time
✓ Generalization across settings	_____ Generalization across people
_____ Generalization across materials	_____ Generalization across cues

	Conditions	Behavior	Criteria
1	In local grocery stores, using a shopping list from home	Chelsea will make family food purchases between $10–$30	With at least 90% accuracy (of items purchased) at least once per week for 4 consecutive weeks
2	In local clothes stores, using a shopping list prepared with her mother	Chelsea will purchase personal clothing costing $20–$50	With 100% accuracy 4 consecutive times over the semester at times that coincide with family needs
3	In a local hair salon	Chelsea will get her hair trimmed/cut (paying for service and tip)	With 100% accuracy appropriately every 5–6 weeks for 5 consecutive times

Choosing Outcomes and Accommodations for Children • © 1998 by Michael F. Giangreco •
Baltimore: Paul H. Brookes Publishing Co.

Step 5
Program-at-a-Glance

Student's Name: *Chelsea Ross*   Date: *9/9/97*

List Educational Program Components

General Supports

1. <u>*Teaching others:*</u> *(a) teach staff emergency procedures to be aware of heart problem symptoms and actions*

2. <u>*Providing Access & Opportunities:*</u> *(a) to general educational classes and activities; (b) needs instructional accommodations to general educ. activities and materials prepared in advance to facilitate multilevel instruction; (c) access to community-based experiences with people without disabilities; (d) access to co-curricular activities with peers.*

3. <u>*Other General Supports:*</u> *(a) Needs time limits extended or waived; (b) needs alternative testing modifications*

Annual Goals
(from Family-Selected Priority Learning Outcomes)

4. *Engages in Personal Fitness Plan when alone and with others*

5. *Prepares meals that are "heart healthy"*

6. *Uses calendar to schedule work, activities with friends and fitness*

7. *Travels safely in the community by public bus and walking*

8. *Makes purchases of goods and services in community stores*

Choosing Outcomes and Accommodations for Children • © 1998 by Michael F. Giangreco •
Baltimore: Paul H. Brookes Publishing Co.

Step 5.   (continued)

Additional Learning Outcomes

9. COMMUNICATION/SOCIALIZATION: (a) follows instructions; (b) asks questions of others; (c) initiates/sustains/terminates social interactions; (d) distinguishes and interacts differently with familiar people, acquaintances, and strangers; (e) advocates for self

10. SELECTED ACADEMICS (Math, English): (a) Reads to get information or follow instructions; (b) reads for leisure; (c) composes sentences/phrases; (d) calculates; (e) uses computer; (f) estimates amounts

11. HOME/HOME ECONOMICS: (a) does chores; (b) cares for clothing; (c) meal planning; (d) budgeting for household expenses

12. SCHOOL: (a) makes purchases in school; (b) participates in extracurricular activities

13. VOCATIONAL: (a) works independently at a task; (b) uses worksite breaktime facilities; (c) applies for job

14. PHYSICAL EDUCATION: (a) fitness routines; (b) hiking; (c) weight training; (d) swimming; (e) aerobics

15. HEALTH: (a) plans for personal health/wellness; (b) knows about types of human relationships; (c) knows health effects of smoking, alcohol, drugs

16. MUSIC: (a) choral singing

Step 7: Organizing and Informing the Instructional Planning Team

Directions: Write date(s) when each item is completed. Team meeting minutes can be used to document team decisions and actions pertaining to the items.

	Date Done
Step 7.1 Reorganize the Team and Clarify Expectations	
1. Clarify any changes in team membership and people's relationship to the team (e.g., core, extended, situational resource).	8/97
2. Establish a team meeting schedule and guidelines (e.g., who needs to attend, dates and time, agenda, rotating roles).	8/97
3. Develop a way to exchange information and ideas among team members about upcoming classroom instructional activities to facilitate lesson planning, instruction, and evaluation.	8/97
4. Clarify who will assume service coordination responsibilities (e.g., information sharing among team members, coordinating paperwork requirements, scheduling, contacting parents).	8/97
5. Clarify who will design and implement the student's instruction.	8/97
6. Clarify who will train, plan for, and supervise paraprofessionals.	8/97
7. Clarify who will make and/or adapt instructional materials.	8/97
8. Clarify who will maintain/care for specialized equipment.	8/97
Step 7.2 Become Familiar with the Student	
9. Ensure that all team members are familiar with the student's Program-at-a-Glance, Annual Goals, and related services.	9/97
10. Share information among team members about student-specific information (e.g., preferred learning styles, arrangements, motivations, instructional strategies, adaptations).	9/97
Step 7.3 Become Familiar with the General Education Program	
11. Ensure that team members are knowledgeable about the general education program and settings (e.g., schedule, typical routines and activities, physical arrangements, curriculum content, class rules, teacher expectations).	9/97
12. Ask general class teachers what support they need from various team members, and how they wish to receive support.	9/97

Choosing Outcomes and Accommodations for Children • © 1998 by Michael F. Giangreco •
Baltimore: Paul H. Brookes Publishing Co.

Step 8.1: Scheduling Matrix

Directions: 1) List the IEP Annual Goals (Step 4), Additional Learning Outcomes categories (Steps 2.1 and 2.2), and class activities in the spaces provided. 2) Use the intersections of the learning outcomes and class activities to note instructional possibilities to assist in scheduling.

Note: General Supports will need to be considered when planning a schedule.

Student name: Chelsea

Grade: 11

Class Activities

		Homeroom 15	English 50	Math 50	Science 50	Social Studies 50	Home Ec. 50	Music 50	Phys. Ed. 50	Health 50	Vocational 100	Community 50	Co-Curricular 60	Homework 90
IEP Annual Goals	Engages in personal fitness	✓	✓	✓	✓			✓	✓		✓	✓	✓	
	Prepares meals (heart healthy)	✓	✓	✓	✓		✓	✓	✓	✓	✓	✓	✓	
	Uses calendar to schedule…	✓	✓	✓	✓	✓	✓			✓	✓	✓	✓	
	Travels safely in community									✓	✓	✓	✓	
	Makes purchases	✓		✓		✓						✓		
Additional Learning Outcomes Categories	Communication/Social	✓	✓	✓	✓	✓	✓	✓	✓	✓	✓	✓	✓	
	Selected Academics	✓	✓	✓	✓	✓	✓	✓	✓	✓	✓	✓	✓	
	Home Economics				✓	✓							✓	
	School	✓												
	Vocational									✓		✓		
	Physical Education							✓	✓			✓		
	Health						✓							
	Music							✓						

Choosing Outcomes and Accommodations for Children • © 1998 by Michael F. Giangreco • Baltimore: Paul H. Brookes Publishing Co.

Step 8.2
Student Schedule

for
Chelsea Ross
(Student Name)

Directions: List classes/activities with corresponding Annual Goals, Additional Learning Outcomes, and General Supports.

EDUCATIONAL PROGRAM COMPONENTS TO BE ADDRESSED IN ALL CLASSES

- *Uses calendar to schedule (G)*
- *Follows instructions (A)*
- *Asks questions of others (A)*
- *Initiates, sustains, terminates social interactions (A)*
- *Reads to get information or to follow instructions (A)*
- *Advocates for self (A)*

- *Access to general classes and activities (S)*
- *Instructional accommodations to facilitate multilevel instruction (S)*
- *Extended or waived time limits (S)*
- *Alternative testing modifications (S)*

GENERAL CLASS OR ACTIVITY	*LEARNING OUTCOMES AND/OR GENERAL SUPPORTS*
HOMEROOM	• *Makes purchases at school store (G)*
PERIOD 1: ENGLISH	• *Reads for leisure (A)* • *Composes sentences (A)* • *Uses computer (A)*
PERIOD 2: PHYS ED (M, W, F)	• *Engages in Personal Fitness Plan (G)* • *Hiking, weight training, swimming, aerobics (A)*
HEALTH (T, Th)	• *Plans for personal wellness (A)* • *Knows about types of human relationships (A)* • *Knows effects of smoking, alcohol, drugs (A)* • *Distinguishes and interacts differently with familiar people, acquaintances, and strangers (A)*

Key: **G** = Annual **Goal**   **A** = **Additional** Learning Outcomes   **S** = General **Supports**

(continued)

Choosing Outcomes and Accommodations for Children • © 1998 by Michael F. Giangreco •
Baltimore: Paul H. Brookes Publishing Co.

HEALTH (T, Th)
(continued)

- Composes sentences and phrases (A)
- Uses computers (A)

PERIOD 3: HOME EC (M, W, F)

- Prepares "heart-healthy" meals (G)
- Makes purchases (G)
- Calculates (A)
- Estimates (A)
- Plans for personal wellness (A)

CHORUS (T, Th)

- Choral signing (A)

PERIOD 4: LUNCH

(purposely unprogrammed)

followed by STUDY HALL

- Begins homework assignments

PERIODS 5, 6, & 7:
COMMUNITY AND
VOCATIONAL

- Travels safely in the community by public bus and walking (G)
- Makes purchases of goods and services in community (G)
- Works independently at a task (A)
- Uses worksite breaktime facilities (A)
- Applies for job (A)

Key: **G** = Annual **Goal**   **A** = **Additional** Learning Outcomes   **S** = General **Supports**

Choosing Outcomes and Accommodations for Children • © 1998 by Michael F. Giangreco •
Baltimore: Paul H. Brookes Publishing Co.

Step 9
Planning and Adapting Instruction

Student: _Chelsea Ross_ Planned by: _Johanna Stiles_ Implemented by: _Donna Huber_

Class Activity/Lesson: _Heart-Healthy Meal Preparation_

Planned by: _Donna Huber & Johanna Stiles_

Short-Term Objective: _Given a choice of fruits and vegetables C. will prepare a "heart-healthy" salad._

Materials Needed: _fruits & vegetables, sharp knife, cutting board, collander, kitchen station, large and small bowls; Heart-Healthy worksheet; nutrition fact labels._

Describe the sequence of what the instructor will do	Describe what the student will do (in observable terms)	Describe the consequences of correct and incorrect student responses	Describe how student progress will be measured and documented
1. Teacher introduces "heart-healthy" concept to class and solicits its characteristics	1. Respond to teacher question with characteristics such as low fat, low salt. All students write the characteristics on paper	1. Teacher walks among students to check work and provide corrective feedback if needed	1 & 2 Quiz on characteristics of heart-healthy food and example is given at the beginning of the next class.
2. Using Heart-Healthy worksheet that lists 20 both positive and negative examples, the teacher reviews 2 examples and asks the students to circle all that meet heart-healthy standards	2. In pairs the students review the list and circle heart-healthy foods, using "nutrition facts" labels to consider fat and salt content	2. Class reviews answers as a large group, soliciting feedback from students (including Chelsea) and self-correct worksheet	
3. Teacher gives directions for each student in a pair to make a salad for partner by: a) preparing b) making the salad c) cleaning up d) evaluating the work e) eating the salad	3. Students follow previously learned procedures to prepare, make the salad, clean up, and judge the quality of the work before taking the salad to eat with lunch	3. Teacher floats among students to provide modeling, feedback, and correction. Partners assist each other	3. Salad judged by partner based on: (a) heart healthy? (b) looks good enough to eat? Partner must give feedback and that feedback will be judged by the teacher.

Choosing Outcomes and Accommodations for Children • © 1998 by Michael F. Giangreco • Baltimore: Paul H. Brookes Publishing Co.

Step 9
Planning and Adapting Instruction

Student: _Chelsea Ross_

Class Activity/Lesson: _Fitness & Cardiovascular Health_

Planned by: _Johanna Stiles_   Implemented by: _Ben Ackert_

Ben Ackert

Short-Term Objective: _C. will use sequence card to engage in her individualized fitness routine (10 min.)._

Materials Needed: _Fitness routine sequence card w/ data recording for activities, heart rates, and time, stop watch, pencil, calculator_

Describe the sequence of what the instructor will do	Describe what the student will do (in observable terms)	Describe the consequences of correct and incorrect student responses	Describe how student progress will be measured and documented
1) Referring to previously designed individualized fitness routines the PE Teacher gives directions to: (a) monitor resting heart rates by counting pulse on neck for 15 sec. and multiplying by 4.; (b) do 5 minutes of stretching warm-ups; (c) follow sequence card of activities; (d) monitor heart rate after 10 minutes; (e) stretch 5 minutes and repeat the previous steps. Teacher will move through stations set up for step aerobics, free weights, walking, & exercises as students work in groups of three.	1) Student will follow the sequence set forth by the teacher. Chelsea's focus will be calculating the heart rates for herself and two classmates using calculator and peer modeling; will also follow the sequence card to move through various activities. Students will record heart rate calculations (e.g. 15 x 4 = 60) on the sequence card and check off activities completed.	1) Chelsea will receive peer and teacher encouragement, feedback, and modeling correction. When she completes an activity, if she does not continue to the next activity, the teacher will use a "step training" procedure by backing up to the last set she did correctly and then using least prompts to guide her to the next steps. Emphasis will be on helping C. recognize the natural cues in her own activity and on the sequence card.	1) Recording of heart rates and activity check off on sequence card 2) Number of instances (per 10 minutes) that "step training" needs to be used 3) Teacher observation and notes about activity participation and quality

Choosing Outcomes and Accommodations for Children • © 1998 by Michael F. Giangreco • Baltimore: Paul H. Brookes Publishing Co.

Step 10.1
Evaluation of Impact Process
for Learning Outcomes

Directions: Answer the following questions to discuss student progress toward IEP Annual Goals or Additional Learning Outcomes categories.

Student name: _Chelsea Ross_   Date of team meeting: _10-30-97_

Team members participating in discussion: _Donna Huber, Johanna Stiles, Chelsea Ross_

---

1. **Annual Goal** or **Additional Learning Outcome(s)** being discussed: _____
   Prepares meals that are "Heart-Healthy"

2. **Valued Life Outcome(s)** being facilitated through the learning outcome(s): _____
   personal health

---

3. When was the last time this learning outcome was discussed by the team?
   Date: _Sept. 17_

4. What has been done to teach the student this learning outcome since it was last discussed? _Chelsea has been learning to discriminate between heart-healthy foods and has been practicing food preparation in home economics class._

5. What progress has the student made on the learning outcome? _She does quite well in class on T & Th but has not generalized well to other days in her cafeteria selections._

6. What changes, if any, has the student experienced on the corresponding Valued Life Outcome(s)? _She has lost pounds but is still significantly overweight (adding more stress to her heart problems)._

7. What changes, if any, need to be made in the educational program to enhance progress or facilitate the corresponding Valued Life Outcome(s)? _Her learning needs to expand to selection of à la carte cafeteria selections and lunches brought from home (as homework)._

Choosing Outcomes and Accommodations for Children • © 1998 by Michael F. Giangreco •
Baltimore: Paul H. Brookes Publishing Co.

Step 10.1
Evaluation of Impact Process
for Learning Outcomes

Directions: Answer the following questions to discuss student progress toward IEP Annual Goals or Additional Learning Outcomes categories.

Student name: _Chelsea Ross_ Date of team meeting: _10-30-97_

Team members participating in discussion: _Ben Ackert, Johanna Stiles, Chelsea Ross_

1. **Annual Goal** or **Additional Learning Outcome(s)** being discussed: _____
   Engages in Personal Fitness Plan . . .

2. **Valued Life Outcome(s)** being facilitated through the learning outcome(s):_____
   Improve health; Expand activities; provide opportunity for interaction with peers

3. When was the last time this learning outcome was discussed by the team?
   Date: _early October_

4. What has been done to teach the student this learning outcome since it was last discussed? _Personal fitness plan was developed and OK'd by physician; program has been implemented since late September (a little over 1 month)._

5. What progress has the student made on the learning outcome? _Chelsea has progressed well making heart rate calculations and knows the mechanics of the various activities_

6. What changes, if any, has the student experienced on the corresponding Valued Life Outcome(s)? _To date, there has been no recorded or noticeable change in her health, but her activities have expanded and she is having increasingly positive peer interactions._

7. What changes, if any, need to be made in the educational program to enhance progress or facilitate the corresponding Valued Life Outcome(s)? _The reason no health effects have been recorded is that Chelsea's rate of activity is too slow to result in an increased heart rate (range established by her doctor). Need to prompt increased rate._

Choosing Outcomes and Accommodations for Children • © 1998 by Michael F. Giangreco •
Baltimore: Paul H. Brookes Publishing Co.

Step 10.2
Evaluation of Impact Process
for General Supports

Directions: Answer the following questions to discuss the student's status regarding the identified General Supports category; use one page for each area.

Student name: _Chelsea Ross_ Date of team meeting: _10-30-97_

Team members participating in discussion: _Chelsea Ross, Mrs. Kensington_ _(school nurse), Johanna Stiles_

---

1. **General Supports** category being discussed: _Teaching others_
   Items: _Teach staff emergency procedures to be aware of heart problem symptoms and actions_

2. **Valued Life Outcome(s)** being facilitated through these general supports: _____
   Personal health and safety

---

3. When was the last time these general supports were discussed by the team?
   Date: _Aug. 1997_

4. What has been done since then related to these general supports? _An in-service was held in which all adults who work with Chelsea were oriented to her heart condition, symptoms, and needed actions by Chelsea & school nurse._

5. What is the current status of these general supports? _The teaching has been accomplished, but a couple of teachers are concened they have forgotten some of what was taught._

6. What changes, if any, has the student experienced on the corresponding Valued Life Outcome(s) as a result of having these general supports provided? _No changes to date since Chelsea has not had any symptoms at school during the first 2 months of school._

7. What changes, if any, need to be made in the educational program regarding these general supports to facilitate the corresponding Valued Life Outcome(s)? _Chelsea's symptoms and needed actions need to be prepared in writing, approved by her physician, and distributed to all appropriate adults. There are also new cafeteria workers who need to be informed._

Choosing Outcomes and Accommodations for Children • © 1998 by Michael F. Giangreco •
Baltimore: Paul H. Brookes Publishing Co.

Step 10.2
Evaluation of Impact Process
for General Supports

Directions: Answer the following questions to discuss the student's status regarding the identified General Supports category; use one page for each area.

Student name: _Chelsea Ross_   Date of team meeting: _10-30-97_
Team members participating in discussion: _Chelsea Ross, Samantha Meade,_ _Johanna Stiles_

---

1. **General Supports** category being discussed: _Providing Access & Opportunities_
    Items: ___(a) access to general educ. activities; (b) needs instructional___ _accommodations; (c) access to community-based instruction; (d) co-_ _curricular_

2. **Valued Life Outcome(s)** being facilitated through these general supports: _____
    expand/improve peer relationships; expand places and activity _opportunities_

---

3. When was the last time these general supports were discussed by the team?
    Date: _9-15-97_

4. What has been done since then related to these general supports? _General class_ _and community-based instruction have begun; teachers are meeting_ _individually with Ms. Stiles to plan accommodations._

5. What is the current status of these general supports? ____Things are going well in_ _general class & community, but co-curricular activities have yet to begin._

6. What changes, if any, has the student experienced on the corresponding Valued Life Outcome(s) as a result of having these general supports provided? _Chelsea has_ _increased the number of classmates she knows by name and has been_ _invited to attend a soccer game with a group of girls; activities/places_ _have expanded modestly._

7. What changes, if any, need to be made in the educational program regarding these general supports to facilitate the corresponding Valued Life Outcome(s)? _Need to_ _work with Chelsea to explore her possible co-curricular activities. She_ _has expressed an interest in being on the yearbook staff and in Pep Club._

Choosing Outcomes and Accommodations for Children • © 1998 by Michael F. Giangreco • Baltimore: Paul H. Brookes Publishing Co.

INDEX

Page numbers followed by an *f* indicate figures.

Order these innovative tools today!

Now you can order the time-saving forms you've found in this book!

Additional forms for **Choosing Outcomes and Accommodations for Children (COACH), 2nd ed.**
Stock #3297 • $23.95 • 1998 • 68 pages each (3 sets per package) • 8 1/2 x 11 saddle-stitched • ISBN 1-55766-329-7

Vermont Interdisciplinary Services Team Approach (VISTA): A Guide to Coordinating Educational Support Services
By Michael F. Giangreco, Ph.D.
This field-tested manual enables your IEP team to fulfill the related services provisions of IDEA as you make effective support services decisions using a collaborative team approach. Ten specific guidelines set forth a problem-solving process that involves families and leads to greater opportunities for students with mild to severe disabilities. With explicit directions, handy reproducible forms, and real-life case examples, it's a perfect complement to the author's widely used COACH manual.
Stock #2304 • **$27.95** • 1996 • 176 pages • 8 1/2 x 11 spiral-bound • ISBN 1-55766-230-4

Quick-Guides to Inclusion: Ideas for Educating Students with Disabilities   *Edited by Michael F. Giangreco, Ph.D.*
This user-friendly guide fits into your busy schedule and your budget! It offers you essential information and brief, to-the-point advice for improving inclusion skills. Inside you'll find five "Quick-Guides" devoted to topics including students with disabilities in the classroom, building partnerships with parents, creating partnerships with paraprofessionals, getting the most out of support services, and creating positive behavioral supports. Effective, yet inexpensive, this classroom tool will help you make inclusion work in any school—on any budget!
Stock #3033 • **$21.95** • 1997 • 160 pages • 8 1/2 x 11 spiral-bound • ISBN 1-55766-303-3

Quick-Guides to Inclusion 2: Ideas for Educating Students with Disabilities   *Edited by Michael F. Giangreco, Ph.D.*
The companion book to *Quick-Guides to Inclusion* features the same easy-to-use format as the first volume and offers pertinent advice on five additional inclusion topics including curriculum adaptations, instructional strategies, augmentative and alternative communication, secondary transition, and administration of inclusive schools. With its easy-to-follow suggestions and tips, this volume offers innovative ideas you can put to use immediately in your own school!
Stock #3351 • **$21.95** • 1998 • 160 pages • 8 1/2 x 11 spiral-bound • ISBN 1-55766-335-1

SAVE MONEY! Order **Quick-Guides to Inclusion** and **Quick-Guides to Inclusion 2** as a set and save. **Stock #336X** • **$39.95**

The Paraprofessional's Guide to the Inclusive Classroom: Working as a Team   *By Mary Beth Doyle, Ph.D.*
This accessible and innovative handbook for the paraprofessional provides basic, practical guidance on important issues in the inclusive classroom. Filled with tips and suggestions such as talking with teachers and team members, reading and using IEPs, maintaining confidentiality, and fostering student independence, this guide will enable school staff to quickly and easily introduce inclusion practices and design appropriate instructional programs for classrooms and individuals. Keep several on hand and eliminate the cost of consultants and formal training programs!
Stock #3122 • **$23.95** • 1997 • 160 pages • 7 x 10 spiral-bound • ISBN 1-55766-312-2

PLACE YOUR ORDER NOW! Free shipping and handling on prepaid check orders.

Please send me ___ copy(ies) of **additional forms** for **COACH, 2nd ed.**/Stock #3297/$23.95
Please send me ___ copy(ies) of **Vermont Interdisciplinary Services Team Approach (VISTA)**/Stock #2304/$27.95
Please send me ___ copy(ies) of **Quick-Guides to Inclusion**/Stock #3033/$21.95
Please send me ___ copy(ies) of **Quick-Guides to Inclusion 2**/Stock #3351/$21.95
Please send me ___ copy(ies) of the set, **Quick-Guides to Inclusion** and **Quick Guides to Inclusion 2**/Stock #336X/$39.95
Please send me ___ copy(ies) of **The Paraprofessional's Guide to the Inclusive Classroom**/Stock #3122/$23.95

___ Bill my institution (purchase order must be attached)   ___ Payment enclosed (make checks payable to Brookes Publishing Co.)

___ VISA   ___ MasterCard   ___ American Express   Credit Card # _____ Exp. date _____

Signature _____ Daytime telephone _____

Name _____

Address _____

City/State/ZIP _____

Yours to review 30 days risk-free. Prices subject to change without notice. Prices may be higher outside the U.S. Maryland orders add 5% sales tax.

Photocopy this form and mail or fax it to Brookes Publishing Co., P.O. Box 10624, Baltimore, MD 21285-0624, Fax 410-337-8539.
Or call toll-free (8 A.M.–5 P.M. ET) 1-800-638-3775. Or e-mail custserv@pbrookes.com.

Source Code: BA3